Writing History, Writing Trauma

PARALLAX RE-VISIONS OF CULTURE AND SOCIETY

Stephen G. Nichols, Gerald Prince, and Wendy Steiner,
SERIES EDITORS

Writing History, Writing Trauma

Dominick LaCapra

The Johns Hopkins University Press
Baltimore and London

The Johns Hopkins University Press
2715 North Charles Street
Baltimore, Maryland 21218-4363
www.press.jhu.edu

Library of Congress Cataloging-in-Publication Data

LaCapra, Dominick, 1939–
Writing history, writing trauma / Dominick LaCapra.
        p.   cm. — (Parallax)
    Includes bibliographical references and index.
    ISBN 0-8018-6495-X (alk. paper)
    ISBN 0-8018-6496-8 (pbk.)
    1. Holocaust, Jewish (1939–1945)—Historiography.
2. Holocaust, Jewish (1939–1945)—Personal narratives—
History and criticism. 3. Holocaust, Jewish (1939–
1945)—Psychological aspects. 4. Psychic trauma. I. Title.
II. Parallax (Baltimore, Md.)
D804.348.L34 2001
940.53′18′072—dc21   00-024994

A catalog record for this book is available from the British
Library.

For Jane and Faye

Contents

Preface

My intention in this book is to provide a broad-ranging, critical perspective on the problem of trauma, notably with respect to major
historical events. This problem has become crucial in modern thought
in general and is especially prominent in post–World War II thought
bearing on the present and the foreseeable future. Trauma and its
symptomatic aftermath pose particularly acute problems for historical
representation and understanding. I explore theoretical and literary-
critical attempts to come to terms with trauma as well as the crucial
role post-traumatic testimonies—notably Holocaust testimonies—
have assumed in recent thought and writing. In doing so, I adapt
psychoanalytic concepts to historical analysis as well as sociocultural
and political critique in elucidating trauma and its aftereffects in culture and in people.

I nonetheless insist that the focus on trauma and the use of concepts derived from psychoanalysis should not obscure the difference
between victims of traumatic historical events and others not directly
experiencing them. Nor should they become a pretext for avoiding
economic, social, and political issues. On the contrary, the very process of working through problems should be closely related to these
issues. The appeal to psychoanalytic concepts such as melancholia and
mourning, acting out and working through adds a necessary dimension to economic, social, and political analyses but does not constitute
a substitute for them. While this book focuses on the theoretical and
historical elucidation of problems related to trauma, its horizon and
the point of certain of its critical analyses are to renew the problem of
the relation between theory and practice by stressing the importance
of linking processes of working through to the reconceptualization of

sociocultural issues and sociopolitical action. Indeed, the very way in which I reconceive certain psychoanalytic concepts is adapted to my understanding of how they may be articulated with both historical analysis and sociocultural, political critique. Thus, I tend to avoid orientations primarily devoted to abstract exploration of internal psychological processes or the sometimes casuistic fine-tuning of concepts and differentiation of schools or models from one another—tendencies that may be justified in other contexts but which depart overmuch from problems I seek to investigate.

In the following pages I take a larger perspective on concerns that I have tried to address in more delimited ways in two earlier books, *Representing the Holocaust: History, Theory, Trauma* and *History and Memory after Auschwitz*.[1] The Nazi genocide remains a crucial concern, but often problems are formulated more broadly as they bear on the role of trauma in and across history. Trauma has been a prevalent preoccupation in recent theory and criticism.[2] At times it has even become an obsession or an occasion for rash amalgamations or conflations (for example, in the idea that contemporary culture, or even all history, is essentially traumatic or that everyone in the post-Holocaust context is a survivor).

There are reasons for the vision of history—or at least modern and, even more, postmodern culture—as traumatic, especially as a symptomatic response to a felt implication in excess and disorientation

1. Dominick LaCapra, *Representing the Holocaust: History, Theory, Trauma* (Ithaca: Cornell University Press, 1994); idem, *History and Memory after Auschwitz* (Ithaca: Cornell University Press, 1998). See also the discussion of related problems in my *History and Reading: Tocqueville, Foucault, French Studies* (Toronto: University of Toronto Press, 2000).

2. See Cathy Caruth, ed., *Trauma: Explorations in Memory* (Baltimore: Johns Hopkins University Press, 1995); Cathy Caruth, *Unclaimed Experience: Trauma, Narrative, History* (Baltimore: Johns Hopkins University Press, 1996); Paul Antze and Michael Lambek, eds., *Tense Past: Cultural Essays in Trauma and Memory* (New York: Routledge, 1996); and Kirby Farrell, *Post-traumatic Culture: Injury and Interpretation in the Nineties* (Baltimore: Johns Hopkins University Press, 1998). See also Ruth Leys' *Trauma: A Genealogy* (Chicago: University of Chicago Press, 2000), a section of which was presented and discussed at engaging sessions sponsored by the Society for the Humanities at Cornell University. Leys' book itself appeared only after my own was in proof.

which may have to be undergone or even acted out if one is to have an experiential or empathic basis for working it through. Indeed, I insist on the need for empathic unsettlement, and the discursive inscription of that unsettlement, in the response to traumatic events or conditions. Moreover, there is an important sense in which the after effects—the hauntingly possessive ghosts—of traumatic events are not fully owned by anyone and, in various ways, affect everyone. But the indiscriminate generalization of the category of survivor and the overall conflation of history or culture with trauma, as well as the near fixation on enacting or acting out post-traumatic symptoms, have the effect of obscuring crucial historical distinctions; they may, as well, block processes that counteract trauma and its symptomatic after effects but which do not obliterate their force and insistence—notably, processes of working through, including those conveyed in institutions and practices that limit excess and mitigate trauma.³ I would distinguish between victims of traumatizing events and commentators (or those born later), but even with respect to the latter I put forth what might paradoxically be termed a limited or framed defense of hyperbole—and even more insistently of empathic unsettlement—as discursive symptom of, and perhaps necessary affective response to, the impact of trauma. Trauma registers in hyperbole in a manner that is avoided or repressed in a complacent reasonableness or bland objectivism, but hyberbole need not, and in my judgment should not, be the unmodulated response to all problems, especially when it takes the form of an all-or-nothing philosophy, typically linked to mimetic

3. After completing this book, I read James Berger's thought-provoking *After the End: Representations of Post-apocalypse* (Minneapolis: University of Minnesota Press, 1999). It takes up and extends in somewhat different directions (notably with respect to postapocalyptic tendencies in recent American history and culture) the conceptualization of problems I tried to develop in my earlier work and to which I return in this book (notably the linkage between trauma, the sublime, and a secular sacred as well as the question of acting out and working through problems). Berger's arguments and my own supplement one another in significant ways. Especially noteworthy are Berger's analyses of the acting-out of trauma in the talk show, the denial of trauma in Reaganism and advertising, and the complex, compelling attempts to come to terms with trauma and its historical aftermath in Toni Morrison's *Beloved* and Thomas Pynchon's *Vineland.*

emulation of one or another variant of critical theory reduced to an all-purpose methodology or stylistic passe-partout.

The dynamic interaction between excess and limits, which I emphasize in my analyses, is, I find, played out in the relation between my principal text and footnotes. Some of my footnotes verge on excess and may well at times give way to it. These little essays on the bottom of the page may perhaps be justified insofar as they open lines of thought which are suggestive yet would be overly digressive if they invaded the principal text. Even the obsessive reader (who, like me, not only reads all footnotes but often begins with them) will perhaps not be consoled by the fact that I showed the ruthlessness of Medea in sacrificing even longer notes to the editorial knife. The comparatively little ones that remain may be more acceptable to the extent they bear witness to the author's vulnerability to the excesses he finds, and at times may be overly critical about, in the work of others.

The first chapter, "Writing History, Writing Trauma" (which also gives its name to the book as a whole), addresses problems from the perspective of history as a discipline, at least in my comprehension of it, at times pushing against its limits and creating or pointing to openings that warrant further exploration (such as the desirable internal relation of the historian to the critical intellectual). I argue that truth claims are necessary but not sufficient conditions that must be cogently related to other dimensions of historiography, including empathic, responsive understanding and performative, dialogical uses of language. I also investigate the role of the middle voice in "writing" trauma and raise the question of its articulation with other uses of discourse, including those operative in truth claims. In the second chapter, "Trauma, Absence, Loss," I further extend the argument of Chapter 1, lay the theoretical groundwork for the book as a whole, and attempt what I hope is a provocative reconceptualization of some very basic issues. I especially try to disclose and criticize the frequent conflation or elision of transhistorical (or structural) and historical trauma. As in the first chapter (and elsewhere in my work), I also try to counteract what I see as a prevalent tendency in professional historiography to resist speculation, even when it is properly framed, and to situate theoretical reworkings or interrogations of prevalent assumptions in strictly confined marginal positions, for example, by relegating them to the so-called think piece or construing them simply as matters of elusive terminology rather than as attempts to rethink historiographical practice in its relation to other disciplines or currents of thought. (Thus, for example, one may marginalize or misunderstand an engagement with psychoanalysis which is addressed to historiographical assumptions and practices or mistakenly see it as a standard form of "psychohistory.")

Simultaneously, I try to create space for historical specificity along with crucial practices of professional historiography which are necessary in accounting for that specificity. In the process, I distinguish historical specificity from what it is at times misleadingly conflated with or derived from, especially in insistently theoretical orientations relying on a more transhistorical notion of trauma which is structural or in some sense originary. Indeed, especially when one or another theory is taught and uncritically assimilated as a primary language or reduced to an all-purpose methodology, there is a tendency to move, via a kind of metametaphysical hyperspace, from the transhistorical to the historical without the crucial mediations provided by careful inquiry, specific knowledge, and critical judgment.[4] (This theoreticist move often comes with a leveling, quasi-transcendental understanding of history which makes it purely illustrative of transhistorical processes, construes it as a "fallen" residue, or puts forward a purely theoretical

---

4. For example, in certain forms of deconstructive criticism, the justifiable deconstruction of absolute origins, implying that the origin is in some sense always already "ruined," may lead immediately to the idea that a given institution, such as the university, is in ruins. Such a seemingly radical—in reality, rather confused—move precludes the necessity for careful, comparative research and informed, discriminating critique. See, for example, Nicolas Royle, "Yes, Yes, the University in Ruins," *Critical Inquiry* 26 (1999), as well as my rejoinder ("Yes, Yes, Yes, Yes . . . Well Maybe") in the same issue. Royle's essay is a critical response to my "The University in Ruins?" (*Critical Inquiry* 25 [1998]: 32–55), which discusses Bill Readings' *The University in Ruins* (Cambridge: Harvard University Press, 1996). See also the participatory, by and large uncritical analysis of Royle's own ecstatic, (post-)apocalyptic *After Derrida* (Manchester: Manchester University Press, 1995) in Sarah Wood, "Let's Start Again," *Diacritics* 29 (1999), 4–19.

conception of it, for example, as trauma, reference, or materiality.)[5] In my account, moreover, not only should transhistorical or structural trauma be distinguished from historical trauma and its attendant losses; it should also be correlated with absence in contrast to loss, notably the absence of undivided origins, absolute foundations, or perfect, totalizing solutions to problems. Failure to make these distinctions eventuates in a misleadingly hypostatized notion of constitutive loss or lack which may well be a secular variant of original sin.

In the third chapter, "Holocaust Testimonies: Attending to the Victim's Voice," I turn to a particular problem with wide-ranging implications and address the role of testimonies in a manner that focuses on the Holocaust but, in its implications, is not restricted to it. Testimonies serve to bring theoretical concerns in sustained contact with the experience of people who lived through events and suffered often devastating losses. They also raise the problem of the role of affect and empathy in historical understanding itself. I would note that "voice" in the title of this chapter is a metaphor that does not exclude the visual. The looks and gestures of survivors also call for reading and understanding. At times nothing could be more graphic and significant than the body language, including the facial expressions, of the survivor-witness in recounting a past that will not pass away. One thinks, for example, of the sweat pouring down the face and head of Paul D., a Jew constrained to convert to Christianity, as he recounts his dream of God with an axe dividing him in two—a dream he does not see in the manner prompted by the interviewer (the self divided between Jew and Christian) but as God's attempt to kill him. One also thinks of the couple (Bessie K. and Jacob K.) who sit on a couch in polar tension—like a diptych whose hinged halves simultaneously strain away from yet nonetheless along with each other—especially in the light of the wife's account of the "bundle" (the baby) hidden under her coat and taken from her at a selection when it

---

5. See, for example, Kevin Neumark, "Traumatic Poetry: Charles Baudelaire and the Shock of Laughter," in Caruth, *Trauma: Explorations in Memory,* 236–55, esp. 250–53.

coughs, a baby whose existence she later disavows or represses and whose story she tells her husband only long after the fact.[6]

In the fourth chapter, "Perpetrators and Victims: The Goldhagen Debate and Beyond," I extend the discussion of victims to include their relation to perpetrators, a problem that came into acute focus in the debate over Daniel Jonah Goldhagen's *Hitler's Willing Executioners: Ordinary Germans and the Holocaust*.[7] Like many others, I tend to believe that the debate stirred up by Goldhagen's book may be of greater significance than the book itself. But I also think that the book, in its own questionable manner, brought up issues that deserve serious examination, issues bearing on the motivation of perpetrators which are often underspecified, overgeneralized, or downplayed.

The penultimate chapter is a 1998 interview that I have edited largely for stylistic purposes and to eliminate certain redundancies. I have, however, kept its oral quality. In it I address many of the problems discussed in earlier chapters, especially with respect to what may seem most open to question but also, I hope, question-worthy and thought-provoking in my recent work. By including both frequently raised queries and my attempt to respond to them, the interview renders basic concepts and arguments more accessible, facilitating their evaluation and constructive critique. The interview, which took place in Jerusalem, also serves to bring up in manifest ways the issue of the globalization of intellectual and existential concerns, particularly with respect to the issue of trauma, its problematic conceptual uses, and its troubled aftermath. In the conclusion I recapitulate certain points and, more important, try to extend them in directions that may prove suggestive for further research and reflection.

A version of the first chapter was initially composed for the lecture series "Writing across the Disciplines," sponsored by the John S. Knight Writing Program at Cornell University, directed by my col-

6. Edited excerpts, including the scenes to which I refer, from the testimonies of Paul D., Bessie K., and Jacob K. are included in *Everything Else Is History*, Yale Fortunoff Archive Tape A67.

7. Daniel Jonah Goldhagen, *Hitler's Willing Executioners: Ordinary Germans and the Holocaust* (New York: Alfred A. Knopf, 1996).

league Jonathan Monroe. Earlier versions of Chapters 2 and 3 were first given to inaugurate the Polonsky Visiting Lectureship in the History of Ideas at the Hebrew University of Jerusalem. I especially thank Gabriel Motzkin for his role in organizing the lectures and serving as a valuable interlocutor. A later version of the second chapter was published in *Critical Inquiry*. A Spanish version of the fourth chapter appears as the introduction to *Los Alemanes, El Holocausto y la culpa colectiva: El Debate Goldhagen*, edited by Federico Finchelstein (Buenos Aires: Eudeba, 1999). The interview that has become the fifth chapter was conducted on June 9, 1998, for a forthcoming CD-Rom, produced by Yad Vashem, on scholarship treating the Holocaust. The interviewer was Amos Goldberg, a research scholar at Yad Vashem. Finally, I thank Tracie Matysik for her help in preparing the index.

Writing History, Writing Trauma

1 | *Writing History, Writing Trauma*

I would initially distinguish between two approaches to historiography. The first is what I would term a documentary or self-sufficient research model, of which positivism is the extreme form. On this first approach, gathering evidence and making referential statements in the form of truth claims based on that evidence constitute necessary and sufficient conditions of historiography. The second approach, which is the negative mirror image of the first, is radical constructivism. For it, referential statements making truth claims apply at best only to events and are of restricted, indeed marginal significance. By contrast, essential are performative, figurative, aesthetic, rhetorical, ideological, and political factors that "construct" structures—stories, plots, arguments, interpretations, explanations—in which referential statements are embedded and take on meaning and significance. As shall become evident, my own view falls at neither extreme represented by these two approaches. It is, however, not simply a *juste-milieu* between the extremes; rather, it attempts to articulate problems and relations in a significantly different manner. In brief, I maintain that referential statements making truth claims based on evidence apply in historiography to both the (problematic) levels of structures and events. Moreover, truth claims are necessary but not sufficient conditions of historiography. A crucial question is how they do and ought to interact with other factors or forces in historiography, in other genres, and in hybridized forms or modes.[1]

A documentary or self-sufficient research model was especially prominent toward the end of the nineteenth and the beginning of the twentieth century, and it may even have been defensible in the attempt to professionalize history under the banner of objectivity and to distance, if not dissociate, it from literature, especially in the form of belles-lettres.[2] Since then that model has to a significant extent persisted in professional historiography, but its value is more questionable, although it has been rendered more sophisticated through its encounter with a radically constructivist position.[3]

In a documentary or self-sufficient research model, priority is often given to research based on primary (preferably archival) documents that enable one to derive authenticated facts about the past which may be recounted in a narrative (the more "artistic" approach) or employed

1. I would note that a self-sufficient research model and radical constructivism form polar opposites, neither of which may adequately characterize the approach of certain historians. But both have played a significant role in the discipline as well as in analyses of it.

2. On this issue, see Peter Novick, *That Noble Dream: The "Objectivity Question" and the American Historical Profession* (Cambridge: Cambridge University Press, 1988). For a discussion of Novick's book by J. H. Hexter, Linda Gordon, David Hollinger, Allan Megill, Peter Novick, and Dorothy Ross, based on a panel at the annual convention of the American Historical Association, see the *American Historical Review* 96 (1991): 673–708. For a discussion that includes an attempt to reconceptualize the problem of objectivity in normative terms, see Thomas Haskell, "Objectivity Is Not Neutrality," in *History and Theory: Contemporary Readings*, ed. Brian Fay, Philip Pomper, and Richard T. Vann (Malden, Mass.: Blackwell Publishers, 1998), 299–319. See also Chris Lorenz's insightful essay in the same volume, "Historical Knowledge and Historical Reality: A Plea for 'Internal Realism'," 342–76. This volume, to which I frequently refer, is in general one of the best sources for contemporary views of historiography on the part of both philosophers and historians. In addition to the essays in it, see as well those in Keith Jenkins, ed., *The Postmodern History Reader* (New York: Routledge, 1997).

3. In the recent past, the affirmation of objectivity may even eventuate in what Hans Kellner has termed "a sort of postmodern literalism, a self-critical (or self-deconstructing, if you will) literalism that points querulously to its own impossibility"—what might also be seen stylistically as a variant of minimalism evidenced, for example, in the work of Berel Lang. See Kellner's "'Never Again' Is Now," in Fay, Pomper, and Vann, *History and Theory*, 235. Kellner's discussion of Hayden White's notion of the middle voice in representing the Holocaust may be compared with what I write later.

in a mode of analysis which puts forth testable hypotheses (the more "social-scientific" approach).[4] On this model, there is a sense in which writing is not a problem. Writing is subordinated to content in the form of facts, their narration, or their analysis. It is thus reduced to writing up the results of research, and style is limited to a restricted notion of mellifluous, immediately readable or accessible, well-crafted prose (or conventional *beau style*) in which form ideally has no significant effect on content. In other words, writing is a medium for expressing a content, and its ideal goal is to be transparent to content or an open window on the past—with figures of rhetoric serving only an instrumental role in illustrating what could be expressed without loss in literal terms. As Nancy Partner puts the point: "Correct modern

4. The social-scientific approach is important for many historians but today not much discussed by philosophers treating historiography (for example, both Chris Lorenz in the analytic tradition and Paul Ricoeur in the continental tradition), who tend to follow Hayden White, even when they criticize him, by focusing on narrative. Although the conception of the relevant social-scientific theories and theorists changes over time, the concern with the relation of history to the social sciences, at times correlated with a deemphasis of the significance of narrative, has been a hallmark of both the Bielefeld school in Germany and the *Annales* in France.

A concern with the relation between history and the social sciences is crucial, but a primary, if not exclusive, orientation in the direction of the social sciences often implies a devaluation of literary studies, rhetoric, and (to a lesser degree) philosophy as relevant for the self-understanding or conduct of historical inquiry (as well as of philosophers and literary theorists as pertinent interlocutors for historians), and it constitutes philosophy and literature largely as *objects* of historical and social-scientific analysis. The unfortunate result is often limited insight into the work and play of philosophical and literary texts or the way they respond—at times critically—to social categories and assumptions, however probing and complex may be the analysis of their social insertion in a collective representation, structure, field, or network. (The mutual reliance of history and the social sciences was in certain respects accentuated by the 1994 change in the title of the journal *Annales ESC* [*Economies Sociétés Civilisations*] to *Annales HSS* [*Histoires, Sciences Sociales*].) Recently this orientation may be changing to allow a broader conception of inter- and cross-disciplinarity in which there is a critical, discriminating opening to the role of philosophy and literary theory as sites that, along with the social sciences, are relevant to a reconceptualization of (or "critical turn" in) history. For the editors' attempt to rethink the journal's approach, see "Histoire et sciences sociales: Un tournant critique?" *Annales ESC* 43 (1988): 291–93, and "Tentons l'expérience," *Annales ESC* 44 (1989): 1317–23. See also *Annales HSS* 49 (1994), *Littérature et histoire*. For a harsh critique of any turn in the *Annales* which would stress theoretical reflection or discourse analysis—much less a mutually thought-provoking interaction with philosophy and literary studies—see Gérard Noiriel, *Sur la "crise" de l'histoire* (Paris: Belin, 1996).

historical style draws attention away from the verbal symbols chosen by the author and directs it to the words of others (or artifacts or natural objects), thus creating by literary convention the illusion [I would rather say, having the regulative ideal—DLC] of transparency, through the text into time."[5]

In its more extreme forms, a documentary or self-sufficient research model *may* bring with it a stress on quantitative methods (prominent in cliometrics), but it generally *does* involve the following features, which add further dimensions to a predominantly, if not exclusively, referential or constative use of language that conveys truth claims based on evidence: (1) a strict separation or binary opposition between subject and object; (2) a tendency to conflate objectivity with objectivism or the objectification of the other which is addressed only in the form of third-person referential statements, direct quotations, and summaries or paraphrases; (3) an identification of historical un-

---

5. Nancy Partner, "Writing on the Writing of History," in Fay, Pomper, and Vann, *History and Theory*, 77. I would note that the suspicion of a plain style and the advocacy of an opaque or at least a difficult style in the modern period are motivated by a number of considerations. One is the general idea that style should respond to the complexity and difficulty of the problems treated, thus that there is something dubious in the attempt to make certain problems easy or deceptively simple and accessible. (One finds this view, combined with a concern for religious intensity and demandingness, in Kierkegaard, for example.) Another is the idea that initiation, with its attendant trials, is necessary to understand and appreciate certain things—or, in Nietzsche's phrase, that all things rare are for the rare. A more democratic variant of this view is the notion that an intricate style may function as a strategy of resistance and ward off the grasp of dominant, oppressive (notably colonial or postcolonial) power. In the words of the Tunisian writer Abdelwahib Meddeb, "We will defend ourselves with arabesque, subversion, labyrinthine constructions, the incessant decentering of the sentence and of language so that the other will lose the way just as in the narrow streets of the *casbah*" (quoted in Jean Dejeux, *Situation de la littérature maghrébine de langue française* [Algiers: Office des publications universitaires, 1982], 103–4).

Still another reason, for writers such as Theodor Adorno and Paul Celan, is that language has been so distorted or corrupted by political and propagandistic uses that it must be made strange, difficult, even resistant to pleasure in order to be used again—a perspective intensified by the deceptions and euphemisms of Nazi discourse. Phrased differently, the last view criticizes a premature return to the pleasure principle in discourse before certain demanding, if not intractable, problems have been confronted and, to some viable extent, worked through in an empathetic, rigorous manner. In a more dubious form, an opaque or convoluted style may become mimetically prevalent when a difficult, demanding approach becomes an all-purpose methodology or stylistic tic.

derstanding with causal explanation or with the fullest possible contextualization of the other (possibly in the form of thick description or narration); (4) a denial of transference or the problem of the implication of the observer in the object of observation; (5) an exclusion or downplaying of a dialogic relation to the other recognized as having a voice or perspective that may question the observer or even place him or her in question by generating problems about his or her assumptions, affective investments, and values. In general, one might say that a self-sufficient research paradigm and, in even more pronounced form, its positivistic extreme confine historiography to constative or referential statements involving truth claims made by an observer about a sharply differentiated object of research.

There are elements of a research paradigm which, extricated from a self-sufficient or autonomous framework, I (along with the overwhelming majority of historians) find indispensable, including the importance of contextualization, clarity, objectivity, footnoting, and the idea that historiography necessarily involves truth claims based on evidence—or what might be called an irreducible "aboutness"—not only on the level of directly referential statements about events but on more structural and comprehensive levels such as narration, interpretation, and analysis. But I think that one has to situate these features in a manner not accommodated by their relatively unproblematic role in a self-sufficient research paradigm.[6]

The note (footnote or endnote) is the correlate of research, and its use as a referential component of research is one criterion that serves

6. The prevalence and importance of such a paradigm or model in the historical profession were perhaps stated in overly restrictive terms by Laurence Veysey when he asserted: "With all this greater sophistication about historical argument, it remains true that the very highest amount of prestige is still awarded to an historian who uncovers (no matter how he does it) some incontestable but previously unknown fact of major importance." "The United States," in *The International Handbook of Historical Studies: Contemporary Research and Theory*, ed. Georg G. Iggers and Harold T. Parker (Westport, Conn.: Greenwood, 1979), 168. Without denying the prevalence and importance of a documentary or self-sufficient research model in the profession, I qualified Veysey's assertion by observing that "the greatest prestige often goes to the historian who revises standard accounts on the basis of massive archival research" (*History and Criticism* [Ithaca: Cornell University Press, 1985], 20).

to differentiate history from fiction. The research paper or monograph is writing replete with referential notes, ideally, in a restricted research paradigm, a note per statement in the principal text. (More subjective moments are confined to a preface or coda or perhaps to notes not serving as references.) Fiction *may* have referential notes, notably when it blends fact and fiction, but historiography to be professional historiography—even beyond a restricted research paradigm—*must* have notes that provide references for statements that function referentially and make truth claims (except when these statements convey what is currently accepted as common knowledge at least among professionals).

For J. H. Hexter, the attitude toward notes distinguishes history not only from fiction but also from physics, and, in almost pastoral tones, he even seems to intimate that, at least in historiography, the note is a case wherein the last shall be first: "One difference becomes manifest in the divergent attitude of the historian and, say, the physicist to the lowly item in their common repertoire—the footnote. It is so lowly, indeed, that it may seem unworthy of notice; but we must remember that the lowly and humble things of the earth may be more instructive than the great and mighty—after all, geneticists learned a good deal more about genetics by considering the fruit fly than they could have learned in an equal span of time from a contemplation of the somewhat more impressive elephant."[7] Hexter unfortunately does not explicate what is implied by his shift from a putative contrast between historiography and physics to an analogy between the historian and the geneticist, and we are left mildly bewildered by the seeming aspersion cast on macrohistory by the allusion to the elephant as object of contemplation. But his affirmation of the importance of the note to historiography is unequivocal and unobjectionable.

Of course, notes may be used in both history and fiction in a manner that questions or even parodies a documentary or self-sufficient research paradigm, and there may be substantive notes that function

---

7. J. H. Hexter, "The Rhetoric of History," in Fay, Pomper, and Vann, *History and Theory*, 60. On the footnote, see also Anthony Grafton, *Footnote: A Curious History* (Cambridge: Harvard University Press, 1997).

not merely as references but as elaborations of points or even as significant qualifications of assertions or arguments in the principal text, at times to the point of establishing a critically dialogic relation between text and note or even something approximating a countertext in the notes.[8] Moreover, with respect to a limit event such as the Holocaust, even the eminent research scholar Raul Hilberg, whose formulation of problems usually tends toward understatement, was led to be hyperbolic and to paraphrase Adorno in posing this seemingly rhetorical question: "I am no poet, but the thought occurred to me that if [Adorno's] statement is true, then is it not equally barbaric to write footnotes after Auschwitz?" Hilberg added:

> I have had to reconstruct the process of destruction in my mind, combining the documents into paragraphs, the paragraphs into chapters, the chapters into a book. I always considered that I stood on solid ground: I had no anxieties about artistic failure. Now I have been told that I have indeed succeeded. And that is a cause of some worry, for we historians usurp history precisely when we are successful in our work, and that is to say that nowadays some people might read what I have written in the mistaken belief that here, on my printed pages, they will find the true ultimate Holocaust as it really happened.[9]

Still, the limit of history and the beginning of fiction is probably reached in the self-referential note (or entry) that goes beyond intertextual indications, related to the research findings or conclusions of other historians, and blocks reference by taking one back into the text with looplike or labyrinthine effects, as one has, for example, in Nabokov's *Pale Fire.* One might also invoke the ping-pong diplomacy of Flaubert's cross-references in *The Dictionary of Received Ideas,* where one has the following entries: "Blondes. Hotter than brunettes. See brunettes. Brunettes. Hotter than blondes. See blondes."

Let us now turn to the second position on historiography to which

8. I think many historians and editors of historical texts get uncomfortable when the latter process occurs, probably because it is a disconcerting departure from the more standard use of footnotes.

9. Raul Hilberg, "I Was Not There," in *Writing and the Holocaust,* ed. Berel Lang (New York: Holmes & Meier, 1988), 25.

I referred earlier: radical constructivism. A radically constructivist position has received its most articulate defenders in such important figures as Hayden White and Frank Ankersmit, who accept the distinction between historical and fictional statements on the level of reference to events but question it on structural levels.[10] For them there is an identity or essential similarity between historiography and fiction, literature, or the aesthetic on structural levels, and their emphasis is on the fictionality of structures in all these areas. At the limit, they present historiography as a closed window so stained by one set of projective factors or another that, at least on a structural level, it reflects back only the historian's own distorted image. Yet at times their work takes them in directions that may go beyond a radically constructivist identification of history with fictionalization, rhetoric, poetics, performativity, or even self-referential discourse. After a brief elaboration of the better-known dimensions of their thought, I spend some time on what I find to be an insufficiently explored, difficult, and thought-provoking initiative in an essay by White, namely, the argument that a discursive analogue of the middle voice is most suitable at least for representing the most extreme, traumatic limit events in history, such as those of the Holocaust.

10. After completing this chapter, I read Chris Lorenz's "Can History Be True?: Narrativism, Positivism, and the 'Metaphorical Turn,'" *History and Theory* 37 (1998): 309–29. It carefully elaborates certain of the points I touch on in terms of a somewhat more restricted frame of reference that focuses on narrative and involves a very limited, if not dismissive, treatment of fiction understood as the opposite of history. See also, in the same volume, John H. Zammito, "Ankersmit's Postmodernist Historiography: The Hyperbole of 'Opacity,'" 330–46. Despite the force and cogency of certain of his arguments, in this essay (as in "Are We Being Theoretical Yet?: The New Historicism, the New Philosophy of History, and 'Practicing Historians,'" *Journal of Modern History* 65 [1993]: 784–814), Zammito shows little appreciation for the ways in which hyperbole and even opacity (or at least difficulty) may be understood and in a qualified manner defended, especially when they are framed in certain ways and are not simply indulged in all contexts. One might provide a limited, contextualized defense of hyperbole as a stylistic indication of one's involvement in the excess of an excessive or extreme (indeed, at times traumatic) context or situation—a response (not a last word or a position) that must be undergone and even to some extent acted out if certain problems are to be understood empathetically and worked through. At the very least, one may argue that there is something questionable in a uniformly benign, mellifluous, blandly reasonable, or conventionally "realistic" response even to the most extreme situations or limit cases.

From what might be seen as a version of a self-sufficient research paradigm which has been rendered more sophisticated by its critical encounter with radical constructivism, Perez Zagorin provides this characterization of a position held by Frank Ankersmit, which Zagorin generalizes to apply to postmodernism and deconstruction in general:

> One of the characteristic moves of postmodern and deconstructionist theory has been to try to obliterate the boundaries between literature and other disciplines by reducing all modes of thought to the common condition of writing. So it maintains that philosophy, like historiography, is merely another kind of writing and subject to its laws, rather than a separate species of reflection concerned with distinctively philosophical questions. Putting aside, however, the identification of language and reality, a thesis construable in different ways (which in any case is well beyond the subject of my discussion), I venture to say that few historians would agree with Ankersmit's consignment of historiography to the category of the aesthetic. Nor would they be likely to approve a characterization that gives preeminence to its literariness. As the Russian formalists and Roman Jakobson have told us, the quality of literariness consists in the way it thrusts language and expression into the foreground and grants them an independent value and importance. Although Ankersmit holds that literary and historical works are similar in this respect, this is surely not the case. In historiography, the attempt by language to draw attention to itself would commonly be regarded as highly inappropriate and an obtrusive breach of the rule of historical writing. In history language is very largely subservient to the historian's effort to convey in the fullest, clearest, and most sensitive way an understanding or knowledge of something in the past.[11]

In his reply, Ankersmit makes a number of points worth taking seriously. He nonetheless seems to agree with important aspects of Zagorin's characterization of his position, although he here shifts or varies his emphasis from aesthetics to politics (as White often does). Ankersmit writes:

---

11. Perez Zagorin, "Postmodernism: Reconsiderations," in Fay, Pomper, and Vann, *History and Theory,* 200.

All that is essential and interesting in the writing of history (both in theory and practice) is not to be found at the level of the individual statements, but at that of the politics adopted by historians when they select the statements that individuate their "picture of the past.". . . Saying *true* things about the past is easy—anybody can do that—but saying *right* things about the past is difficult. That truly [*sic*] requires historical insight and originality. . . . I have elsewhere called these "pictures of the past" narrative substances. The question everything turns on, then, is whether or not we are prepared to recognize these narrative substances as logical entities *next* to the logical entities like subject, predicate, theoretical concept, statement, and so on, we already know from philosophical logic. . . . If we take seriously the text and its narrative substances we will become postmodernists; if we see only the statement we will remain modernist. Or, to put it in a slogan, the statement is modernist, the (historical) text is postmodernist.[12]

By narrative substance, Ankersmit means what White discussed in terms of prefigurative tropes and meaning-endowing, projective narrative structures. Like White, he also sees the narrative substance or structure as fictive and politically or ideologically motivated, and he infers from the evident fact that "we can never test our conclusions by comparing the elected text with 'the past' itself" the questionable conclusion that "narrative substances do not refer to the past" (212). He also asserts that "we can only speak of causes and effects at the level of the statement" and that "narrative language is metaphorical (tropological)"; indeed, that "the historical text is a substitute for the absent past" (220).

One may certainly agree with Ankersmit (or White) that it is of pressing importance to attend to current ideological and political dimensions or functions of historical accounts. Moreover, all narratives "construct" or shape and some narratives more or less drastically distort their objects. But, without adopting Zagorin's limited frame of reference, one might still argue that the historical text becomes a

12. Frank Ankersmit, "Reply to Professor Zagorin," in Fay, Pomper, and Vann, *History and Theory*, 209.

substitute for the absent past only when it is construed as a totalized object that pretends to closure and is fetishized as such. (Put in somewhat ironic psychoanalytic terms, the historical text as fetish would become an avatar of the phallic mother giving birth to total history— at one time the dream of the *Annales* school.) One might also maintain that, although a past reality or object is for historians an inference from textual traces in the broad sense, the inference, while not exhausted by, nonetheless necessarily and crucially involves reference and truth claims with respect to both events and structures or general interpretations and explanations. In other words, saying the right things may not be limited to but does constitutively require saying true things on the levels of both statements referring to events and broader narrative, interpretive, or explanatory endeavors. How to adjudicate truth claims may differ in significant ways with respect to events and to broader endeavors (such as interpretations or readings of the past), but truth claims are at issue on both levels.

For example, in the debate about the Holocaust, in which White and Ankersmit have recently participated, reference and truth claims pertain not only to statements such as "the Wannsee conference took place on January 20, 1942." They also apply to broader considerations such as those at issue in the debate between intentionalists (who stress the role of an intentional policy of genocide formulated by Hitler as well as the importance of that policy in a dictatorship) and functionalists (who stress the role of the "polycratic" or decentered nature of the Nazi regime, more impersonal bureaucratic processes, and the activities of middle- to low-level functionaries in implementing and even at times initiating the "final solution"). Most historians of the Holocaust would now argue that an account both true and right is found neither in an intentionalist nor in a functionalist approach but in a more complex combination of their emphases as well as in a partial shift of attention to other factors not sufficiently accounted for by either. The more recent terms of the debate include facts (or statements of fact referring to events) that were important for both intentionalists and functionalists (notably the facts of the genocide itself as recounted by Raul Hilberg and others). But the debate is now about the relative weight to be given to (1) bureaucratic processes (including medicalized and hygienic concerns based on purportedly scientific race theory) linked to what Hilberg termed the "machinery of destruction," perhaps in relation to a broader concept such as modernization (with Zygmunt Bauman), a technological frame of reference (Heidegger's *Gestell*), and instrumental rationality (Horkheimer and Adorno's "dialectic of Enlightenment"), and (2) anti-Semitism as an ideology and practice, perhaps in relation to an expanded conception of victimization which would differentially refer to such groups as the handicapped, "Gypsies," homosexuals, and Slavs, including such issues as the prevalence in Germany and elsewhere of rabid (or what Daniel Jonah Goldhagen terms *eliminationist*) anti-Semitism and its relation to fears of degeneration, quasi-ritual anxiety about contamination, and a quasi-sacrificial desire for purification of the *Volksgemeinschaft* as well as its regeneration or even redemption through violence. Of course, there are still more issues involved in contemporary debates— including in intricate ways rhetorical, political, affective, and ideological matters—but these indications are enough to demonstrate that truth claims are nonetheless at issue on levels other than that of discrete statements referring to events.

When one moves from Ankersmit to White, it is important to note that the former's opposition between modernism and postmodernism is replicated in the latter's opposition between nineteenth-century realism and modernism.[13] This very displacement might indicate that

---

13. In his most recent work, Ankersmit has moved from a constructivist aestheticism to the concept of experience to which I turn in a somewhat different way later in this essay. Experience—conceived perhaps in too foundational and undifferentiated a form—is a key concept in John Toews, "Intellectual History after the Linguistic Turn: The Autonomy of Meaning and the Irreducibility of Experience," *American Historical Review* 92 (1987): 879–907. See also Zammito, "Are We Being Theoretical Enough Yet?" as well as my "History, Language, and Reading: Waiting for Crillon," *American Historical Review* 100 (1995): 799–828 (a version of which is republished as chap. 1 of my *History and Reading: Tocqueville, Foucault, French Studies* [Toronto: University of Toronto Press, 2000] and in shortened form in Fay, Pomper, and Vann, *History and Theory*, 90–118). Curiously, neither Toews nor

the oppositions are less secure than they seem to either thinker and that both nineteenth-century realism and modernism may be more internally complex than either allows in employing one or the other for purposes of contrast and polemics. One might also observe that White tends to identify narrativization with fictionalization in a questionable manner.[14] As I have intimated, narrative structures may involve truth claims, either in terms of "correspondence" to lived narrative structures (such as those involved in more or less realized plans and projects) or in terms of references (for example, concerning patterns or more or less varied repetitions) that may retrospectively be seen to inform processes or activities in ways that may not have been entirely conscious to participants. (Here one may, for example, point to the role of secularization as a complex, often at least partly unconscious, displacement of the religious in the secular.)

The comparison of historiography and fiction may be taken in a different direction than that prominent in White. One might argue that narratives in fiction may also involve truth claims on a structural or general level by providing insight into phenomena such as slavery or the Holocaust, by offering a reading of a process or period, or by giving at least a plausible "feel" for experience and emotion which may be difficult to arrive at through restricted documentary methods. One

---

Zammito discusses the problem of empathy, which would seem to be crucial for any attempt to relate historiography and experience, particularly one that insists on the distinction between the differentiated experience of those studied and the differentiated experience of the historian. One may also note that utopian projects are always to some extent situated beyond historical experience even when they invoke a mythological golden age.

14. I would note that one should not simply conflate the contrast between the literal and the figurative with that between the factual and the fictive. Assertions of fact or truth claims may be conveyed in figurative language (for example, "war is hell" or "she has a heart as big as all outdoors"). Conversely, fiction may be written in nonfigurative, "literal" language, indeed in language that tries to eliminate or render banal all metaphors (as, in different ways, in the writing of Flaubert, Kafka, or Beckett). Of course, in ordinary language "literal" may be used as the correlate of "factual" or in a seemingly pleonastic manner ("the literal truth"). The correlation, if not identification, of the figurative and the fictional (or, even more broadly, the literary) is an aspect of a special theory of language which is open to question.

might, for example, make such a case for Toni Morrison's *Beloved* with respect to the aftermath of slavery and the role of transgenerational, phantomlike forces that haunt later generations, or for Albert Camus's *The Fall* with respect to the reception of the Holocaust.[15] (Indeed, the more pertinent contrast between historiography and fiction might be on the level of events, where historians, as distinguished from writers of fiction, may not imbricate or treat in the same way actual events and ones they invent.)

At the very least, the complex relation of narrative structures to truth claims might provide a different understanding of modern and postmodern realism (including what has been termed *traumatic realism*) wherein correspondence itself is not to be understood in terms of positivism or essentialism but as a metaphor that signifies a referential relation (or truth claim) that is more or less direct or indirect (probably generically more indirect in fiction than in historiography). Furthermore, one might maintain that truth claims coming from historiography, on the levels of both events and structures, may be employed in the discussion and critique of art (including fiction) in a manner that is especially pressing with respect to extreme events that still particularly concern people at present. For example, one might justifiably criticize a work of art on historical as well as aesthetic and normative grounds if it treated the Third Reich in a manner that excluded or marginalized the Nazi genocide or even if it addressed the latter in terms of a harmonizing narrative that provided the reader or viewer with an unwarranted sense of spiritual uplift (as does the ending of *Schindler's List,* for example). On similar grounds, one might also criticize a work of art that addressed the relation between perpetrator and victim largely in terms of erotic titillation within the acting-out of a repetition compulsion (as *Night Porter* might be argued to do).[16]

15. For a discussion of *The Fall* (as well as of Art Spiegelman's *Maus*) from the perspective suggested here, see my *History and Memory after Auschwitz* (Ithaca: Cornell University Press, 1998), chaps. 3 and 5.

16. Here one may mention the more difficult case of Roberto Benigni's 1998 film *Life Is Beautiful.* I think this film tends to break into two parts—the pre–concentration camp and the camp experiences. The film does not recognize the break and is, if anything, too

Truth claims are neither the only nor always the most important consideration in art and its analysis. Of obvious importance are poetic, rhetorical, and performative dimensions of art which not only mark but also make differences historically (dimensions that are differentially at play in historical writing as well). But my general point is that truth claims are nonetheless relevant to works of art both on the level of their general structures or procedures of emplotment—which may offer significant insights (or, at times, oversights), suggesting lines of inquiry for the work of historians (for example, with respect to transgenerational processes of "possession" or haunting)—and on the level of justifiable questions addressed to art on the basis of historical knowledge and research. In brief, the interaction or mutually interrogative relation between historiography and art (including fiction) is more complicated than is suggested by either an identity or a binary opposition between the two, a point that is becoming increasingly forceful in recent attempts to reconceptualize the study of art and culture.[17]

One might also make explicit what is not thematized as such in White: narrativization is closest to fictionalization in the sense of a dubious departure from, or distortion of, historical reality when it con-

---

continuous in its techniques and approach to problems. The "magical realism" and humor that work wonderfully in the first, pre–concentration camp part (for example, in creating and sustaining the relationship between the couple or in protecting the child from harsh realities) become in many ways inappropriate in the context of the concentration camp. Life in the camp demanded more and is an unsuitable context for benign humor and the stylizations (or games) of protective denial. The second part of the film tends to be either too implausible or not implausible enough, and it discloses both the possibilities and limits of Benigni's type of humor and realism. (The camp itself remains a rather "utopian" space or nowhere land, underspecified in terms of location, duration of stay, and operation—itself magically stylized in questionable ways—and the uplifting end of the film might be seen as the Italian mother-and-child analogue of a Hollywood ending.)

17. This perspective has informed my own approach to problems. See especially my *"Madame Bovary" on Trial* (Ithaca: Cornell University Press, 1982) or, more recently, my discussion of Claude Lanzmann's *Shoah* in *History and Memory after Auschwitz*, chap. 4. For an early attempt to rethink French studies in a manner relating history and art, see Maurice Crubellier, *Histoire Culturelle de la France XIXe–XXe siècle* (Paris: A. Colin, 1974). For a recent attempt, see Kristin Ross, *Fast Cars, Clean Bodies: Decolonization and the Reordering of French Culture* (Cambridge: MIT Press, 1995). See also the final chapter of my *History and Reading*.

veys relatively unproblematic closure (or what Frank Kermode terms a sense of an ending).[18] Indeed, White sometimes tends to identify narrative with conventional or formulaic narrative involving closure and to move from this limited identification to a general critique of narrative. (This move is pronounced in Sande Cohen's *Historical Culture*.[19]) Yet White also defends what he sees as modernist narrative and argues that historiography would do better to emulate its resistance to closure and its experimentalism in general rather than rely on nineteenth-century realism in its putative modes of representation and emplotment. Hans Kellner has attempted to show how Fernand Braudel's study of the Mediterranean at the time of Philip II does just that by enacting a satiric and carnivalesque interaction of various levels of meaning, interpretation, and explanation.[20] In any case, White's critiques of narrative are most convincing when applied to conventional narratives (or the conventional dimension of narrative) seeking resonant closure, and his claims about the possible role of experimental narrative with respect to historiography are often thought-provoking even when he does not show precisely how they might be applied or enacted.

Rather than track further White's movements that have already been extensively discussed in the literature and, if anything, have overly predetermined the terms of debate even for his critics, I would like to turn to a relatively recent essay of his in which he discusses the Holocaust.[21] In it he relates what he sees as an appropriately modernist

18. Frank Kermode, *The Sense of an Ending: Studies in the Theory of Fiction* (New York: Oxford University Press, 1967).

19. Sande Cohen, *Historical Culture: On the Recoding of an Academic Discipline* (Berkeley: University of California Press, 1986).

20. Hans Kellner, "Disorderly Conduct: Braudel's Mediterranean Satire," *History and Theory* 18 (1979): 187–222, reprinted in *Language and Historical Representation: Getting the Story Crooked* (Madison: University of Wisconsin Press, 1989), 153–89. See also Philippe Carrard, *Poetics of the New History: French Historical Discourse from Braudel to Chartier* (Baltimore: Johns Hopkins University Press, 1992).

21. Hayden White, "Historical Emplotment and the Story of Truth," in *Probing the Limits of Representation: Nazism and the "Final Solution,"* ed. Saul Friedlander (Cambridge: Harvard University Press, 1992), 37–53. I shall mention points at which White himself turns to the concept of experience in this essay.

representation with a discursive analogue of the middle voice as discussed by Roland Barthes in his famous essay "To Write: An Intransitive Verb?"[22] White seems to pull back somewhat from radical constructivism and an "endowment" or projective theory of meaning involving the idea that a historian could choose to plot any series of (inherently meaningless or chaotic) events with any given plot structure or mode. He continues to assert that "narrative accounts do not consist only of factual statements (singular existential propositions) and arguments; they consist also of poetic and rhetorical elements by which *what would otherwise be a list of facts is transformed into a story* [my emphasis]." Furthermore, "this raises the question of the relation of the various generic plot types that can be used to endow events with different kinds of meaning—tragic, epic, comic, romance, pastoral, farcical, and the like—to the events themselves" (39). White also asserts: "We can confidently presume that the facts of the matter set limits on the *kinds* of stories that can *properly* (in the sense of both veraciously and appropriately) be told about them only if we believe that the events themselves possess a 'story' kind of form and a 'plot' kind of meaning" (40).

In light of his earlier work, one might have expected White to argue that the latter presumption is untenable, whether entertained confidently or not, since plot structures are purportedly projective and fictive, perhaps politically or ideologically motivated, constructs that "endow" inherently meaningless events with meaning and structure. In the terms he borrowed from Sartre's *Nausea,* life (or reality) as lived is inherently chaotic or meaningless—one damned thing after another—and it is transformed retrospectively into a meaningful story only when told in a narrative. A lived story or a life with a determinate ("plotted") meaning, much less a true story, simply becomes a contradiction in terms. The reader might well do a double-take when White, contrary to expectations, writes: "In the case of an emplotment of the events of the Third Reich in a 'comic' or 'pastoral' mode, we would

22. Included with a discussion in *The Structuralist Controversy: The Languages of Criticism and the Sciences of Man,* ed. Richard Macksey and Eugenio Donato (Baltimore: Johns Hopkins Press, 1970), 134–56.

be eminently justified in appealing to 'the facts' in order to dismiss it from the lists of 'competing narratives' of the Third Reich" (40). White goes on to make an exception for an ironic, metacritical twist on a comic or pastoral story, but how he is able to put forward the earlier dismissal as "eminently justified" is puzzling in terms of his earlier postulates. I would add that the possibility is not purely hypothetical, for some attempts to normalize the Nazi period rely on nostalgic, pastoral forms, as is the case, for example, in Edgar Reitz's monumental docudrama *Heimat*. In it a pastoral evocation of life in the provinces both airbrushes the Third Reich and marginalizes its treatment of the Jews.[23]

In responding to White's essay, Martin Jay exclaimed: "In his anxiety to avoid inclusion in the ranks of those who argue for a kind of relativistic 'anything goes,' which might provide ammunition for revisionist skeptics about the existence of the Holocaust, [White] undercuts what is most powerful in his celebrated critique of naive historical realism."[24] The problem encountered by White is not, however, unique to his treatment of the Holocaust. One might argue that the Holocaust raises in an accentuated form problems that arise with respect to other series of events, especially other extreme, traumatic series of events that are of particular concern at present because they

---

23. See the excellent discussion of Reitz in Eric Santner, *Stranded Objects: Mourning, Melancholia, and Film in Postwar Germany* (Ithaca: Cornell University Press, 1990).

24. "Of Plots, Witnesses, and Judgments," in Friedlander, *Probing the Limits of Representation*, 97. A further question is whether the writer of fiction, in contrast to the historian, may assume the victim's voice. I think that when this happens in an unmediated manner (for example, through identification) one tends to have confessional literature or perhaps the dubious *faux mémoire*, whose literary qualities are quite limited. (Insofar as a text is taken as the expression of the actual victim's voice, notably as memoir, one may be inhibited from a rigorous critical examination of its literary qualities, an inhibition evident in the treatment of Elie Wiesel's *Night* or, at first, of Binjamin Wilkormirski's *Fragments: Memories of a Wartime Childhood*, which I discuss later. In the case of a text written by a victim, this inhibition, which probably exists only for a time, may be partially defended in that it places the reader in a double bind between the desire to criticize and the fear of its inappropriateness—a bind analogous in some small way to that in which victims were placed by their experiences.) By contrast, in more significant literature, the relation of the author to the victim and the victim's voice is mediated and stylistically qualified, for example, by embodying the victim's voice in narrators or characters as well as in modulations of free indirect style.

are highly "cathected" or invested with affect and considerations of value. As I indicated earlier, one such problem is the manner in which truth claims are at issue not only on the level of statements referring to events but on structural levels such as narrative plots, interpretations, and explanations.

I have alluded to the particularly difficult and knotty twist in White's argument represented by his appeal to the middle voice, which he takes as the appropriate way to "write" trauma. Modern languages do not have a middle voice in grammar but may at best allow for a discursive analogue of it. Barthes sees as a primary task of modern writing the attempt to recuperate discursively what has been lost grammatically by working or playing out a middle-voiced alternative to the active and passive voices. White, however, tends to conflate the middle voice with intransitive writing and to ignore the question mark in Barthes's title. Still, one may distinguish two movements in Barthes's essay itself which White tends to follow. The first is to take writing as intransitive or to see it as self-referential, thereby bracketing the question of reference and focusing exclusively on the relation of speaker and discourse (or signifier and signified). Thus Barthes writes: "Modern literature is trying, through various experiments, to establish a new status in writing for the agent of writing. The meaning or the goal of this effort is to substitute the instance of discourse for the instance of reality (or of the referent), which has been, and still is, a mythical 'alibi' dominating the idea of literature" (144). This formulation, which enjoins bracketing the referential function of language, is dubious with respect to historiography, which involves referential statements and truth claims, and I have indicated that I think it would even be questionable, in certain respects, for fiction and, more generally, literature and art.[25]

The second tendency in Barthes is different, for it situates the

25. White does not comment on the fact that, while Barthes postulates a homology between the sentence and discourse, thus taking linguistics as an adequate model for discourse analysis, White himself asserts a dichotomy between the referential sentence in historiography and narrative structure. I would argue that both moves are deceptive and that the relation between the sentence and discourse is more complex and warrants differential analysis.

middle voice not as homologous with intransitive or self-referential writing but as undecidable with respect to the opposition between the transitive and the intransitive. As Barthes succinctly puts it, "we place ourselves at the very heart of a problematic of *inter*locution" (144). In this sense the middle voice, as White suggests, would enact the play of Derridian *différance*—play resisting seemingly dichotomous binary opposites (such as transitive and intransitive, active and passive, past and present, or masculine and feminine) that effect something like a dubiously purifying, scapegoating process and repress an anxiety-ridden middle area of undecidability as well as the manner in which seeming opposites displace and internally mark each other. The middle voice would thus be the "in-between" voice of undecidability and the unavailability or radical ambivalence of clear-cut positions. It might, of course, also be seen as the voice Heidegger seeks in his "step back" from the history of metaphysics in a thinking that recalls more "originary" possibilities.[26]

Barthes himself relates the middle voice to the problem of the relation between the present and the past, notably in terms of one's relation as speaker to one's discourse in the present in contradistinction to one's account of a past discourse or phenomenon. More precisely, he appeals to Benveniste's argument that many languages "have a double system of time. The first temporal system is that of the discourse itself, which is adapted to the temporality of the speaker [*énonciateur*] and for which the *énonciation* [speech act—DLC] is always the point of origin [*moment générateur*]. The second is the system of history or narrative, which is adapted to the recounting of past events without any intervention by the speaker and which is consequently deprived of present and future (except periphrastically)" (137).

As Derrida notes in his intervention, the distinction as posited by Barthes seems to function as a misleading binary opposition and, I would add, applies as such, in a manner open to criticism, only to a

26. For an interesting discussion of the middle voice in Derrida and Heidegger which came to my attention after I wrote this chapter, see Thomas Pepper, *Singularities: Extremes of Theory in the Twentieth Century* (Cambridge: Cambridge University Press, 1997), chap. 2.

self-sufficient research paradigm in positivistic form.[27] I would further note that the deconstruction of binary oppositions does not automatically entail the blurring of all distinctions. In resisting the latter tendency, one may argue that deconstruction and undecidability, in casting doubt on binaries, raise the related issues of both the actual (often very important) role of binary oppositions in empirical reality (an issue demanding research) and the elaboration of nonbinary distinctions as well the attribution to them of relative strength or weakness in fact and in right. In this sense distinctions are articulations (at times related to institutions) that counteract the "free" play of *différance* (or dissemination) and more or less problematically bind it by generating limits that resist that play in its unregulated form. They are to thought what judgments and decisions are to evaluation and practice.

I would make a correlation that will be significant in my later argument—a correlation that indicates the desirability of relating deconstructive and psychoanalytic concepts. I would argue, or at least suggest, that undecidability and unregulated *différance,* threatening to disarticulate relations, confuse self and other, and collapse all distinctions, including that between present and past, are related to transference and prevail in trauma and in post-traumatic acting out in which one is haunted or possessed by the past and performatively caught up in the compulsive repetition of traumatic scenes—scenes in which the past returns and the future is blocked or fatalistically caught up in a melancholic feedback loop. In acting out, tenses implode, and it is as if one were back there in the past reliving the traumatic scene. Any duality (or double inscription) of time (past and present or future) is experientially collapsed or productive only of aporias and double binds. In this sense, the aporia and the double bind might be seen as marking a trauma that has not been worked through. Working

27. Derrida questioned Barthes's opposition particularly with respect to a notion of the full presence of discursive time unmarked by the past, and he asserted that "the distinction between discursive time and historical time becomes fragile, perhaps" (155). I later argue that the problematic, perhaps fragile, distinction between discursive and historical time, or between present and past, is nonetheless especially significant with respect to acting out and working through. This distinction, of course, does not deny that the present is marked by the past and, in certain ways, haunted by revenants.

through is an articulatory practice: to the extent one works through trauma (as well as transferential relations in general), one is able to distinguish between past and present and to recall in memory that something happened to one (or one's people) back then while realizing that one is living here and now with openings to the future. This does not imply either that there is a pure opposition between past and present or that acting out—whether for the traumatized or for those empathetically relating to them—can be fully transcended toward a state of closure or full ego identity. But it does mean that processes of working through may counteract the force of acting out and the repetition compulsion. These processes of working through, including mourning and modes of critical thought and practice, involve the possibility of making distinctions or developing articulations that are recognized as problematic but still function as limits and as possibly desirable resistances to undecidability, particularly when the latter is tantamount to confusion and the obliteration or blurring of all distinctions (states that may indeed occur in trauma or in acting out post-traumatic conditions).[28]

Those traumatized by extreme events, as well as those empathizing with them, may resist working through because of what might almost be termed a fidelity to trauma, a feeling that one must somehow keep faith with it. Part of this feeling may be the melancholic sentiment that, in working through the past in a manner that enables survival or a reengagement in life, one is betraying those who were overwhelmed and consumed by that traumatic past. One's bond with the dead, especially with dead intimates, may invest trauma with value and make its reliving a painful but necessary commemoration or memorial to which one remains dedicated or at least bound. This situation may

28. One may also correlate acting out and working through with Walter Benjamin's notions of *Erlebnis* and *Erfahrung*—at least if these concepts are understood in a certain way. Trauma and its post-traumatic acting act, reliving, or reenactment are modes of *Erlebnis*—"experience" that is often radically disorienting and chaotic. Working through is a mode of *Erfahrung* which need not be seen in stereotypically Hegelian terms as implying full dialectical transcendence or narrative closure.

create a more or less unconscious desire to remain within trauma. It certainly invalidates any form of conceptual or narrative closure, and it may also generate resistances to the role of any counterforces, for example, those involved in mourning understood not simply as isolated grieving or endless bereavement but as a social process that may be at least partly effective in returning one to the demands and responsibilities of social life. Moreover, on a somewhat different level, there has been an important tendency in modern culture and thought to convert trauma into the occasion for sublimity, to transvalue it into a test of the self or the group and an entry into the extraordinary. In the sublime, the excess of trauma becomes an uncanny source of elation or ecstasy. Even extremely destructive and disorienting events, such as the Holocaust or the dropping of atomic bombs on Hiroshima and Nagasaki, may become occasions of negative sublimity or displaced sacralization. They may also give rise to what may be termed founding traumas—traumas that paradoxically become the valorized or intensely cathected basis of identity for an individual or a group rather than events that pose the problematic question of identity.

Various modes of signification provide relatively safe havens for exploring the complex relations between acting out and working through trauma. Some of the most powerful forms of modern art and writing, as well as some of the most compelling forms of criticism (including forms of deconstruction), often seem to be traumatic writing or post-traumatic writing in closest proximity to trauma. They may also involve the feeling of keeping faith with trauma in a manner that leads to a compulsive preoccupation with aporia, an endlessly melancholic, impossible mourning, and a resistance to working through. I think one is involved here in more or less secularized displacements of the sacred and its paradoxes. The hiddenness, death, or absence of a radically transcendent divinity or of absolute foundations makes of existence a fundamentally traumatic scene in which anxiety threatens to color, and perhaps confuse, all relations. One's relation to every other—instead of involving a tense, at times paradoxical, interaction of proximity and distance, solidarity and criticism, trust and wariness—

may be figured on the model of one's anxiety-ridden "relation without relation" to a radically transcendent (now perhaps recognized as absent) divinity who is totally other. This is, of course, precisely the situation of everyone as described in Derrida's *Gift of Death*.[29]

Sacrifice—what Derrida discusses as the gift of death—is a mode of performatively reenacting traumatic scenes in which victimization is combined with oblation or gift giving (typically with the victim as the gift), a type of activity which, in its undisplaced or unsublimated form, involves actual killing.[30] Derrida stresses the excess of generosity or gift giving and elides the problem of the victim in *The Gift of Death*. But disseminatory writing, as a supplement of the deconstruction of binaries which undercuts the basis of a scapegoating process, might be seen as a symbolic displacement of sacrifice which distributes the disarticulated, torn-apart, or fragmented self in a radically decentered discourse, perhaps in the hope of symbolically playing out a sacrificial process devoid of a differentiated, discriminated-against scapegoat or victim. The deconstruction of binary oppositions that subtend and are regenerated in sacrifice would thus be supplemented by their general displacement and the attempt to undo sacrifice, requiring a discrete victim—an attempt made in and through disseminatory writing that generalizes (rather than projectively localizing) anxiety, enacts (in the dual sense of both acting out and in part working through) transference, and scatters seeds of the self in signifying practices. Open to

29. Jacques Derrida, *Gift of Death*, trans. David Wells (1992; Chicago: University of Chicago Press, 1995).

30. Sacrifice itself can be seen as a relatively safe haven only on the problematic assumption that the institution of sacrifice, by localizing anxiety and projecting blame onto a particular victim—a scapegoat who is often an outsider to the community or one of its weak members not having the support of a potentially vengeful group—functions to limit a more generalized sacrificial crisis involving indiscriminate violence. Yet the scapegoating in sacrifice is bound up with binary oppositions (self and other, insider and outsider) that, in their putatively pure form, can become extremely unstable, as "suspect" insiders are projected to the outside and violence returns to characterize relations within the community that seemed to protect itself by selecting a discrete victim or set of victims. On these problems, compare the views of René Girard, *Violence and the Sacred*, trans. Patrick Gregory (1972; Baltimore: Johns Hopkins University Press, 1977) and *Things Hidden since the Foundation of the World*, trans. Stephen Bann and Michael Metteer (1978; Stanford: Stanford University Press, 1987).

question is the manner in which this process may be related to the elaboration of problematic but nonarbitrary distinctions, judgments, and decisions required for responsible thought and practice as well as to the generation of alternative institutions necessary for an ongoing society and polity.

In any case, it is significant that in his primary "performative" example of the middle voice as distinguished from the active voice, Barthes himself invokes sacrifice, something White mentions without commentary in a footnote. Barthes writes (and here writing may, in a rather analytic, affectless manner, seem to be implicated in traumatization and to displace sacrifice):

> According to the classic example, given by Meillet and Benveniste, the verb *to sacrifice* (ritually) is active if the priest sacrifices the victim in my place for me, and it is middle voice if, taking the knife from the priest's hands, I make the sacrifice for myself. In the case of the active, the action is accomplished outside the subject, because, although the priest makes the sacrifice, he is not affected by it. In the case of the middle voice, on the contrary, the subject affects himself in acting; he always remains inside the action, even if an object is involved. The middle voice does not, therefore, exclude transitivity. Thus defined, the middle voice corresponds exactly to the state of the verb *to write.* (142)

Hayden White proposes the middle voice in undifferentiated terms as the proper way of representing the Holocaust. In a seeming performative contradiction, he even writes that the middle voice is the way to represent realistically not only the Holocaust but modern experience in general:

> The best way to represent the Holocaust and the experience of it may well be by a kind of "intransitive writing" which lays no claim to the kind of realism aspired to by the nineteenth-century historians and writers. But we may want to consider that by intransitive writing we must intend something like the relationship to that event expressed in the middle voice. This is not to suggest that we will give up the effort to represent the Holocaust realistically, but rather that our notion of what constitutes realistic representation must be revised to take account of experiences that are unique to

our century and for which older modes of representation have proven inadequate. (52)

Notions of uniqueness aside, perhaps the most generous way to interpret this passage is to see in it both an attempt to evoke the question of truth claims in historiography (as well as in fiction) and a call for a traumatic realism that somehow attempts to come to terms, affectively and cognitively, with limit experiences involving trauma and its aftereffects. What nonetheless remains questionable is White's indiscriminate affirmation of the middle voice as the only mode of representation suitable for the Holocaust and modernity in general, an affirmation that would seem to prescribe an insufficiently modulated rhetoric or mode of discourse and rule out or undermine the pertinence of third-person referential statements, direct quotations, and summaries or paraphrases. One may even ask in what sense it is possible to make truth claims in the middle voice and to what extent that question is suspended by its use. In any case, without further qualification, White's generalized middle voice would seem to imply a basically similar or at least insufficiently differentiated treatment of Hitler, Jewish Councils, victims of concentration and death camps, and others in significantly different subject positions.

What is also elided in White's account, as in Barthes's (or in Derrida's *Gift of Death*), is the problem of the victim and the force of the distinction between victim and perpetrator. A rashly generalized middle voice would seem to undercut or undo systematically not only the binary opposition but any distinction, however problematic in certain cases, between victim and perpetrator, as it would seem to undercut the problems of agency and responsibility in general (except insofar as one is willing to identify responsibility with decisionism or an ungrounded, if not blind, leap of faith). Moreover, it would accord with White's dubious tendency to envision the Holocaust as an undifferentiated scene of horror and negative sublimity, a scene beneath or beyond ethical considerations and calling for representation in the middle voice. What would seem to be required (but lacking in White) is an account of relations of the middle voice to other uses of language as well as a subtle exploration of actual and desirable modulations of the middle voice itself in discourse addressing various, at times very different, topics or others.

One may further note that White's approach is facilitated, and its dubiousness concealed, by something implicit in Barthes's account and made explicit, but not recognized as dubious, in White's. The problem of the victim and the distinction between victim and perpetrator (or sacrificer) may be readily elided or obscured if one assumes the unproblematic identification of perpetrator and victim—or at least of observer or secondary witness and victim.[31] This identification is most plausible in the case of self-sacrifice. It is altogether dubious in the case of the sacrifice of another, whatever the bond between the sacrificer and sacrificed or between the sacrificed and the secondary witness. It is noteworthy that White cites as a case of middle voice Berel Lang's example, which (at least in White's rendering) involves unproblematic identification: "Lang explicitly commends intransitive writing (and speech) as appropriate to individual Jews who, as in the recounting of the story of the Exodus at Passover, 'should tell the story of the genocide as though he or she had passed through it' and in an exercise of self-identification specifically Jewish in nature" (48). I would observe that this form of identification is not specific to Jews. In fact, it has been criticized by some Jews—one may recall the title of Hilberg's article from which I quoted earlier: "I Was Not There." And the analogy between the Holocaust and ritual recounting

31. By identification I mean the unmediated fusion of self and other in which the otherness or alterity of the other is not recognized and respected. It may involve what Melanie Klein treats as projective identification, in which aspects not acknowledged in the self are attributed to the other. It may also involve incorporation, in which aspects of the other are taken into or encrypted in the self. Projective identification and incorporation may be necessary and inevitable processes in the relation of self and other—processes bound up with transference which are both particularly active with respect to highly "cathected" objects and especially pronounced in trauma and its aftermath. But counterforces to projective identification and incorporation may be generated in the self and society, and such counterforces are crucial for critical processes of inquiry, judgment, and practice. Moreover, empathy may be contrasted with identification (as fusion with the other) insofar as empathy marks the point at which the other is indeed recognized and respected as other, and one does not feel compelled or authorized to speak in the other's voice or take the other's place, for example, as surrogate victim or perpetrator.

of the Exodus at Passover would seem pertinent only within a frame of reference that uncritically makes the Holocaust the sacralized center of a civil religion.[32]

Unchecked identification implies a confusion of self and other which may bring an incorporation of the experience and voice of the victim and its reenactment or acting out. As in acting out in general, one possessed, however vicariously, by the past and reliving its traumatic scenes may be tragically incapable of acting responsibly or behaving in an ethical manner involving consideration for others as others. One need not blame the victim possessed by the past and unable to get beyond it to any viable extent in order to question the idea that it is desirable to identify with this victim, or to become a surrogate victim, and to write (or perform) in that incorporated voice. At least in its ability to question a rash generalization of the middle voice as a mode of writing or representation, Jean-Pierre Vernant's intervention after the delivery of Barthes's essay is worth quoting:

> [The middle voice designates] the type of action where the agent remains enveloped in the released action. Barthes considers that this furnishes a metaphorical model for the present state of writing. Then I would ask, is it by accident that the middle voice disappeared in the evolution of Indo-European? Already in ancient Greece the opposition was no longer situated between the active and the middle voice but between the active and the passive voice, so that the middle voice became a sort of vestige with which linguists wondered what to do. . . . In thought as expressed in Greek or ancient Indo-European there is no idea of the agent being the *source* of his action. Or, if I may translate that, as a historian of Greek civilization, there is no category of the *will* in Greece. But what we see in the Western world, through language, the evolution of law, the creation of a vocabulary of the will, is precisely the idea of the human subject as agent, the source of actions, creating them, assuming them, carrying responsibility for them. Therefore, what I

---

32. On these issues, see Charles Maier, "A Surfeit of Memory?: Reflections on History, Melancholy, and Denial," *History and Memory* 5 (1992): 136–51; Anson Rabinbach, "From Explosion to Erosion: Holocaust Memorialization in America since Bitburg," *History and Memory* 9 (1997): 226–55; and Peter Novick, *The Holocaust in American Life* (Boston: Houghton Mifflin, 1999).

ask you, Barthes, is this: Are we seeing, in the literary domain, a complete reversal of this evolution and do you believe that we are going to see, on the literary level, the reappearance of the middle voice in the linguistic domain? (152)

One may refer to the text for Barthes's answer, which I do not believe is up to the question (however contestable some of the latter's features may be).[33] Vernant's question suggests the manner in which the middle voice and issues connected with it may be further related to the way the Heideggerian "step back" (at times figured as a recourse to the pre-Socratic) converts the seemingly vestigial middle voice into a returning repressed, eventuates in a mode of discourse which, in insistently remaining undecidable, is suspicious of will as the most recent avatar of the metaphysical foundation, and simultaneously undercuts ethical discourse as superficial with respect to the call of Being (a call presumably to be answered in some discursive or poetic variant that recalls the middle voice). The larger question, as I suggested, is that of the possibilities and limits of the middle voice with respect to a wide range of issues, including the legitimate role of distinctions and the problems of agency and ethical responsibility, including the ability to distinguish among accounts that are more or less true as well as among degrees of responsibility or liability in action.

In a sense one's response to the role of the middle voice may be intimately bound up with one's response to reenacting or acting out trauma in relation to attempts to work it through. In my own tentative judgment, the use in historiography of some discursive analogue of the middle voice might be most justified with respect to one's most tangled and difficult relations of proximity and distance with regard to the other, notably when one is moved, even shaken or unsettled, in

33. Vernant seems to have an unproblematic notion of the agent as creative source of his or her action as well as of the will as a category. I would further note that the free indirect style (or *Erlebte Rede*) is one more or less guarded mode of returning discursively to the middle voice. It is, in my judgment, an internally dialogized mode of discourse involving varying degrees of proximity and distance—not necessarily identification—between narrator and narrated objects or characters, and it approaches undecidability at the limit. I also think there are problems in its indiscriminate use or rash generalization. For a discussion of free indirect style, see my *"Madame Bovary" on Trial*, chap. 6.

such a manner that one is unable or unwilling to judge or even to predicate with any degree of confidence. Hence something like a middle voice that suspended judgment or approached it only in the most tentative terms might be called for with respect to ambiguous figures in Primo Levi's gray zone, for example, certain well-intentioned but deceived and at times self-deceived members of Jewish Councils (such as Adam Czerniakow of the Warsaw Ghetto) who were indeed caught in double binds not of their own making.[34] It might also be pertinent—and extremely difficult of attainment—in the case of certain victims who were also perpetrators, notably someone like Tadeusz Borowski, who reacted to his experience in an excruciating, unsettling manner both demanding and repelling the empathy of the reader.[35] The fate of certain victims in even more dire and less compromising circumstances is often such that it makes the use of any voice problematic for the historian, notably including a voice that enacts identification. In any event, the use of the middle voice would require modulations of proximity and distance, empathy and irony with respect to different "objects" of investigation, and it need not be understood as ruling out all forms of objectivity and objectification.

In yet another, more affirmative register, there is a sense in which the middle voice may be related to an unheard-of utopia of generosity or gift giving beyond, or in excess of, calculation, positions, judgment, and victimization of the other. It may also exceed both delimited conceptions of justice and historiography in any form we would now recognize. The question is whether one can immediately leap to that utopia discursively (even deny that it is a utopia) or, assuming at least its partial value, whether it has to be approached or approximated in a different, more modulated and qualified fashion requiring the countervailing force of normative limits and the role of critical thought and practice. In realistic terms, the further question is whether or to what

34. Levi recommends caution in judgment even with respect to the very compromised Chaim Rumkowski, whose story "sums up in itself the entire theme of the gray zone and leaves one dangling." (1986; *The Drowned and the Saved* [New York: Random House, 1989], 66–67).

35. See *This Way for the Gas, Ladies and Gentlemen,* selected and trans. Barbara Vedder, intro. Jan Kott (1959; New York: Penguin Books, 1976).

extent the unqualified enactment of what strives to be an affirmative middle-voiced (a)positionality attests to, or even furthers, a movement away from a binary, sacrificial logic and any totalizing belief that a regulative ideal (such as justice) may be fully realized (a movement that is in my judgment desirable) toward a problematic condition of social emergency or crisis marked by the generalization of trauma as trope, arbitrary decision (or leaps of secular faith across antinomic or anomic abysses), extreme anxiety, and disorientation, if not panic. It is unclear whether discourse in the middle voice, particularly when it is not supplemented and checked by other uses of language, is able to provide viable indications of desirable social and cultural articulations, including institutions and practices, other than in the generalized terms of a state of crisis or excess and open-ended hope (or messianicity without a messiah) that may induce indiscriminate hyperbole and undecidability (as well as a "contagiously" manneristic style at times verging on preciosity) in the face of proliferating aporias or double binds.[36] In any case, to the extent that the notion of a discursive analogue of the middle voice does indeed harbor an affirma-

36. Derrida himself rejects the applicability of the notion of "utopianism" to his thought with respect to "messianicity" (even to the point of seemingly denying in this crucial instance the displacement of the religious in the secular). However, he does so in questionable terms that might be read as affirming utopianism in another, "here-now" sense: "Messianicity (which I regard as a universal structure of experience, and which cannot be reduced to religious messianism of any stripe) is anything but Utopian: it refers, in every here-now, to the coming of an eminently real, concrete event, that is, to the most irreducibly heterogeneous otherness. Nothing is more 'realistic' or 'immediate' than this messianic apprehension, straining forward toward the event of him who/that which is coming. I say 'apprehension,' because this experience, strained forward toward the event, is at the same time a waiting without expectation [*une attente sans attente*] (an active preparation, anticipation against the backdrop of a horizon, but also exposure without horizon, and therefore an irreducible amalgam of desire and anguish, affirmation and fear, promise and threat). . . . This is an ineluctability whose imperative, always here-now, in singular fashion, can in no case yield to the allure of Utopia, at least not to what the word literally signifies or is ordinarily taken to mean." "Marx and Sons," in *Ghostly Demarcations: A Symposium on Jacques Derrida's Specters of Marx,* ed. Michael Sprinker (London: Verso, 1999), 248–49. The question, however, is the role of thought and practice in transitional or intermediate zones that fall neither at the extreme of universality nor at that of singularity (or "the most irreducibly heterogeneous otherness") as well as whether Derrida, especially in his more recent work ostensibly concerned with social and political issues, devotes to it the sustained attention it merits.

tive or even utopian dimension, it would be desirable to explicate that dimension as clearly and fully as possible in order to facilitate informed attempts to evaluate it and submit it critically to reality testing without which affirmation becomes empty and utopianism is tantamount to wishful thinking.[37]

Without prejudging other possibilities, I would like to evoke a recent case in which the middle voice and undecidability are at issue in a particularly troubling and dubious manner. I am referring to Binjamin Wilkomirski's *Fragments: Memories of a Wartime Childhood.*[38] First thought to be the memoir of a child survivor of a concentration camp, the book has been called into question in that its author may never have been in a camp—indeed, may have been born not in 1938 in Latvia but in 1941 in Switzerland. Problems of Holocaust denial and recovered memory make this case particularly controversial. And recent revelations concerning the retention and concealment of victims' wealth in Swiss banks have made Switzerland an object of special scrutiny.

I would enumerate at least four possibilities in the writing and reading of Wilkomirski's book. First, one may take it as a memoir, and this is the way it frames itself. It contains certain skeptical notes that may be read retrospectively to raise the question of whether the book at rare moments signals its fictionality, for example, the narrator's confused memories ("I was maybe ten or twelve, I just don't know" [139]) or the statement—ironic in different ways before and after the

37. See the rather utopian, "deconstructive" approach to the "other" and trust in Derek Attridge, "Innovation, Literature, Ethics: Relating to the Other," *PMLA* 114 (1999): 20–31 (special issue, *Ethics and Literary Study,* ed. Lawrence Buell). Attridge tries to combine the notion (derived from Derrida and Levinas) that every other is totally other with an affirmation of total trust in that other, who is an unknown stranger and may be a "monster." His argument includes the idea that responsibility for the other is not obligation, nor is it codified in any way: instead it is total openness and trust. This idea of trust seems devoid of all reality testing and is other-worldly in the sense that it would require a total transformation of historical conditions to enable one to distinguish it from utter gullibility. The context of German-Jewish relations in the Shoah casts an especially uncanny light on Attridge's argument. (The issue of *PMLA* in which Attridge's essay appears includes an interesting set of instances of the state of reflection on ethics in literary studies today.)

38. Binjamin Wilkomirski, *Fragments: Memories of a Wartime Childhood,* trans. Carol Brown Janeway (1995; New York: Schocken Books, 1996).

charges of imposture—that, in Switzerland, "everyone keeps saying I'm to forget, that it never happened, I only dreamed it" (129). But the doubts could readily be attributed to the confusion and disarray of a traumatized child from whose perspective the book is written. And certain events recounted in the book (such as tiny babies eating their own frozen fingers down to the bone [70–71]) may be seen with twenty-twenty hindsight as implausible. Still, what is plausible or implausible in events of the Holocaust is notoriously difficult to determine. And the book was initially accepted by many Holocaust experts and even by survivors and former hidden children (such as Saul Friedlander, who is an author of a memoir concerning his own childhood experiences). The book was obviously taken as authentic by those who granted it numerous awards, including the Jewish Book Award and the Prix de la Mémoire de la Shoah. The back cover of the paperback edition includes quotations from reviews that indicate how it was read. Jonathan Kozol wrote in the *Nation:* "This stunning and austerely written work is so profoundly moving, so morally important, and so free from literary artifice of any kind at all that I wonder if I even have the right to try to offer praise." And the blurb states unequivocally: "An extraordinary memoir of a small boy who spent his childhood in the Nazi death camps. Beautifully written, with an indelible impact that makes this a book that is not read but experienced." Indeed, the passionate nature (but certainly not the existence or even the strength) of the negative reaction to the disclosure of Wilkomirski's possible, if not probable, imposture is related to the initial widespread acceptance of the book as a genuine memoir and the feeling of trust betrayed in the event it is not.

Second, one may take the book as fiction, but, as I have noted, this is not the way it is framed or presents itself. If it were explicitly framed as fiction, one might marvel at its ability to evoke certain feelings and states of mind in a remarkably empathetic fashion (although, once it is removed from actual experience of life in the camps, one might also see the book not as "austerely written" but at least at times as somewhat overwritten). Still, one might understand it as involving truth claims not in terms of certain individual statements (such as those involving the identity of the author-narrator) but on more general levels, for example, with respect to how children in the camps might well have experienced certain events.

Third, one may take the book as a pathological case history of someone who may actually imagine or believe he was in a concentration camp as a child even if he was not. This reading might conceivably be justified, but it could easily function to eliminate disconcerting questions raised by the relation of the book to history and fiction. (Briefly put, my own view here is that one should have empathy for the author but provide criticism of the book as it bears on the public sphere—a distinction easily collapsed in a "clinical" approach to problems.)

Fourth, one can simply moot or bracket the question of the book's author or the status of his experience and see the text as undecidable with respect to its status as fiction or memoir. One might then analyze it either along with other works of fiction or with other memoirs. (Or perhaps one might see it as belonging to an emerging hybridized genre: the *faux mémoire*.) This as-you-like-it response seems to be recommended by Wilkomirski himself, who stated in an interview: "It was always left freely up to readers to regard my book either as literature or as a personal document."[39]

But this affirmation of the undecidability of the text which leaves any decision or choice concerning its status up to the reader does not seem acceptable, and it may well be that some hybrids (such as the *faux mémoire*) are, in certain instances, undesirable. Indeed, Wilkomirski's is a case in which the appeal to undecidability seems inappropriate even if one were to claim that Wilkomirski was traumatized in a displaced or secondary manner by events of the Holocaust (or, as may be suggested at one point in the narrative, by a documentary film about it [148]) and wrote his book while reliving an imaginary or phantasmatic past he had never experienced in historical reality.[40]

My own views have partially emerged in my discussion and critique

39. Quoted in *Newsweek*, November 16, 1998, 84.
40. After I completed this chapter, there appeared Ellen Lappin's "The Man with Two Heads," *Granta* 66 (1999): 7–65, whose extensive analysis of Wilkomirski and his book may be compared with the brief one I offer.

of others. Since I have written extensively on them in other places, I shall be brief in stating them in condensed form here. I would begin by noting that the position I defend puts forth a conception of history as tensely involving both an objective (not objectivist) reconstruction of the past and a dialogic exchange with it and other inquirers into it wherein knowledge involves not only the processing of information but also affect, empathy, and questions of value.[41] This third position is not a straightforward dialectical synthesis of the other two, for it involves a critical and self-critical component that resists closure. Moreover, it does not simply eliminate hyperbole for a middling or *juste-milieu* reasonableness, if not complacency. It involves the recognition of the possibly thought-provoking and fruitful role of hyperbole in emphasizing what one believes is given insufficient weight at a given time in the ongoing attempt to articulate possibilities in a discipline or in the broader culture. (In this sense it may be justifiable, at a certain point in the history of historiography, to stress the role of rhetoric and performativity insofar as they are indeed largely ignored or downplayed and one does not see them as the exclusive generative or self-referential basis of a conception of the past.)[42] There may even be a legitimate role for polemic and parody as dialogic modes in a larger contest or agon of points of view or discourses. Hyperbole enacts stylistically the fact that one is affected by excess and trauma, but one can be excessive in many ways, prominently including a penchant for blandly generalized, unearned judiciousness that harmonizes problems and may even signal a numbing insensitivity to their import and implications. Still, the position I am defending does not entail a simple insertion within, or unrestrained enactment or acting-out of, hyperbole and excess. Instead it affirms the value of a difficultly achieved interaction between limits and excess, including the idea that

41. For the importance of self-contextualization of the historian in a contemporary context of exchange and debate with other inquirers, see my *Representing the Holocaust: History, Theory, Trauma* (Ithaca: Cornell University Press, 1994), chap. 3.

42. In this respect, see my "Rhetoric and History," in *History and Criticism*, 15–44. The argument there should be seen as complementing and supplementing the approach I develop in the present chapter. It should not be conflated with the radically constructivist positions taken by Hayden White or Frank Ankersmit.

hyperbole should in certain ways be framed as hyperbole (hence to some extent limited) and distinguished from other modes of address—including more understated and balanced ones—which may be called for in certain situations.

Truth claims are at issue in differential ways at all levels of historical discourse. But the writings of Ankersmit, White, and others have, I think, made it evident that one cannot affirm a conventional stereotype of transparent representation or even a self-sufficient research paradigm. I think one begins investigation already inserted in an ongoing historical process, a positioning toward which one may attempt to acquire some transformative perspective or critical purchase. A crucial aspect of this positioning is the problem of the implication of the observer in the observed, what in psychoanalytic terms is treated as transference. Indeed, there is a sense in which transference indicates that one begins inquiry in a middle-voiced "position," which one engages in various ways. In historiography there are transferential relations between inquirers (especially pronounced in the relations between professor and graduate student) and between inquirers and the past, its figures, and processes. The basic sense of transference I would stress is the tendency to repeat or reenact performatively in one's own discourse or relations processes active in the object of study. I think transference in this sense occurs willy-nilly, and the problem is how one comes to terms with it in ways involving various combinations, more or less subtle variations, and hybridized forms of acting out and working through.

As I have intimated, the question of experience (to which several historians have recently turned) is important in these respects—but experience not as an uncritically invoked, foundational concept or as an undifferentiated ground of historiography.[43] Rather, one has a se-

---

43. For some caveats about the concept of experience, see my "History, Language, and Reading," 822–24. In his diary entry for April 25, 1937, Victor Klemperer makes this chilling observation: "An always recurring word: 'Experience.' Whenever some Gauleiter or SS leader, one of the minor and most minor subordinate gods speaks, then one does not hear his speech, but "experiences" it. Eva [Klemperer's non-Jewish wife] rightly says it was already there before National Socialism. Certainly, it is to be found in the currents that

ries of interrelated problems involving the question of experience. For example, what is the relation between experience and nonexperiential aspects of history such as demographic movements, price fluctuations, and objectified structural processes in general? How may one criticize a methodology focused only on objectified processes or employing only objectified modes of representation yet raise the question of objectivity in a postpositivist and postdeconstructive way?[44] What is the relation between the differentiated experience of agents or subjects in the past and the differentiated experience of observers or secondary witnesses, including historians in one of their roles, in a present marked in complicated ways by that past? How does one relate actual and imaginary or virtual experience? How is experience related to truth claims and to critical value judgments? How does trauma or traumatic "experience" disrupt experience and raise specific problems for representation and writing? What is the gap or even the abyss between historical experience and utopian projects, including that intimated in certain discursive analogues of the middle voice?[45]

I shall not pretend to answer these important questions. Rather, I would conclude by contending that the problem of experience should

created it." *I Will Bear Witness: A Diary of the Nazi Years, 1933–1941,* trans. Martin Chalmers (1995; New York: Random House, 1998), 216. Klemperer was a German Jew (converted to Protestantism) who managed to live in Dresden through various forms of oppression throughout the Third Reich, and he strongly affirmed Enlightenment values. His observation should be seen as applying to one possible, important use (or abuse) of the concept of experience. It nonetheless serves to indicate that experience should not indiscriminately be seen as positive. See also Bernard Lepetit, ed., *Les formes de l'expérience: Une autre histoire sociale* (Paris: Albin Michel, 1995), and Jacques Revel, ed., *Jeux d'échelles: La micro-analyse à l'expérience* (Paris: Gallimard-Le Seuil, 1996). The turn to microhistory involves a concern for a history of experience, notably in figures such as Carlo Ginzburg and Giovanni Levi.

44. Satya Mohanty provides insight into this question in *Literary Theory and the Claims of History* (Ithaca: Cornell University Press, 1997).

45. Compare Nietzsche: "Ultimately, nobody can get more out of things, including books, than he already knows. For what one lacks access to from experience one will have no ear. Now let us imagine an extreme case: that a book speaks of nothing but events that lie altogether beyond the possibility of any frequent or even rare experience—that it is the first language for a new series of experiences. In that case, simply nothing will be heard, but there will be the acoustic illusion that where nothing is heard, nothing is there." *Ecce Homo* ("Why I Write Such Good Books," pt. 1) in *The Genealogy of Morals and Ecce Homo,* ed. Walter Kaufmann (1967; New York: Vintage Books, 1989), 261.

lead to the question of the role of empathy in historical understanding. This question was, at least in restricted ways, important for such figures as Dilthey and Collingwood but has by and large been stricken from the historical agenda in the more recent past.[46] One reason for the eclipse of concern with empathy was the relation of the ideal of objectivity to the professionalization of historiography along with the tendency to conflate objectivity with objectification.[47] A closely related tendency, which facilitated the dismissal of empathy, was to conflate it with intuition or unproblematic identification implying the total fusion of self and other. Any attempt, however qualified, to rehabilitate a concern with empathy in historical understanding must distinguish it from these traditional conflations (as well as from patronizing sympathy). It must also critically engage professional identities or research strategies that marginalize or even eliminate the role of empathy along with dialogic exchange and affective (in contrast to

46. I employ the term *empathy* while trying to distance it from conventional or traditional associations with identification leading to a putative identity between self and other, whether through projection or incorporation. I am not employing *sympathy* both because that term has to some degree the connotation of condescension or pity (at least a superior position of the sympathizer) and because it has been commodified through its use in greeting cards and other relatively affectless or evacuated modes of expressing sorrow or fellow feeling. Moreover, *empathy* is the term that has a history both in historiography (or metahistory) and in psychoanalytic literature.

47. In *That Noble Dream* Peter Novick, in treating the role of objectivity in the historical profession, tends to replicate his sources in largely ignoring an explicit treatment of the problem of empathy, and the term does not appear in his index. Nor is Dilthey mentioned in the book. There are a few references to R. G. Collingwood. But it is significant that Collingwood's notion of historical explanation as rethinking or reexperiencing the past had little to do with affect and trauma. Collingwood praised Dilthey for conceiving of "the historian as living in his object, or rather making his object live in him." See *The Idea of History* (1946; New York: Oxford University Press, 1956), 172. But he criticized Dilthey for positivistically understanding knowledge on the model of natural scientific universals and reducing history to psychology. Collingwood's idea of historical knowledge as the reenactment of past experience in the historian's own mind was, however, largely focused on rethinking (or reawakening in the present) particular, reflective (or purposive), often rather elevated processes of deliberation such as an emperor's dealing with a certain situation or a philosopher's seeking a solution to a problem (283). Hence William Dray could plausibly be seen as taking up Collingwood's heritage in elaborating a "rational action" model of explanation explicitly linked to a libertarian metaphysical position. (See Novick, *That Noble Dream*, 397.)

narrowly cognitive) response in general. Especially open to question is a strategy of objectification and sustained ironic distance allowing only for unargued subjective asides—a strategy that both induces a denial of transferential implication in the object of study and obviates the problem of the actual and desirable interactions between self and other, including the possibilities and limits of a discursive middle voice.[48] Such an objectifying strategy may well posit or assume a radical divide between objectivity and subjectivity (as well as between research and dialogic exchange) and lead to an either/or conception of the relation between empathy and critical analysis. When this occurs, objectification may be confined to treatment of the other, and subjectivity (or even radical constructivism) attributed to contemporaries or even the historian's own self, thereby obscuring the voices of the dead and the problem of one's own subject positions, projective tendencies, and investments. The historian may even eliminate or overly alleviate the diachronic weight of the past, including the after effects of trauma, by seeing the past only in terms of contemporary uses and abuses, for example, as symbolic capital in memory politics.[49]

I think historiography involves an element of objectification, and objectification may perhaps be related to the phenomenon of numb-

48. Of the many works relying on such a strategy, I would mention only Richard J. Evans, *In Defense of History* (New York: W. W. Norton, 1997). The principal text, an objectifying, rapid survey of recent developments in historiography and metahistory, is supplemented by a section entitled "Further Reading," in which opinionated, subjective asides are adorned by a generous assortment of bouquets for some and barbs for others.

49. Such an orientation may be found even in Peter Novick's important *Holocaust in American Life,* in which—rather than being seen as possibly complementary to his concerns—the investigation of the problem of trauma, except in survivors, is "overall" seen as irrelevant in the case of Americans and opposed to a presentist, constructivist, at times debunking notion of historical understanding in terms of the uses and abuses of the Holocaust in "memory politics" (3–5). This orientation prevents Novick from elaborating a sufficiently complex and nuanced account of the transgenerational transmission of trauma (especially with respect to the children of survivors), the various (at times problematic) functions of trauma in the larger culture, and the role of empathy in historical understanding itself. Still, when detached from binarist, radically constructivist assumptions, inquiry into contemporary uses and "constructions" of the past is significant, including the constitution of the Holocaust as an identity-building icon and center of a civil religion—inquiry that Novick's book undertakes in a thought-provoking (indeed, intentionally controversial and at times debatable) manner.

ing in trauma itself. As a counterforce to numbing, empathy may be understood in terms of attending to, even trying, in limited ways, to recapture the possibly split-off, affective dimension of the experience of others. Empathy may also be seen as counteracting victimization, including self-victimization. It involves affectivity as a crucial aspect of understanding in the historian or other observer or analyst. As in trauma, numbing (objectification and splitting of object from subject, including self-as-subject from self-as-object) may function for the historian as a protective shield or preservative against unproblematic identification with the experience of others and the possibility of being traumatized by it. But objectivity should not be identified with objectivism or exclusive objectification that denies or forecloses empathy, just as empathy should not be conflated with unchecked identification, vicarious experience, and surrogate victimage. Objectivity requires checks and resistances to full identification, and this is one important function of meticulous research, contextualization, and the attempt to be as attentive as possible to the voices of others whose alterity is recognized. Empathy in this sense is a form of virtual, not vicarious, experience related to what Kaja Silverman has termed *heteropathic identification,* in which emotional response comes with respect for the other and the realization that the experience of the other is not one's own.[50]

Hence the experience, including the affective response, of the historian is at issue in a number of complicated ways with respect to understanding (or knowledge in a broad sense that includes cognition but is not limited to it). It helps to define the subject positions of the historian and may serve as an initial warrant to speak in certain voices. In discussing the Holocaust, for example, it makes a difference—at least an initial difference—whether the historian is a survivor, the child of survivors, a Jew, a Palestinian, a German or an Austrian, a child of perpetrators, someone born later, and so forth, with subtle distinctions and variations that it would take very long even to touch upon.

50. See Kaja Silverman, *The Threshold of the Visible World* (New York: Routledge, 1996).

But part of the process of inquiry, involving both research and an attempt at dialogic exchange with the past and other inquirers into it, is to work over and through initial subject positions in a manner that may enable one to write or say certain things that one would not have been able or inclined to write or say initially. Identity politics in a necessary sense may be defined in terms of subject positions and one's work with and on them. Identity politics in a dubious sense may be defined as simply repeating and further legitimating or acting out the subject positions with which one begins without subjecting them to critical testing that may either change or in certain ways validate them.

The import of my comments is that experience in relation to historical understanding should not be seen in a narrowly cognitive way that involves only a processing of information. Without diminishing the importance of research, contextualization, and objective reconstruction of the past, experience as it bears on understanding involves affect both in the observed and in the observer. Trauma is a disruptive experience that disarticulates the self and creates holes in existence; it has belated effects that are controlled only with difficulty and perhaps never fully mastered. The study of traumatic events poses especially difficult problems in representation and writing both for research and for any dialogic exchange with the past which acknowledges the claims it makes on people and relates it to the present and future. Being responsive to the traumatic experience of others, notably of victims, implies not the appropriation of their experience but what I would call empathic unsettlement, which should have stylistic effects or, more broadly, effects in writing which cannot be reduced to formulas or rules of method. (With respect to perpetrators, who may also be traumatized by their experience, I would argue that the historian should attempt to understand and explain such behavior and experience as far as possible—even recognize the unsettling possibility of such behavior and experience in him- or herself—but obviously attempt to counteract the realization of even its reduced analogues.) At the very least, empathic unsettlement poses a barrier to closure in discourse and places in jeopardy harmonizing or spiritually uplifting accounts of extreme events from which we attempt to derive reassurance or a benefit (for example, unearned confidence about the ability of the human spirit to endure any adversity with dignity and nobility).[51] The question is whether historiography in its own way may help not speciously to heal but to come to terms with the wounds and scars of the past. Such a coming-to-terms would seek knowledge whose truth claims are not one-dimensionally objectifying or narrowly cognitive but involve affect and may empathetically expose the self to an unsettlement, if not a secondary trauma, which should not be glorified or fixated upon but addressed in a manner that strives to be cognitively and ethically responsible as well as open to the challenge of utopian aspiration. Trauma brings about a dissociation of affect and representation: one disorientingly feels what one cannot represent; one numbingly represents what one cannot feel. Working through trauma involves the effort to articulate or rearticulate affect and representation in a manner that may never transcend, but may to some viable extent counteract, a reenactment, or acting out, of that disabling dissociation.

51. Anne Frank is a recent figure who has been subjected to representation that attempts to bring to the reader or viewer unearned and incongruous spiritual uplift. For a recent biography that ends in this manner, see Melissa Mueller, *Anne Frank: The Biography* (New York: Henry Holt, 1998).

2 ∎ *Trauma, Absence, Loss*

A recent conference at Yale brought together scholars, journalists, and public intellectuals working on the Holocaust or on the South African Truth and Reconciliation Commission (TRC), as well as members of the latter body. The New Haven Hotel, in which many participants stayed, had a floor that was indicated on the elevator by the initials TRC, standing for Trauma Recovery Center. At first the encounter with the acronym on the elevator created an uncanny impression, especially on recently arrived guests from South Africa. But it belatedly became evident that the TRC in the hotel had an elective affinity with the TRC at the conference. The Truth and Reconciliation Commission was in its own way a trauma recovery center. Its awe-inspiring and difficult, if not impossible, project was to provide a quasi-judicial setting in which the truth was sought and some measure of justice rendered (at least retrospectively) in a larger context in which former victims were now rulers who were trying to find ways and means of reconciling themselves with former rulers and at times with perpetrators of oppression. The TRC also provided a forum for the voices—often the suppressed, repressed, or uneasily accommodated voices—of certain victims who were being heard for the first time in the public sphere. Indeed, as a force in the public sphere the TRC itself was attempting to combine truth seeking in an open forum with a collective ritual, requiring the acknowledgment of blameworthy and at times criminal activity, in the interest of working through a past that had severely divided groups and caused damages to victims (including damages inflicted by victims on other victims). This complicated past was now to be disclosed truthfully in order for a process of working it through to be historically informed and to have some chance of being effective ritually and politically in creating both a livable society and a national collectivity. Perhaps the most salient dimension of the TRC has been its attempt to engage this collective ritual process of mourning losses in order to create conditions for a more desirable future. It might even be seen as attempting what others have repeatedly called for in postwar Germany in the 1986 Historians' Debate and again in the controversy stirred up a decade later by responses to Daniel Jonah Goldhagen's *Hitler's Willing Executioners: Ordinary Germans and the Holocaust.*[1]

I begin with this anecdote and my reflections about it in order to indicate the stakes of a distinction I would like to draw and elaborate—the distinction between absence and loss. These stakes certainly include intellectual clarity and cogency, but they also have ethical and political dimensions. Postapartheid South Africa and post-Nazi Germany face the problem of acknowledging and working through historical losses in ways that affect different groups differently. Indeed, the problem for beneficiaries of earlier oppression in both countries is

1. See Daniel Jonah Goldhagen, *Hitler's Willing Executioners: Ordinary Germans and the Holocaust* (New York: Alfred A. Knopf, 1996). On these issues, see Peter Baldwin, ed., *Reworking the Past: Hitler, the Holocaust, and the Historians' Debate* (Boston: Beacon Press, 1990), and Robert R. Shandley, ed., *Unwilling Germans?: The Goldhagen Debate* (Minneapolis: University of Minnesota Press, 1998), as well as my *Representing the Holocaust: History, Theory, Trauma* (Ithaca: Cornell University Press, 1994) and *History and Memory after Auschwitz* (Ithaca: Cornell University Press, 1998). The recent electoral successes of the right-wing populist Jörg Haider, who has been prone to make blatantly apologetic statements about Hitler and the Nazi regime, may in part be attributed to the widespread denial in Austria of the need for an effective process of coming to terms with the past.

how to recognize and mourn the losses of former victims and simultaneously to find a legitimate way to represent and mourn for their own losses without having a self-directed process occlude victims' losses or enter into an objectionable balancing of accounts (for example, in such statements as "Don't talk to us about the Holocaust unless you are going to talk about the pillage, rape, and dislocation on the eastern front caused by the Russian invasion toward the end of the war" or "Don't talk to us about the horrors of apartheid if you say nothing about the killing of civilians and police by antiapartheid agitators and activists"). A crucial issue with respect to traumatic historical events is whether attempts to work through problems, including rituals of mourning, can viably come to terms with (without ever fully healing or overcoming) the divided legacies, open wounds, and unspeakable losses of a dire past.[2]

Of course, the situations in Germany and South Africa have their historical particularity, not least of which is the near total elimination of Jews in Germany as opposed to the majority status, as well as the rise to power, of blacks in South Africa. Without slighting this difference or other significant differences, a basic point is that individuals and groups in Germany and South Africa (as well as in other countries) face particular losses in distinct ways, and those losses cannot be adequately addressed when they are enveloped in an overly generalized

2. One may relate trauma in collectivities to what René Girard discusses as sacrificial crisis accompanied by the threat or occurrence of generalized mimetic violence, which sacrifice, at times unsuccessfully, functions to stabilize by concentrating violence on one (or a delimited set of) scapegoated victim(s). See especially his *Violence and the Sacred,* trans. Patrick Gregory (1972; Baltimore: Johns Hopkins University Press, 1977), and *Things Hidden since the Foundation of the World,* trans. Stephen Bann and Michael Metteer (1978; Stanford: Stanford University Press, 1987). Girard, however, remains committed to reductionism and monocausal explanations. In his brief discussion of mourning, he follows his general practice of moving from a possible connection (for example, with respect to the tomb as the site of the victim of stoning) to a necessary derivation, and he presents mourning as the result of mimetic reconciliation polarized around the sacrificial victim; see *Things Hidden since the Foundation of the World,* 81. He usefully stresses the interaction between life and death in mourning but does not explore the broader problem of the relation of mourning to ways of working through the past. Moreover, he provides little insight into the process of secularization in terms of displacements of the sacred and sacrifice, including their role in the Nazi genocide, about which he is surprisingly silent.

discourse of absence, including the absence of ultimate metaphysical foundations.[3] Conversely, absence at a "foundational" level cannot simply be derived from particular historical losses, however much it may be suggested or its recognition prompted by their magnitude and the intensity of one's response to them. When absence is converted into loss, one increases the likelihood of misplaced nostalgia or utopian politics in quest of a new totality or fully unified community. When loss is converted into (or encrypted in an indiscriminately generalized rhetoric of) absence, one faces the impasse of endless melancholy, impossible mourning, and interminable aporia in which any process of working through the past and its historical losses is foreclosed or prematurely aborted.[4]

To blur the distinction between, or to conflate, absence and loss may itself bear striking witness to the impact of trauma and the posttraumatic, which create a state of disorientation, agitation, or even confusion and may induce a gripping response whose power and force of attraction can be compelling. The very conflation attests to the way one remains possessed or haunted by the past, whose ghosts and shrouds resist distinctions (such as that between absence and loss). Indeed, in post-traumatic situations in which one relives (or acts out) the past, distinctions tend to collapse, including the crucial distinction between then and now wherein one is able to remember what happened to one in the past but realizes one is living in the here and now

3. Eric Santner touches on a similar point when he indicates his reservations concerning certain responses (including Jacques Derrida's) to the discovery of Paul de Man's World War II journalistic writings: "Central to all of these texts is the notion that to attend to, and even in a certain sense to mourn, the death that de Man has explicitly identified as a fundamentally 'linguistic predicament,' is an adequate mode of coming to terms with one's complicity, however indirect or ambivalent, in a movement responsible for the extermination of millions" (Eric L. Santner, *Stranded Objects: Mourning, Memory, and Film in Postwar Germany* [Ithaca: Cornell University Press, 1990], 19).

4. The distinction between absence and loss would also apply critically to Bill Readings' *The University in Ruins* (Cambridge: Harvard University Press, 1996). In it the current, putative university in ruins is contrasted with a university of culture that is conceived as a (welcome) loss but which would more accurately be understood as an absence—a status that places in doubt the idea of ruins which is its correlate and raises questions about the rather empty utopia that is proposed as its alternative. See my discussion in "The University in Ruins?" *Critical Inquiry* 25 (1998): 32–55.

with future possibilities. I would argue that the response of even secondary witnesses (including historians) to traumatic events must involve empathic unsettlement that should register in one's very mode of address in ways revealing both similarities and differences across genres (such as history and literature). But a difficulty arises when the virtual experience involved in empathy gives way to vicarious victimhood, and empathy with the victim seems to become an identity. And a post-traumatic response of unsettlement becomes questionable when it is routinized in a methodology or style that enacts compulsive repetition, including the compulsively repetitive turn to the aporia, paradox, or impasse. I would like to argue that the perhaps necessary acting-out of trauma in victims and the empathic unsettlement (at times even inducing more or less muted trauma) in secondary witnesses should not be seen as foreclosing attempts to work through the past and its losses, both in victims or other agents and in secondary witnesses, and that the very ability to make the distinction between absence and loss (as well as to recognize its problematic nature) is one aspect of a complex process of working through.

It should be emphasized that complex, problematic distinctions are not binaries and should be understood as having varying degrees of strength or weakness.[5] Without conceiving of it as a binary opposition, I am pointing to the significance, even the relative strength, of the distinction between absence and loss. (I later elaborate the relation of this distinction to two further distinctions: between structural trauma and historical trauma, onto which it may perhaps be mapped, and between acting out and working through the past, to which it is connected in complex ways that resist mapping.) My contention is that the difference (or nonidentity) between absence and loss is often

5. Of course, distinctions may operate ideologically as binaries and have important social and political functions, for example, in shoring up identity and fostering exclusion of those deemed outsiders. Indeed, binaries may be seen as excessively rigid defenses against the incidence or recurrence of trauma—defenses that are always dubious and which become especially fragile when they do not have institutional support. A scapegoat mechanism both depends on and performatively generates binary oppositions by localizing alterity (involving things one resists recognizing in oneself) and projecting it, as well as attendant anxiety, onto discrete others, and it may conceal both absences and losses in oneself or one's group.

elided, and the two are conflated with confusing and dubious results. This conflation tends to take place so rapidly that it escapes notice and seems natural or necessary. Yet, among other questionable consequences, it threatens to convert subsequent accounts into displacements of the story of original sin wherein a prelapsarian state of unity or identity, whether real or fictive, is understood as giving way through a fall to difference and conflict. As I have intimated, it also typically involves the tendency to avoid addressing historical problems, including losses, in sufficiently specific terms or to enshroud, perhaps even to etherealize, them in a generalized discourse of absence. Still, the distinction between absence and loss cannot be construed as a simple binary because the two do interact in complex ways in any concrete situation, and the temptation is great to conflate one with the other, particularly in post-traumatic situations or periods experienced in terms of crisis.[6]

In an obvious and restricted sense losses may entail absences, but the converse need not be the case. Moreover, I would situate the type of absence in which I am especially (but not exclusively) interested on a transhistorical level, while situating loss on a historical level.[7] In this

6. Absence and loss could not form a binary in that the opposite of absence is presence and that of loss is gain. Presence is, of course, often identified or correlated with gain, and presence/gain may be opposed to absence/loss in a broader binary configuration. The problem, which cannot be formulated in binary terms, is the mutual interaction and marking of presence/absence and gain/loss in what Derrida terms a larger economy, and the difficult issue is to elaborate distinctions that do not function as binaries or sheer dichotomies.

7. There are, of course, absences on an ordinary or historical level as well as ambivalently situated absences. Moreover, by transhistorical I do not mean absolute or invariant. I mean that which arises or is asserted in a contingent or particular historical setting but which is postulated as transhistorical. In a different setting, the terms of the postulation may vary even though the postulation is meant as transhistorical. An open question requiring further inquiry is whether the transhistorical is also universal. Do all cultures and societies have some modality or intimation of absence at the origin, along with an attendant anxiety, with which they come to terms in different—at times very different—ways (related to the modes of discourse and practice, including ritual, available in them)? Or is this kind of absence limited to, or at least distinctive of, certain cultures or societies in a manner that is nonetheless transhistorical in that it is not confined to a given period of time but reappears in different forms over time and whose recurrent inflections may even be defining characteristics of the culture? Then again, does one need a more subtle, complex formulation that would accommodate both of these seeming options? In another register, is the transhistori-

transhistorical sense absence is not an event and does not imply tenses (past, present, or future). By contrast, the historical past is the scene of losses that may be narrated as well as of specific possibilities that may conceivably be reactivated, reconfigured, and transformed in the present or future. The past is misperceived in terms of sheer absence or utter annihilation. Something of the past always remains, if only as a haunting presence or symptomatic revenant. Moreover, losses are specific and involve particular events, such as the death of loved ones on a personal level or, on a broader scale, the losses brought about by apartheid or by the Holocaust in its effects on Jews and other victims of the Nazi genocide, including both the lives and the cultures of affected groups. I think it is misleading to situate loss on a transhistorical level, something that happens when it is conflated with absence and conceived as constitutive of existence.

When absence itself is narrativized, it is perhaps necessarily identified with loss (for example, the loss of innocence, full community, or unity with the mother) and even figured as an event or derived from one (as in the story of the Fall or the oedipal scenario). Here there is a sense in which such narrative, at least in conventional forms, must be reductive, based on misrecognition, and even close to myth.[8] But this also suggests a reason why nonconventional narratives addressing the problem of absence, for example, those of Samuel Beckett or Maurice Blanchot, tend not to include events in any significant way and seem to be abstract, evacuated, or disembodied.[9] In them

---

cal postulated in a performative or regulative fashion, whatever may be its empirical status? These questions indicate the problematic status of the concept of the transhistorical. Still, the concept is in my judgment useful in drawing a distinction that serves to counteract certain misleading conflations or confusions.

8. I would define this form of myth as the attempt to derive a structure (for example, the structure of guilt in the story of the Fall from Eden or in Freud's primal crime) from an event that performatively enacts it.

9. Maurice Blanchot's *The Writing of the Disaster,* trans. Ann Smock (1980; Lincoln: University of Nebraska Press, 1986), tends to treat absences and losses (such as those of the Shoah) in relatively undifferentiated terms. This is to some extent in contrast with the more complex treatment of absence in Blanchot's *L'Entretien infini* (Paris: Gallimard, 1969), trans. Susan Hanson under the title *The Infinite Conversation* (Minneapolis: University of Minnesota Press, 1993), or in narratives such as his *Death Sentence,* trans. Lydia Davis (1948;

"nothing" happens, which makes them devoid of interest from a conventional perspective.

Absence appears in all societies or cultures, yet it is likely to be confronted differently and differently articulated with loss. In terms of absence, one may recognize that one cannot lose what one never had. With respect to the critique of foundations, one may argue that absence (not loss) applies to ultimate foundations in general, notably to metaphysical grounds (including the human being as origin of meaning and value).[10] In this sense, absence is the absence of an absolute that should not itself be absolutized and fetishized such that it becomes an object of fixation and absorbs, mystifies, or downgrades the

---

Barrytown, N.Y.: Station Hill Press, 1978). I have noted that the mingling of absence and loss may bear witness to experience in closest proximity to trauma wherein confusion itself may be a telling post-traumatic sign or symptom of radical disorientation. On the other hand, the ability to distinguish (without simply opposing) absence and loss may be related to at least a partial working through of problems related to trauma or extreme disruption.

10. Absence would also apply to the penis in woman (in critical contrast to its interpretation as loss or lack within the context of the oedipal complex) and to the phallus as a transcendental signifier. One might argue that it also applies to all forms of radical transcendence. It is debatable whether separation from the mother after the rupture or dissolution of the putative pre-oedipal unity of mother and child—as it is played out, for example, in the *fort/da* game—should be seen as an absence or a loss. Freud observed this much discussed game in the behavior of his one-and-a-half-year-old grandson. In it the child compensates for the uncontrolled comings and goings of the mother by playing with a bobbin attached to a string which it throws over the side of its crib while uttering the sound "ooo" and retrieving it with the sound "aaa." Sometimes the first gesture (throwing) takes place without the second. Freud interprets the sounds as meaning "fort" and "da" and speculates that the child is substituting the bobbin (which might perhaps be seen as a transitional object, in the words of D. W. Winnicott) for the mother; see Sigmund Freud, "Beyond the Pleasure Principle," *The Standard Edition of the Complete Psychological Works of Sigmund Freud,* trans. and ed. Strachey, 24 vols. (London: Hogarth Press, 1958), 18:14–16. One might speculate that the game would seem to combine a compulsive repetition that is acted out as well as an attempt to achieve some control over events and, to some extent, work through them. It would thus be suspended between melancholia and mourning with respect to an absent object that is easily experienced or interpreted as lost. (Insofar as the pre-oedipal symbiosis or bond is a fictive projection from a postoedipal position, one may argue that, in the separation from the mother, one is dealing with an absence that is readily misperceived or experienced as a loss that can somehow be recuperated or made good.) When the first part of the game is autonomized, one would seem caught up in a melancholic loop that comes close to endless grieving. If these speculations are correct, the game is a crucial instance of what Clifford Geertz refers to as "deep play"—play that is quite serious and even a matter of life and death (Clifford Geertz, *The Interpretation of Cultures* [New York: Basic Books, 1973], 432).

significance of particular historical losses. The conversion of absence into loss gives rise to both Christian and oedipal stories (the Fall and the primal crime)—stories that are very similar in structure and import (for example, in attempting to explain the origin of guilt). When understood as lost, divinity becomes hidden or dead, lost because of some sin or fault that could be compensated for in order for redemption or salvation to occur, allowing a return to unity with the godhead. Paradise lost could be regained, at least at the end of time. One might ask whether the conversion of absence into loss is essential to all fundamentalisms or foundational philosophies. In any case, the critique of ultimate or absolute foundations is best understood as related to an affirmation or recognition of absence, not a postulation of loss.[11]

Within the oedipal complex, the penis in woman is fantasized as lacking or even as having been once present in a totalized, fully integral or intact phallic mother; it would have been lost through some mishap that may also occur to men if they do not overcome castration anxiety in the "proper" way by finding a substitute for the mother. A golden or paradisiac age fulfills a similar function to the divinity or the phallic mother in that, either as a putative reality or a fiction, it is situated at a point of origin that could be recuperated or regained in an ideal future. The fully unified community or *Volksgemeinschaft* in which there is no conflict or difference is another avatar of the essential foundation, and anti-Semitism or comparable forms of prejudice against so-called polluters of the city are projective modes of dis-

---

11. Note that, in contrast to the famous assertion "God is dead" (whose relation to Nietzsche's voice is complex), one may argue that one finds an affirmation of absence as absence in the final passage of Nietzsche's "How the 'True World' Finally Became a Fable," in *Twilight of the Idols:* "The true world—we have abolished. What world has remained? The apparent one perhaps? But no! *With the true world we have also abolished the apparent one.* (Noon; moment of the briefest shadow; end of the longest error; high point of humanity; INCIPIT ZARATHUSTRA" (Friedrich Nietzsche, "How the 'True World' Finally Became a Fable," *Twilight of the Idols,* in *The Portable Nietzsche,* trans. and ed. Walter Kaufmann [New York: Viking Press, 1954], 486). One would have to read closely the entire section that concludes with this passage, including the interplay of principal text and parentheses in which what is included as seemingly marginal in the parentheses becomes increasingly insistent and important. The implications of the passage are explored, as Nietzsche intimates, in *Thus Spake Zarathustra.*

placing anxiety away from the self. The oceanic feeling, correlated with the presymbolic, pre-oedipal imaginary unity (or community) with the mother, would presumably also be lost by separation from the (m)other with the intervention of (the name of) the father and the institution of the symbolic under the sway of the phallus.[12] When they are interpreted in a certain way, a similar conflation of absence and loss occurs with respect to the passage from nature to culture, the entry into language, the traumatic encounter with the "real," the alienation from species-being, the anxiety-ridden thrownness and fallenness of *Dasein,* the inevitable generation of the aporia, or the constitutive nature of melancholic loss in relation to the genesis of subjectivity.

Eliding the difference between absence and loss is also crucial to conventional narrative structure, dialectical sublation (or *Aufhebung*), and sacrifice (which might be seen as displacements of one another). In a conventional narrative, a putatively naive or pure beginning—something construed as a variant of full presence, innocence, or in-tactness—is lost through the ins and outs, trials and tribulations, of the middle only to be recovered, at least on the level of higher insight, at the end. In speculative dialectics, an original identity is lost as it is dismembered or torn apart through contradiction and conflict, to be recovered on a higher level through *Aufhebung*—the movement of negation, preservation, and lifting to a higher level. In sacrifice an innocent or purified victim is violently torn apart in order that communicants may be regenerated or redeemed and attain a higher unity

12. This is, of course, the story Freud tells in *Civilization and Its Discontents,* at points in ways that render it problematic, and which Jacques Lacan repeats and further problematizes in his own register. In *Civilization and Its Discontents,* the coherence of the story, beginning with the oceanic feeling and seeking the origin of civilization and its discontents, is continually disrupted by the indirections and interrupted movements of the narrative, and in Lacan the pre-oedipal unity with the mother is explicitly situated as imaginary. Even if the oceanic feeling relates to a misrecognition (of absence as loss) and an imaginary union with the (m)other, Freud's assertion that he "cannot discover this 'oceanic feeling'" in himself remains suspect. It is nonetheless significant that he remarks that the oceanic feeling "seems something rather in the nature of an intellectual perception, which is not, it is true, without an accompanying feeling-tone" and that he "could not convince" himself of "the primary nature of such a feeling" (Freud, *Civilization and Its Discontents* [1930], trans. and ed. James Strachey [New York: W. W. Norton, 1962], 12).

or proximity to the godhead. Regeneration through violence may, of course, itself be displaced or find a substitute in secular scenarios that disguise, or even deny, their relation to sacrifice.

Loss is often correlated with lack, for as loss is to the past, so lack is to the present and future. A lost object is one that may be felt to be lacking, although a lack need not necessarily involve a loss. Lack nonetheless indicates a felt need or a deficiency; it refers to something that ought to be there but is missing. Just as loss need not be conflated with absence, for example, by not construing historical losses as constitutive of existence or as implying an original full presence, identity, or intactness, so lack may be postulated without the implication that whatever would fill or compensate for it was once there. But, I would argue, this inference is commonly drawn, and lack is frequently understood as implying a loss, especially in conventional narrative, dialectical, and sacrificial scenarios. Moreover, absence may be converted into a lack, a loss, or both.

Here an example may be useful. Martha Nussbaum writes: "Saul Bellow's rhetorical question—where would we find 'the Tolstoy of the Zulus, the Proust of the Papuans'—has been widely repeated as a normative statement critical of the cultural achievements of these societies. The person who repeats it in this spirit is to a degree observing accurately; many non-Western cultures do lack a form comparable to the novel."[13] Nussbaum goes on to criticize the attempt to privilege

---

13. Martha Nussbaum, *Cultivating Humanity: A Classical Defense of Reform in Liberal Education* (Cambridge: Harvard University Press, 1997), 132. I would also mention a singularly objectionable example of invoking lack instead of absence. It is found in Keith Windschuttle, *The Killing of History: How a Discipline Is Being Murdered by Literary Critics and Social Theorists* (Paddington, Australia: Macleay Press, 1996), 276–77. For Windschuttle, the fact that the Maori were devastated by invading Europeans proves that the Maori lacked something, to wit, a historical sense that would have enabled them to recognize the effects of "contact" with Europeans. Here the putative absence of a historical sense is construed as lack and inserted into an "argument" that amounts to blaming the victim. One might further observe that the sense of absence pertinent to the foregoing cases is not quite the same as that of absence at the origin. But the two are related in that the absence of absolute foundations should foster hesitancy in making cross-cultural judgments concerning a putative lack or deficiency. In cases more controversial than that invoked by Nussbaum, in which one is indeed inclined to make cross-cultural judgments—for example,

the novel and is manifestly trying to counter forms of ethnocentrism and chauvinism. But her formulation threatens to incorporate what she is opposing or to be implicated in a transferential repetition. It would clearly be more accurate to say that forms comparable to the novel are absent rather than lacking in other cultures (if indeed they are in fact absent). Such a formulation might be best for all cross-cultural comparisons unless one is willing to argue that the absence represents a lack. How to make this argument concerning lack in nonethnocentric terms, which do not simply privilege something presumably distinctive of, or unique to, one's own culture, poses a difficult problem in normative thinking. Of course, on an empirical level, an absence may be experienced as lack if members of the culture in question come to hold that position, for example, as a result of their contact with another culture and perhaps through the need to express, more or less ambiguously, resistance to the domination of that culture by making critical use of its forms (such as the novel).

One may observe that there are forms of narrative which do not unproblematically instantiate the conventional beginning-middle-end plot, which seeks resonant closure or uplift and tends to conflate absence with loss or lack. In fact, there are forms that both contest it and suggest other modes of narration which raise in probing and problematic ways the question of the nature of the losses and absences, anxieties and traumas, that called them into existence. Most signifi-

---

cases involving women's or human rights—I would argue (as Nussbaum is herself inclined to do) that one should begin by listening attentively to voices in the culture or society in question. It is possible that groups or individuals in that society will be making arguments (for example, concerning so-called female circumcision) that are well worth attending to and may go in the same direction as the argument one is inclined to make. It may also be the case that their argument will be more cogent or convincing because it comes from people having greater familiarity with the culture. Moreover, as I intimate in the text, the society or culture in question is not an isolate and will have already had various kinds of interaction with the "West," including an opportunity for groups within it to confront the type of argument one is likely to make. And the present scene includes many individuals who are themselves in complex, diasporic positions between a variety of cultures and whose views are already worked over by multiple perspectives. These considerations do not deprive one of a voice in cross-cultural arguments or judgments, but they do make it more likely that that voice will be better informed.

cant novelists from Flaubert through Joyce, Musil, Woolf, and Beckett to the present experimentally explore alternative narrative modalities that do not simply rely on a variant of a conventional plot structure, and their novels have earlier analogues, especially in the picaresque and carnivalesque traditions (novels such as *Don Quixote* and *Tristram Shandy*, for example). (One may suggest that narratives in other cultures which differ from the conventional narrative may show more striking resemblances to experimental, open-ended novels than to the stereotypical conventional novel.) In a somewhat comparable fashion, one may point to a dialectic that does not reach closure but instead enacts an unfinished, unfinalizable interplay of forces involving a series of substitutions without origin or ultimate referent, an interplay that may enable more desirable configurations that cannot be equated with salvation or redemption.[14] With respect to sacrifice, which typically combines oblation and victimization, one may distinguish the element of gift giving from victimization and attempt to valorize the former while situating it in possible modes of interaction and subject positioning which do not entail victimization or the construction of the victim as the gift to a deity or godlike being.[15]

14. This type of open dialectic was sought by Maurice Merleau-Ponty and, in more insistently negative terms, allowing for an impossibly utopian or redemptive hope-against-hope, by Theodor Adorno. It may also be found in an important dimension of Marx's work. On Marx in this respect, see my *Soundings in Critical Theory* (Ithaca: Cornell University Press, 1989), chap. 6. One should, of course, also be wary of simplistic oppositions between conventional and experimental novels. It might be better to refer to conventional and experimental dimensions of novels that are developed to a greater or lesser extent in actual novels. Harlequin novels come close to instantiating a conventional or formulaic extreme, while experimental texts may at times leave conventional expectations up to the reader.

15. The work of Derrida is crucially concerned with the problem of absence and would seem to valorize the gift as distinguished from victimization. But, in his important *The Gift of Death*, trans. David Wills (1992; Chicago: University of Chicago Press, 1995), Derrida's analysis of sacrifice is limited by the fact that he focuses on the gift without thematizing the question of its relation to victimization. (For example, he has nothing significant to say about Isaac as victim and his relation to his father.) The result may be a vision of relations in terms of supererogatory virtues (perhaps even a secular analogue of grace) in which generosity (or gift giving) beyond all calculation is extended to every other figured as totally other (on the model of a radically transcendent divinity). (In the phrase Derrida repeatedly employs, "tout autre est tout autre" [every other is totally other]. And as he puts it in rendering his understanding of Kierkegaard's view, with which he seems to agree: "What

The affirmation of absence as absence rather than as loss or lack opens up different possibilities and requires different modes of coming to terms with problems. It allows for a better determination of historical losses or lacks that do not entail the obliteration of the past (often a past seen as subsequent to a fall or hyperbolically construed as sheer absence or as utterly meaningless).[16] Historical losses or lacks

---

can be said about Abraham's relation to God can be said about my relation without relation to *every other (one) as every (bit) other* [*tout autre comme tout autre*], in particular my relation to my neighbor or my loved ones who are as inaccessible to me, as secret and transcendent as Jahweh" [77–78, 78].) One may initially contest this view by arguing that, whatever one's relation to a radically transcendent divinity, one's relation to others in society is based on a variable combination of distance or strangeness and intimacy, solidarity, or proximity, as Kierkegaard himself seemed to intimate when he restricted lifelong indirect communication to the God-man and asserted that "we human beings need each other, and in that there is already directness" (Søren Kierkegaard, *Søren Kierkegaard's Journals and Papers*, trans. and ed. Howard V. Hong and Edna H. Hong, 5 vols. [Bloomington: Indiana University Press, 1970], 2:384). In addition, from the perspective Derrida here elaborates, one has little basis to investigate victimization and its relation to the gift, including the difficult problem of distinguishing between the two and valorizing the latter while criticizing the former. One may also be ill equipped to pose the problem of the tense relation between ethics (based on justice, normative limits, and reciprocity) and what "generously" exceeds ethics—with the possibility that a vision focused, if not fixated, on excess relates to a society of saints or an elect group who may not have limiting norms that interact with and, to some extent, check excess, perhaps including the excess of violence and the gift of death.

One may further note that one of the early Derrida's most quoted statements is "il n'y a pas de hors-texte" [there is no outside-the-text], wherein the text is not the book or the written word in the ordinary sense but a relational network of instituted traces (Derrida, *Of Grammatology*, trans. Gayatri Chakravorty Spivak [1967; Baltimore: Johns Hopkins University Press, 1974], 158). The apparent contradiction between this statement and the assertion that every other is totally other (which one might understand to signify that every other, in a relation without relation, is "hors-texte") may be addressed in two ways. First, the early statement may be read to mean that there is nothing outside the text, that is to say, radical transcendence or total otherness indicates an absence. Second, the apparent contradiction might be converted into a necessary paradox if one affirmed, on a very basic (erased or quasi-foundational?) level, both the transcendence (infinite distance) and the immanence (closest proximity) of the other. One enters here into paradoxes related to displacements of the sacred, which Lacan treated in terms of *extimité* (external intimacy of the traumatic Thing) and Derrida explored in terms of the elusive, internal-external center in "Structure, Sign, and Play in the Discourse of the Human Sciences," *Writing and Difference*, trans. Alan Bass (1967; Chicago: University of Chicago Press, 1978).

16. This entailment may at times be found in Hayden White's more hyperbolic moments, for example, in "The Politics of Historical Interpretation: Discipline and Desublimation," *Critical Inquiry* 9 (1982): 128–29; reprinted in *The Content of the Form: Narra-*

can be dealt with in ways that may significantly improve conditions—indeed, effect basic structural transformation—without promising secular salvation or a sociopolitical return to a putatively lost (or lacking) unity or community. Paradise absent is different from paradise lost: it may not be seen as annihilated only to be regained in some hoped-for, apocalyptic future or sublimely blank utopia that, through a kind of creation *ex nihilo,* will bring total renewal, salvation, or redemption. It is not there, and one must therefore turn to other, nonredemptive options in personal, social, and political life—options other than an evacuated past and a vacuous or blank, yet somehow redemptive, future.[17]

For Freud, anxiety had the quality of indefiniteness and absence or indeterminacy of an object; for Kierkegaard and Heidegger, it was the fear of something that is nothing. In these conceptions, the idea that there is nothing to fear has two senses. There is no particular thing to fear. And anxiety—the elusive experience or affect related to absence—is a fear that has no thing (nothing) as its object. A crucial way of attempting to allay anxiety is to locate a particular or specific thing that could be feared and thus enable one to find ways of eliminating or mastering that fear. The conversion of absence into loss gives anxiety an identifiable object—the lost object—and generates the hope that anxiety may be eliminated or overcome. By contrast, the anxiety attendant upon absence may never be entirely eliminated or overcome but must be lived with in various ways. It allows for only limited

---

tive Discourse and Historical Representation (Baltimore: Johns Hopkins University Press, 1987), 72–73. The vision of the past as utterly meaningless may be conjoined with a radical constructivism (at times in decisionist form) that presents the human being as "endowing" the past or the other with meaning and value. Radical constructivism might be interpreted as a form of secular creationism in which the human being becomes an ultimate foundation and the displaced repository of quasi-divine powers. I would argue that the attempt to annihilate the past, along with putative creation *ex nihilo,* may well engender processes of traumatization and even terrorism which blind one to the (postrevolutionary or postconversion) symptomatic return of the repressed in displaced, disguised, or distorted forms.

17. In part as a defense against the equivocal threat (and allure) of the total community, one finds blank or empty utopian (or messianic) longing in the early Walter Benjamin as well as in recent figures such as Fredric Jameson. See Fredric Jameson, *The Political Unconscious: Narrative as a Socially Symbolic Act* (Ithaca: Cornell University Press, 1981), 11.

control that is never absolutely assured; any cure would be deceptive. Avoidance of this anxiety is one basis for the typical projection of blame for a putative loss onto identifiable others, thereby inviting the generation of scapegoating or sacrificial scenarios. In converting absence into loss, one assumes that there was (or at least could be) some original unity, wholeness, security, or identity that others have ruined, polluted, or contaminated and thus made "us" lose. Therefore, to regain it one must somehow get rid of or eliminate those others—or perhaps that sinful other in oneself.

Acknowledging and affirming, or working through, absence as absence requires the recognition of both the dubious nature of ultimate solutions and the necessary anxiety that cannot be eliminated from the self or projected onto others. It also opens up empowering possibilities in the necessarily limited, nontotalizing, and nonredemptive elaboration of institutions and practices in the creation of a more desirable, perhaps significantly different—but not perfect or totally unified—life in the here and now. Absence is in this sense inherently ambivalent, both anxiety producing and possibly empowering, or even ecstatic.[18] It is also ambivalent in its relation to presence, which is never full or lost in its plenitude but in a complex, mutually marking interplay with absence.[19]

---

18. The unconscious and the drives might be apprehended as active or generative absences that are ambivalent. They may not be recovered as if they were losses or lacks and made fully present to consciousness. Rather, they may be best construed as destructive and enabling absences—potentiating and nihilating forces—which are recurrently displaced. They create gaps or vortices in existence which both threaten to consume the self or others and may be sources of activity, even sublimity or elation and *jouissance*. In this sense, the most telling, disorienting instance or effect of the so-called death drive is in the endlessly compulsive repetition of traumatic scenes—scenes in which the distinction between absence and loss, as well as between structural and historical trauma, threatens to be obliterated. Moreover, the status of one's own—in contrast to another's—death and of the unconscious as absences may be a reason why Freud believed one could never accept one's own death on an unconscious level. Such an acceptance might not make any sense, since nothing—no ego—could do the accepting.

19. This relationship of mutual marking which places in question notions of full being, pure identity, and binary opposition is crucial to Derrida's notion of *différance*. In line with Derrida's thought, one may also observe that the ambivalence of absence and its interinvolvement with nonfull presence prevent the absolutization or reification of absence in

Desire has a different impetus and configuration with respect to absence and to loss or lack. In terms of loss or lack, the object of desire is specified: to recover the lost or lacking object or some substitute for it. If the lost object is divine or Edenic, the goal may be a new god or heavenly city, possibly a secular hero or a utopia that will save the people and legitimate the self as well as confirm the identity of the follower. Especially with respect to elusive or phantasmatic objects, desire may be limitless and open to an infinite series of displacements in quest of a surrogate for what has presumably been lost. Moreover, desire may give way to melancholic nostalgia in the *recherche du temps perdu*. By contrast, the object or direction of desire is not specified in relation to absence. The problem and the challenge become how to orient and perhaps limit desire, which is inherently indeterminate and possibly limitless. Desire may again become infinite (as the desire of or for desire). But the foregrounding of the question of desire and the problematization of its objects may at least enable a distinction between desire and desirability (or the normative articulation of desire) as well as the attempt to generate a viable interplay between desirable limits to desire and the role of excess, ecstatic transgression, or transcendence of those limits. It would also require the specification of historical losses or lacks and the differential ways they may be addressed, for example, through structural change in the polity, economy, and society.[20]

---

some analogue of negative theology. One may, however, maintain that absence implies neither existence nor nonexistence: it remains neutral or undecided with respect to the question of existence. In any event, the assertion of nonexistence is more determinate than, and requires a step beyond, the recognition of absence.

20. Here one might suggest that in Lacan desire is related to absence, although the oedipal scenario and the status of the phallus as the ultimate, elusive object of desire may induce a slippage of desire in the direction of loss or lack (the absence or gap in being [*béance*] deceptively being misrecognized as a constitutive lack [*manque à être*]). Desire would more definitely be related to loss or lack as well as to future possibilities when it is specified in terms of demand (which Lacan distinguishes from desire). It is worth noting that in Émile Durkheim's work the key problem is the generation and establishment of legitimate limits to desire which are themselves normatively desirable and able to turn desire back upon or against itself in the interest of collective morality and the mutual articulation of rights and duties. Desirable normative limits would define legitimate demands but be

I have intimated that, especially in a secular context, a commonly desired ultimate foundation or ground is full unity, community, or consensus, which is often, if not typically, figured as lost or perhaps lacking, usually because of the intrusive presence of others seen as outsiders or polluters of the city or the body politic. One may, however, insist that such unity, community, or consensus is absent and that the sociopolitical problem is how to deal with that absence as well as the differences and forms of conflict which accompany it. In the terms suggested by Jean-Luc Nancy, this is a problem of being in common without common being.[21] Not acknowledging this problem is quite compatible with an ideology of consensus in which differences and conflicts are not recognized and groups or individuals who are in fact not part of the presumed consensus are excluded or drastically under-represented in the political arena. A related problem is how to provide a means of symbolizing and expressing difference and conflict, thereby making possible the limiting or lessening of violence that may increasingly become an option to the extent that other options are not available. In other words, violence in unmediated form may be more likely when there are no accepted or legitimated modes of symbolizing difference and conflict in an effective manner that enables them to be addressed and to some extent dealt with.[22] One could even argue that the provision of modes of symbolizing difference and conflict—not full consensus or community—is basic to democracy and that the dialogic itself in a democratic context must have an agonistic component.

One may contend that the absence of absolute or essential founda-

---

open to anomic excess or transgressive challenge, ideally in terms that both tested and reinvigorated or renewed limits. Mikhail Bakhtin's notion of the functioning of the carnivalesque in a relatively stable and legitimated society might be argued to share similar assumptions, but with a different stress than Durkheim's more "serious" and ethically motivated conception of desirable social life.

21. See Jean-Luc Nancy, *The Inoperative Community*, trans. Peter Connor et. al., ed. Connor (1986; Minneapolis: University of Minnesota Press, 1991).

22. On this issue, see Françoise Gaillard, "The Terror of Consensus," trans. Jennifer Curtis Gage, in *Terror and Consensus: Vicissitudes of French Thought*, ed. Jean-Joseph Goux and Philip R. Wood (Stanford: Stanford University Press, 1998), 65–74. Gaillard seems to assume that consensus is always absent and functions as an ideology, but she does not explicitly make this point.

tions, including consensus, does not eliminate all room for agreement or all possibility of good (in contrast to absolute or ultimate) grounds for an argument. But one need not confound agreement with full consensus, a uniform way of life, an avoidance of strenuous argument, or the exclusion or elimination of all significant differences. One form of agreement which would seem important has as its object a (written or unwritten) constitution that sets certain ground rules that would be transgressed only when differences become so pronounced, and conflict so great, as to lead to a civil war. Especially in the current neoconservative and conservative-liberal context, one might also advocate agreement at least on the essentials of the welfare state as well as the attempt to make its role compatible with internationalism.[23] Still, even short of a situation of extreme crisis, grounds would be contestable and would have to be developed in and through discussion and argument involving dialogic relations both to others and within the self. Dialogic relations are agonistic and nonauthoritarian in that an argument is always subject to a response or counterargument; it may be answered or criticized in an ongoing give-and-take (in contrast to an authoritarian command or to what may be termed a hit-and-run riposte that evasively flees dialogic engagement with the other).[24] Criticism may be telling and entail the need for basic change, but it may also reinvigorate or validate an argument able to withstand it.

Given the force of narcissism and the limits of insight into the self, concrete others are crucial in discussing the bases of certain judgments, policies, and practices. Indeed, a particularly contestable object of discussion and argument is precisely the kinds of difference one judges desirable (or possibly preferred, or at least permitted) and those one judges undesirable (but not necessarily subject to exclusion) in a collectivity or a life. Such debate might go on within the self as well as between selves, and one might not be able to reach agreement with others or a unified position within the self on all important issues. But

---

23. On this issue, see Bruce Robbins, *Feeling Global: Internationalism in Distress* (New York: New York University Press, 1999).

24. The nondialogic riposte has become typical of such genres as the talk show, the letter to the editor, and the book review.

incommensurability in the sense of non-negotiable difference (what Jean-François Lyotard terms a *différend*) need not be prematurely generalized as characteristic of all relations between groups, positions, or issues. Non-negotiable difference might, rather, be seen as the limit case of incommensurability in another sense: that of the ability to translate from perspective to perspective and perhaps to reach agreement or decision on certain issues without having some superordinate master language, absolute foundation, or final arbiter (divinity, the sovereign, the community, reason, or what have you). Hence relativism (at least if it is understood either as absolute noncommunication or non-negotiability of perspectives or as "anything goes") need not be inevitable on a normative level.[25]

Nor need relativism be seen as inevitable on a cognitive level. The idea that there are no pure facts and that all facts have interpretive (or narrative) dimensions does not entail the homogeneity of interpretation. In other words, one might agree that there is in some sense interpretation all the way down but argue that interpretation is not homogeneous all the way down. Indeed, some dimension of fact may be so basic that one might argue that any plausible or even any con-

---

25. Recently, Lyotard has seemed to postulate a *différend* (or antinomy) between writing as a sublimely impossible, ultimately solitary, indeed abject and terrorized encounter with excess or the unrepresentable and politics as the art of the collectively possible. As he puts it,

> terror and the abjection that goes hand in hand with it should be excluded from the political dispensation of the community to the very extent that it should be undergone and singularly embraced in writing, as the condition of the latter. . . . We are asked to help settle the injustices that abound in the world. We do it. But the anguish that I am talking about is of a different caliber than worrying about civics. It resists the Republic and the system; it is more archaic than either; it both protects and flees from the inhuman stranger that is in us, the "rapture and terror," as Baudelaire said. (Jean-François Lyotard, "Terror on the Run," trans. Philip R. Wood and Graham Harris, in Goux and Wood, *Terror and Consensus*, 32, 35)

Lyotard (like Adorno in this respect) formulates problems in their limit form, and one can recognize the value of his remarks even if one resists seeing problems only in terms of the extreme limit (or excess) and argues for a greater variety of possible and legitimate relations between politics and writing. One may also raise doubts about the ability of Lyotard's thought to ward off political terrorism and his tendency at times (as in the ironic reference to civics) to situate political problems that are open to some measure of resolution on a seemingly inferior level as compared with writing or avant-garde art.

ceivable interpretation (or narrative) addressing a problem or series of events (such as the Holocaust) would have to accommodate it, hence that it would make little sense even to refer to this level as interpretive. Generally this is the level of simple declarative statements involving observations ("Hitler had a moustache") or well-validated assertions ("The Wannsee conference was held in January 1942"). These statements are often banal and depend on conventions that may in certain contexts be questioned (for example, the role of a calendar oriented around the birth of Christ), but they are nonetheless important and indispensable in discourse and life. (For example, it is not acceptable to justify being late for an appointment on the grounds that one objects to the hegemony of a certain calendar, although different conceptions of time may indeed be crucial in cross-cultural misunderstandings.) Moreover, such statements or assertions may at times bear on extremely significant issues that are resolvable in principle but difficult to resolve in fact (for example, whether and when an explicit, top-down decision on genocide was made in Nazi Germany and who made it).

As noted earlier, not all narratives are conventional, and the history of significant modern literature is in good part that of largely nonconventional narratives—narratives that may well explore problems of absence and loss. It is curious that theorists who know much better nonetheless seem to assume the most conventional form of narrative (particularly nineteenth-century realism read in a rather limited manner) when they generalize about the nature of narrative, often to criticize its conventionalizing or ideological nature.[26] Moreover, not all discourse is narrative, and a crucial problem is the relation of narrative

26. The view of narrative as conventionalizing is crucial to Sande Cohen's argument in *Historical Culture: On the Recoding of an Academic Discipline* (Berkeley: University of California Press, 1986). One might, however, contend both that historiography has stricter theoretical limits than the novel in experimenting with narrative (for example, with respect to inventing events, as well as on more structural levels, such as the use of free indirect style) and that it probably has not been as experimental as it could be. On these issues, see White, *Content of the Form;* Philippe Carrard, *Poetics of the New History: French Historical Discourse from Braudel to Chartier* (Baltimore: Johns Hopkins University Press, 1992); Robert J. Berkhofer Jr., *Beyond the Great Story: History as Text and Discourse* (Cambridge: Harvard University Press, 1995); and my *History and Criticism* (Ithaca: Cornell University Press, 1985).

to other modes of discourse. Indeed, nonconventional narratives often explore in critical ways their relation to myth as well as to non-narrative genres or modes such as the lyric, image, conceptual analysis, argument, or essay.[27] In my judgment, it is dubious to assert with Fredric Jameson or Paul Ricoeur (who themselves paradoxically often write in an essayistic form) that narrative is *the* basic instance of the human mind or that all discourse (at least all historical discourse) is ultimately narrative in nature. Such assertions usually rely on a very attenuated or overly expansive notion of narrative and are interesting as hyperbole only when they enable a far-ranging inquiry into the different possibilities and modalities of narrative (as they do in the work of Jameson and Ricoeur).

By contrast to absence, loss is situated on a historical level and is the consequence of particular events. The nature of losses varies with the nature of events and responses to them. Some losses may be traumatic while others are not, and there are variations in the intensity or devastating impact of trauma. There are, of course, also particular losses in all societies and cultures, indeed in all lives, but the ways in which they might be confronted differ from the responses more suited to absence. When absence and loss are conflated, melancholic paralysis or manic agitation may set in, and the significance or force of particular historical losses (for example, those of apartheid or the Shoah) may be obfuscated or rashly generalized. As a consequence one encounters the dubious ideas that everyone (including perpetrators or collaborators) is a victim, that all history is trauma, or that we all share a pathological public sphere or a "wound culture."[28] (As a recent public service message would have it, "Violence makes victims of us all.")[29] Further-

27. Here it would be useful to return to and try to develop further the reflections on the essay found in the work of Georg Lukács, Adorno, and Robert Musil.

28. For a critical investigation of the latter concepts, see Mark Seltzer, *Serial Killers: Death and Life in America's Wound Culture* (New York: Routledge, 1998). For an account of uses and abuses of the concept of trauma in the 1890s and the 1990s, see Kirby Farrell, *Post-Traumatic Culture: Injury and Interpretation in the Nineties* (Baltimore: Johns Hopkins University Press, 1998). See also Ruth Leys, *Trauma: A Genealogy* (Chicago: University of Chicago Press, 2000).

29. I thank Richard Schaefer for this example.

more, the conflation of absence and loss would facilitate the appropriation of particular traumas by those who did not experience them, typically in a movement of identity formation which makes invidious and ideological use of traumatic series of events in foundational ways or as symbolic capital.

Losses occur in any life or society, but it is still important not to specify them prematurely or conflate them with absences. Historical losses can conceivably be avoided or, when they occur, at least in part compensated for, worked through, and even to some extent overcome. Absence, along with the anxiety it brings, could be worked through only in the sense that one may learn better to live with it and not convert it into a loss or lack that one believes could be made good, notably through the elimination or victimization of those to whom blame is imputed. Conversely, it is important not to hypostatize particular historical losses or lacks and present them as mere instantiations of some inevitable absence or constitutive feature of existence. Indeed, specific phantoms that possess the self or the community can be laid to rest through mourning only when they are specified and named as historically lost others. And particular, at times interacting, forms of prejudice (such as anti-Semitism, racism, or homophobia) can be engaged ethically and politically only when they are specified in terms of their precise, historically differentiated incidence (including the different ways in which they may involve the conversion of absence into loss with the identity-building localization of anxiety that is projected onto abjected or putatively guilty others).

I would also distinguish in nonbinary terms between two additional interacting processes: acting out and working through, which are interrelated modes of responding to loss or historical trauma. As I have intimated, if the concepts of acting out and working through are to be applied to absence, it would have to be in a special sense. I have argued elsewhere that mourning might be seen as a form of working through, and melancholia as a form of acting out.[30] Freud, in comparing melancholia with mourning, saw melancholia as characteristic of

---

30. See my *Representing the Holocaust* and *History and Memory after Auschwitz*.

an arrested process in which the depressed, self-berating, and traumatized self, locked in compulsive repetition, is possessed by the past, faces a future of impasses, and remains narcissistically identified with the lost object. Mourning brings the possibility of engaging trauma and achieving a reinvestment in, or recathexis of, life which allows one to begin again. In line with Freud's concepts, one might further suggest that mourning be seen not simply as individual or quasi-transcendental grieving but as a homeopathic socialization or ritualization of the repetition compulsion that attempts to turn it against the death drive and to counteract compulsiveness—especially the compulsive repetition of traumatic scenes of violence—by re-petitioning in ways that allow for a measure of critical distance, change, resumption of social life, ethical responsibility, and renewal. Through memory work, especially the socially engaged memory work involved in working through, one is able to distinguish between past and present and to recognize something as having happened to one (or one's people) back then which is related to, but not identical with, here and now. Moreover, through mourning and the at least symbolic provision of a proper burial, one attempts to assist in restoring to victims the dignity denied them by their victimizers.[31] In any case, I am suggesting that the broader concepts that include, without being restricted to, melancholia and mourning are acting out and working through— concepts whose applicability must, of course, be further specified in different contexts and with respect to different subject positions.[32]

31. A particularly vexed problem for perpetrators and those benefitting from, or burdened by, their legacy is the estimation of victims such that they may become valued objects of mourning. In immediate postwar Germany, effective mourning was blocked or impeded by confusion or insufficient specificity about the object of mourning, for example, whether and how it referred to oneself, the lost glories of Hitler and the *Hitlerzeit,* or the victims of the Nazi genocide, victims who might still not be properly valued. This point does not imply, in the case of a sufficiently removed later generation, the desirability of a simple repudiation of one's historical relation to perpetrators and the identification with, and assumption of the status of, the victims. (This process of simple repudiation of the Nazi past and identification with the victim played, I think, a role in the admittedly overdetermined success in Germany of Goldhagen's *Hitler's Willing Executioners.*)

32. See Freud, "Remembering, Repeating and Working-Through (Further Recommendations on the Technique of Psycho-Analysis II)" (1914), in *Standard Edition of the*

Mourning is not the only modality of working through, although it is a very important one. Among a variety of possible modalities, one may mention certain forms of nontotalizing narrative and critical, as well as self-critical, thought and practice. For example, Beckett may be read as a novelist and dramatist of absence and not simply loss, as a writer whose works deploy ways of both acting out and working through absence. One might perhaps say that his world is one of paradise absent, not paradise lost. He is the non-Milton, not simply the anti-Milton, of narrative. In Beckett, any intimation of a lost or a future utopia becomes evanescent and insubstantial. Seen in a certain light, deconstruction is itself a way of working through and playing (at times acting) out absence in its complex, mutually implicated relations to nonfull presence. (In this respect it may be similar to Buddhism.)[33] The distinction between absence and loss would permit the rereading of many figures and movements in order to understand their relations to these concepts and related processes.[34]

Complete Psychological Works of Sigmund Freud, 12:145–56, and "Mourning and Melancholia," (1917) *Standard Edition of the Complete Psychological Works of Sigmund Freud,* 14:237–60. I would agree with Judith Butler that "in *The Ego and the Id* [Freud] makes room for the notion that melancholic identification may be a *prerequisite* for letting the object go" (Judith Butler, *The Psychic Life of Power: Theories in Subjection* [Stanford: Stanford University Press, 1997], 134). But I think this is already implied by the analysis of the complex, ambivalent relation of melancholia and mourning in "Mourning and Melancholia." Moreover, acting out in general may be a prerequisite of working through, at least with respect to traumatic events, although, as I later argue, I do not think that melancholia should be given an originary position as constitutive of the socialized psyche.

33. Wood notes the resemblance between Derrida's notion of *différance* and the Buddhist notion of "dependent arising" or "dependent cooriginication" in which the "emptiness" or nonfull presence of each thing implies its interinvolvement with others and the absence of any ultimate ground, foundation, or *sub-jectum* (metaphysical subject as foundation) (Wood, "'Democracy' and 'Totalitarianism' in Contemporary French Thought: Neoliberalism, the Heidegger Scandal, and Ethics in Post-Structuralism," in Goux and Wood, *Terror and Consensus,* 98). He quotes Nagarjuna, the second-century founder of the Madhyamika school, as stating: "When emptiness 'works,' then everything in existence 'works' " (ibid., 98 n. 48).

34. I would also note that, on the level of belief and practice, the line of thought I am suggesting might lead to a seemingly paradoxical, nonfanatical religious atheism that is not the simple negation, opposite, or reversal of established religions (as most atheisms tend to be). Instead, it might indicate the value of elements of religion (for example, certain rituals) and even seek to honor the name of God in God's absence. An important tendency in both

Poststructuralism in general, and deconstruction in particular, often involve forms of traumatic writing or post-traumatic writing in closest proximity to trauma, and they variably engage processes of acting out and working through. In one sense, however, deconstruction is misunderstood when it is applied to historical losses. Historical losses call for mourning—and possibly for critique and transformative sociopolitical practice. When absence, approximated to loss, becomes the object of mourning, the mourning may (perhaps must) become impossible and turn continually back into endless melancholy. The approximation or even conflation of absence and loss induces a melancholic or impossibly mournful response to the closure of metaphysics, a generalized "hauntology," and even a dubious assimilation (or at least an insufficiently differentiated treatment) of other problems (notably a limit event such as the Holocaust and its effects on victims) with respect to a metaphysical or metametaphysical frame of reference.

In another sense, deconstruction in certain of its registers may also be understood as a form of immanent critique which is applicable to historical phenomena and practices, including losses. It is especially significant politically in undoing pure binary oppositions that subtend and are generated by a scapegoat mechanism involving the constitution as well as the victimization of the other as a totally external, impure contaminant or pollutant; it also enables one to pose more precisely the problem of distinctions that are not pure binary opposites.[35] In this sense it does not entail a homogenizing reprocessing of all texts and phenomena or the blurring of all distinctions (including that between absence and loss) but instead the recognition that the problem of

---

religious and secular thought might be seen as going in this direction, for example, in Heidegger, Levinas, and Derrida. See also the discussion of post-Holocaust Jewish theology in Zachary Braiterman, *(God) after Auschwitz* (Princeton: Princeton University Press, 1998). Braiterman's emphasis is, however, on the critique of theodicy, an issue already rehearsed in pre-Holocaust thought.

35. As indicated earlier, theoretical or discursive undoing is not in and of itself tantamount to practical transformation, and it should not blind one to the empirically effective role of binary oppositions.

distinctions becomes more—not less—pressing in light of the un-availability or dubiousness of binary oppositions. Moreover, decon-struction may be extended in the direction of modes of social and political practice which address losses, lacks, and possibilities that are neither conflated with absence nor taken to imply a redemptive full presence in the past or future.[36] If it is so understood, the mourning that deconstruction enables, especially in post-traumatic contexts, need not merge with quasi-transcendental, endless grieving, which becomes altogether impossible. Even in terms of absence, deconstruc-tion may open other possibilities of response, including more affirma-tive, carnivalesque, and generally complex ones (for example, in terms of a displaced wake in which the carnivalesque has a role in mourning itself). In any case, losses would have to be specified or named for mourning as a social process to be possible. (This point may provide some insight into the desire of intimates to locate the bodies and deter-mine the names of victims so that they may be given a proper burial.)

When mourning turns to absence and absence is conflated with loss, then mourning becomes impossible, endless, quasi-transcen-dental grieving, scarcely distinguishable (if at all) from interminable melancholy. If mourning applies to absence in a manner that resists conflation with loss, it would have to be in some unheard-of, radically unfamiliar sense that does not simply foster an indiscriminate, un-modulated rhetoric (in which loss blurs vertiginously into absence, and apartheid or the Shoah presents no resistance to an all-purpose reading practice) or fold back into interminable (even originary or constitutive) melancholy or quasi-transcendental grieving. In any

36. Here one may refer to the deconstruction and critique of humanism in its histori-cally specific form that represents the human being as the absolute center of meaning and value and justifies any practice insofar as it serves human interests. This critique does not amount to a simple antihumanism, nor does it entail a rejection of agency, subjectivity, or responsible action, as some critics seem to assume. See, for example, Luc Ferry and Alain Renaut, *French Philosophy of the Sixties: An Essay on Antihumanism,* trans. Mary H. S. Cattani (1985; Amherst: University of Massachusetts Press, 1990). It does, however, situate these important concerns differently, and it is open to a reconception of human rights in relation to the claims of other beings and the environment.

case, the relation of deconstruction to problems of absence and loss (as well as to structural and historical trauma) should be posed and explored as an explicit object of inquiry.[37]

In acting out, the past is performatively regenerated or relived as if it were fully present rather than represented in memory and inscription, and it hauntingly returns as the repressed. Mourning involves a different inflection of performativity: a relation to the past which involves recognizing its difference from the present—simultaneously remembering and taking leave of or actively forgetting it, thereby allowing for critical judgment and a reinvestment in life, notably social and civic life with its demands, responsibilities, and norms requiring respectful recognition and consideration for others. By contrast, to the extent someone is possessed by the past and acting out a repetition compulsion, he or she may be incapable of ethically responsible behavior. Still, with respect to traumatic losses, acting out may well be a necessary condition of working through, at least for victims. Possession by the past may never be fully overcome or transcended, and working through may at best enable some distance or critical perspective that is acquired with extreme difficulty and not achieved once and for all. In some disconcertingly ambivalent form, trauma and one's (more or less symbolic) repetition of it may even be valorized, notably when leaving it seems to mean betraying lost loved ones who were consumed by it—as seemed to be the case for Charlotte Delbo, who resisted narrative closure and engaged in hesitant post-traumatic writing as an act of fidelity to victims of the Holocaust.

Moreover, the secondary witness (including the historian) who

---

37. In *Mourning Becomes the Law: Philosophy and Representation* (Cambridge: Cambridge University Press, 1996), Gillian Rose writes: "Post-modernism in its renunciation of reason, power, and truth identifies itself as a process of endless mourning, lamenting the loss of securities which, on its own argument, were none such. Yet this everlasting melancholia accurately monitors the refusal to let go, which I express in the phrase describing post-modernism as despairing rationalism without reason.' One recent ironic aphorism for this static condition between desire for presence and acceptance of absence occurs in an interview by Derrida: 'I mourn, therefore I am'" (11). I do not agree with all aspects of Rose's analysis and critique, but I share her concern about an insistence on impossible mourning that continually loops back into inconsolable melancholy, thereby providing little room for even limited processes (including political processes) of working through problems.

resists full identification and the dubious appropriation of the status of victim through vicarious or surrogate victimage may nonetheless undergo empathic unsettlement or even muted trauma. Indeed, the muting or mitigation of trauma that is nonetheless recognized and, to some extent, acted out may be a requirement or precondition of working through problems. Acting out and working through are in general intimately linked but analytically distinguishable processes, and it may be argued that a basis of desirable practice is to create conditions in which working through, while never fully transcending the force of acting out and the repetition compulsion, may nonetheless counteract or at least mitigate it in order to generate different possibilities—a different force field—in thought and life, notably empathic relations of trust not based on quasi-sacrificial processes of victimization and self-victimization.

There is at times a tendency in certain contemporary approaches to eliminate or obscure the role of problematic intermediary or transitional processes (including the very interaction between limits and excess) and to restrict possibilities to two extremes between which one may oscillate or be suspended: the justifiably rejected or criticized phantasm of total mastery, full ego identity, definitive closure, "totalitarian" social integration, redemption, and radically positive transcendence (whether poetic or political), on the one hand, and endless mutability, fragmentation, melancholia, aporias, irrecoverable residues or exclusions, and double binds, at times with the acting-out of repetition compulsions, on the other. I find this all-or-nothing tendency in different ways in the works of Paul de Man, Lawrence Langer, and Slavoj Žižek, among others.[38] Even Judith Butler, in her important and thought-provoking book *Bodies That Matter: On the Discur-*

---

38. The all-or-nothing tendency (including the somewhat histrionic idea that one should "never say never") also appears in the assumption that any critique of excess must eventuate in an indiscriminate affirmation of a *juste milieu* or a blandly general belief that one must never exaggerate, be hyperbolic, or go too far. On the contrary, one may recognize that, in certain contexts (notably post-traumatic ones), one must undergo at least the temptation of excess and even engage in forms of hyperbole but still attempt to signal the importance of, and help bring about, a viable interaction between excess and legitimate normative limits.

sive Limits of "Sex," at one point delineates theoretical possibilities in terms of phantasmatic total mastery and the disruptive repetition compulsion when she stresses the "difference between a repetition in the service of the fantasy of mastery (i.e., a repetition of acts which build the subject, and which are said to be the constructive or constituting acts of a subject) and a notion of repetition compulsion, taken from Freud, which breaks apart that fantasy of mastery and sets its limits."[39] In this formulation, the repetition compulsion sets limits to the fantasy of total mastery, but there is no indication of forms of working through which check or generate counterforces to compulsive repetition but are not tantamount to total mastery or definitive closure. Is one confined to two extremes—total mastery and the shattering effect of an endless repetition compulsion—extremes that attest to the predominance of an all-or-nothing logic? Are critical theory and conceptions of performativity confined to impossible mourning and modalities of melancholic or manic acting-out of post-traumatic conditions (at times including a belief in creation *ex nihilo*)?

Butler returns to these problems in her recent *The Psychic Life of Power: Theories in Subjection.* If it is taken as a "stark and hyperbolic construction" (as she puts it in passing), I find persuasive her account of the formation of (rigid) heterosexual identity on the basis of a "melancholic" repudiation of homosexual desire which involves an inability to mourn abjected losses (such as victims of AIDS) (136). But I would question the tendency, especially in her final chapter, to generalize an account of the formation of subjectivity on the basis of a constitutive or originary melancholy.[40] Moreover, for Butler

---

39. Judith Butler, *Bodies That Matter: On the Discursive Limits of "Sex"* (New York: Routledge, 1993), 10 n. 7. See also 22 n. 19, where she further elaborates her view. Relevant to the issues I discuss is the analysis in Peter Starr, *Logics of Failed Revolt: French Theory after May '68* (Stanford: Stanford University Press, 1995), which I read only after completing this chapter. Of special interest is Starr's discussion of Lacan (chap. 3).

40. Here her strategy is one of reversal in the form of metaleptic performativity: melancholy, which would seem to be the effect of the superego insofar as melancholia (as analytically distinguished from mourning) involves self-criticism and even self-berating, is the cause of the superego—indeed, a terroristic superego as a vehicle of the death drive—in its distinction from the ego.

melancholia itself is the disguised precipitate of social power as a lost object.[41] Although one may certainly recognize the importance of (always already) internalized (and often occulted) social power in the generation of subjectivity and subjection, one may ask whether Butler's analysis is overly restricted or insufficiently specific in its one-sided view of the superego, its rather unmediated derivation of the psyche from occulted social power, and its minimal account of critical judgment (seemingly a sort of residue with respect to internalized social power). Her account may even represent one of the latest avatars of the long story of conflating absence with loss that becomes constitutive instead of historical: the notion of loss related to melancholia as originary or constitutive of the subject and of the socialization of the psyche.[42] This account would seem to be in some sense yet another secular displacement of the Fall or original sin. An absence, gap, or structural trauma (related to anxiety and perhaps to radical ambivalence) is converted into, or equated with, a constitutive or originary loss (of social power and homosexual desire) as an unexamined presupposition for the postulation of melancholy as the origin or source of subjectivity. As Butler at points seems to intimate, absence not conflated with loss would not entail the postulation of melancholy as the source of subjectivity; by contrast, it would allow for various modes of subjectivity (of course including melancholy, which may indeed be especially pronounced in moder-

41. "By withdrawing its own presence, power becomes an object lost–'a loss of a more ideal kind.' . . . The subject is produced, paradoxically, through this withdrawal of power, its dissimulation and fabulation of the psyche as a speaking topos. Social power vanishes, becoming the object lost, or social power makes vanish, effecting a mandatory set of losses. Thus, it effects a melancholia that reproduces power as the psychic voice of judgment, addressed to (turned upon) oneself, thus modeling reflexivity on subjection" (*Psychic Life of Power,* 197–98).

42. In the penultimate chapter, by contrast, melancholia is more dynamically related to arrested mourning without being given an originary or constitutive status. Adam Phillips' critique, which was addressed to a version of the penultimate chapter and which separates the two last chapters in the book, may have prompted a change in Butler's argument—a questionable change, in my judgment. Phillips justifiably objects to facile, redemptive ideas of mourning but, in the process, almost threatens to foreclose working through and simultaneously to see melancholia as the more radical option.

nity).[43] In any event, if a special status were to be claimed for melancholy as a mode of subjectivity, this claim would be sociocultural and would have to be investigated and substantiated not in seemingly universalistic but in differentiated historical terms.[44]

Sometimes evident as well in recent thought is a perspective fixated on failed transcendence or irremediable, even inconsolable and constitutive, loss or lack, in which any mode of reconstruction or renewal is seen as objectionably totalizing, recuperative, optimistic, or

43. As Butler puts it in her penultimate chapter,
I would argue that phenomenologically there are many ways of experiencing gender and sexuality that do not reduce to this equation [of melancholic gender identity derived from the repudiation of homosexual desire and its incorporation as a lost identity], that do not presume that gender is stabilized through the installation of a firm heterosexuality, but for the moment I want to invoke this stark and hyperbolic construction of the relation between gender and sexuality in order to think through the question of ungrieved and ungrievable loss in the formation of what we might call the gendered character of the ego. (*Psychic Life of Power,* 136)
The difficulty is that the "stark and hyperbolic construction" tends to govern the entire analysis and may severely restrict or even foreclose the attempt to "think through" other possibilities that may, to a greater or lesser extent, even constitute countervailing forces in existing society. Among these possible modes of subjectivity is trust, which, of course, applies differently with respect to a subject's relations with different others and groups of others. Along with working through, trust is a category that may not hold a sufficiently prominent place in certain forms of critical theory. To avoid certain inferences, I would note that trust is not purely positive or related to a Pollyanna view of existence. The attitude of trust, which is, I think, common in people and especially evident in children, opens one to manipulation and abuse. The prevalence of the confidence man (or, more generally, the trickster figure) as a social type in both history and literature is one sign of the openness of trust to abuse. Yet trust also has other possibilities in child care and in social relations more generally. Indeed, one might suggest that the intensity and prevalence (not the mere existence) of melancholia may be related to the abuse or impairment of trust, and melancholia is often pronounced in those who have experienced some injury to trust.

44. On these problems, see, for example, Juliana Schiesari, *The Gendering of Melancholia: Feminism, Psychoanalysis, and the Symbolics of Loss in Renaissance Literature* (Ithaca: Cornell University Press, 1992); Winfried Schleiner, *Melancholy, Genius, and Utopia in the Renaissance* (Wiesbaden: O. Harrassowitz, 1991); Mitchell Robert Breitwieser, *American Puritanism and the Defense of Mourning: Religion, Grief, and Ethnology in Mary White Rowlandson's Captivity Narrative* (Madison: University of Wisconsin Press, 1990); and especially Wolf Lepenies, *Melancholy and Society,* trans. Jeremy Gaines and Doris Jones (1969; Cambridge: Harvard University Press, 1992). One may, of course, argue that Butler is postulating melancholic loss in transhistorical terms comparable to those I employ for absence. This is, however, a postulation I am trying to question and resist.

naive.[45] What is not theorized in this frame of reference is the possibility of working through in which totalization (as well as redemption—whether putatively successful or failed) is actively resisted and the repetition compulsion counteracted, especially through social practices and institutions generating normative limits that are not conflated with normalization—limits that are affirmed as legitimate yet subject to disruption, challenge, change, and even radical disorientation.[46] Without this notion of working through, mourning may be treated only as endless grieving and not as a social process involving not

45. After completing the present chapter, I read a work that parallels this line of argument: Allison Weir's *Sacrificial Logics: Feminist Theory and the Critique of Identity* (New York: Routledge, 1996). Weir, however, tends to use interchangeably the concepts of the sacrificial and the binary without further elucidating their relationship. On de Man, see my "The Temporality of Rhetoric," in *Soundings in Critical Theory*, 90–124.

46. Normalization involves the postulation of the statistical average (or perhaps the dominant) as normative. This postulation is certainly open to criticism, but its critique does not imply the avoidance or delegitimation of all normativity, including alternative normativities. Indeed, a crucial problem with respect to homophobia would be the development of a normativity that did not "abjectify" homosexual desire and practice—for example, a normativity that engaged the problems of commitment and trust without simply taking the conventional family as its model. It may be noted that Derrida, while recognizing that "there is nothing but" normativity, also states his suspicion of normativity "in the ordinary sense of the term" and observes that what he suggests about responsibility "signals instead in the direction of a law, of an imperative injunction to which one must finally respond *without norm*" (Derrida, "A 'Madness' Must Watch over Thinking," interview with François Ewald, *Points . . . Interviews, 1974–1994*, trans. Peggy Kamuf et al., ed. Elisabeth Weber [1992; Stanford: Stanford University Press, 1995], 361–62). He also asserts that "each time a responsibility (ethical or political) has to be taken, one must pass by way of antinomic injunctions, which have an aporetic form, by way of a sort of experience of the impossible" (ibid., 359). One may agree with him yet also insist (as he sometimes does) on the tense interaction between norms (distinguished from normalization) and what escapes or exceeds them, thereby calling for something like "an imperative injunction" that leads to a "responsible" decision in the context of "antinomic injunctions"—a decision that cannot be convincingly justified through normatively based reasoning. But this eventuality, which exists to some extent in every moral decision and is particularly accentuated in extreme cases, does not diminish the importance of norms setting legitimate limits that are crucial in ethico-political education and reasoning. Without a countervailing stress on limiting norms that articulate social and political relations, one's concern with an "experience of the impossible" may become all-consuming, and tension may be resolved or distended in the direction of a decisionist messianism (or messianicity) without a messiah—an ethics or politics of "imperative injunctions" that come from nowhere (like leaps of religiously atheistic faith) and repeatedly point to the promise of a blank, ever-to-come future (an *avenir* that is always *à-venir* and never in any sense a present, however limited or marked by absence).

simply alterity in the abstract but actual others—possibly empathic, trustworthy others. I have noted that mourning, if linked to an originary or constitutive loss, would necessarily seem to merge with endless, quasi-transcendental grieving that may be indistinguishable from interminable melancholy.[47] The possibility of even limited working through may seem foreclosed in modern societies precisely because of the relative dearth of effective rites of passage, including rituals or, more generally, effective social processes such as mourning. But this historical deficit should neither be directly imputed as a failing to individuals who find themselves unable to mourn nor generalized, absolutized, or conflated with absence, as occurs in the universalistic notion of a necessary constitutive loss or lack or an indiscriminate conflation of all history with trauma.[48]

A related point bears on the problematic but, I think, important distinction between structural trauma and historical trauma, a distinction that enables one to pose the problem of relations between the two in other than binary terms.[49] One may argue that structural trauma is

47. Walter Benjamin's *The Origin of German Tragic Drama,* trans. John Osborne (1928; London: Verso, 1977), may have provided an important model for what has become a prevalent move in recent theory. *Trauerspiel* would be better translated as "mourning play" and understood in terms of an impossible mourning in closest proximity to interminably melancholic grieving. In my judgment, Benjamin's thought is not restricted to a framework that valorizes melancholy and resists mourning (as a mode of working through), but this framework does play an important role especially in his early work. (See Martin Jay, "Against Consolation: Walter Benjamin and the Refusal to Mourn," in *War and Remembrance in the Twentieth Century,* eds. Jay Winter and Emmanuel Sivàn [Cambridge: Cambridge University Press, 1999], 221–39.) Benjamin might be reread against the grain to elicit forms of mourning and working through intricately related to melancholy as well as for indications of absence not conflated with loss and blank messianic hope. Indeed, a distinctive appreciation of his turn to Marxism would be significant in this rereading.

48. This conflation tends to occur in Shoshana Felman's contributions to the work she coauthored with Dori Laub, M.D., *Testimony: Crises of Witnessing in Literature, Psychoanalysis, and History* (New York: Routledge, 1992).

49. Structuralists such as Claude Lévi-Strauss or Ferdinand de Saussure tended to confine their interest in events to that which could indeed be informed by structures (for example, *la langue,* or language, as an abstract, systematic structure of differences). Whatever structure did not encompass or inform was seen as merely contingent or particular (for example, *la parole,* or the particular, contingent spoken word). One move of poststructuralism was to focus on the contingent or particular as supplement that could not be seen as

related to (even correlated with) transhistorical absence (absence of/at the origin) and appears in different ways in all societies and all lives. As I indicated earlier, it may be evoked or addressed in various fashions— in terms of the separation from the (m)other, the passage from nature to culture, the eruption of the pre-oedipal or presymbolic in the symbolic, the entry into language, the encounter with the "real," alienation from species-being, the anxiety-ridden thrownness of *Dasein,* the inevitable generation of the aporia, the constitutive nature of originary melancholic loss in relation to subjectivity, and so forth. I would reiterate that one difficulty in these scenarios is the frequent conversion of absence into loss or lack, notably through the notion of a fall from a putative state of grace, at-homeness, unity, or community. One can nonetheless postulate, hypothesize, or affirm absence as absence and recognize the role of something like untranscendable structural trauma without rashly rendering its role in hyperbolic terms or immediately equating it with loss or lack. By not conflating absence and loss, one would historicize and problematize certain forms of desire, such as the desire for redemption and totality or, in Sartre's words, the desire to be in-itself-for-itself or God.[50] One would also help prevent the indiscriminate generalization of historical trauma into the idea of a wound culture or the notion that everyone is somehow a victim (or, for that matter, a survivor).

---

mere refuse or negligible residue with respect to structures and the "scientific" structuralism focused on them. Yet the result was at times an extreme stress on contingency, particularity, or singularity in a manner that induced nominalism and a repetitive return to the aporetic interplay of structure and event. More fruitful is the notion that seeming binaries interact and mutually mark each other in ways involving "internal" differences—a perspective that enables the recognition of the actual role of binaries (for example, in more or less repressive or oppressive hierarchies), allows for a critique of that role, and raises the question of nonbinaristic distinctions, including their relative strength or weakness (both in fact and in right). As I intimated earlier, one form of myth is the symmetrical opposite of structuralism: the latter accounts for myth through structures or codes that inform it, while myth attempts to "explain" the genesis of structure from an event that performatively enacts it.

50. At least in one movement of his argument in *Being and Nothingness: An Essay on Phenomenological Ontology,* trans. Hazel E. Barnes (1943; New York: Washington Square Press, 1953), Sartre did historicize this desire.

Historical trauma is specific, and not everyone is subject to it or entitled to the subject position associated with it. It is dubious to identify with the victim to the point of making oneself a surrogate victim who has a right to the victim's voice or subject position.[51] The role of empathy and empathic unsettlement in the attentive secondary witness does not entail this identity; it involves a kind of virtual experience through which one puts oneself in the other's position while recognizing the difference of that position and hence not taking the other's place. Opening oneself to empathic unsettlement is, as I intimated, a desirable affective dimension of inquiry which complements and supplements empirical research and analysis. Empathy is important in attempting to understand traumatic events and victims, and it may (I think, should) have stylistic effects in the way one discusses or addresses certain problems. It places in jeopardy fetishized and totalizing narratives that deny the trauma that called them into existence by prematurely (re)turning to the pleasure principle, harmonizing events, and often recuperating the past in terms of uplifting messages or optimistic, self-serving scenarios. (To some extent the film *Schindler's List* relies on such a fetishistic narrative.)

Empathic unsettlement also raises in pointed form the problem of how to address traumatic events involving victimization, including the problem of composing narratives that neither confuse one's own voice or position with the victim's nor seek facile uplift, harmonization, or closure but allow the unsettlement that they address to affect the narrative's own movement in terms of both acting out and working through. Without discounting all forms of critical distance (even numbing "objectivity") that may be necessary for research, judgment, and self-preservation, one may also appeal to the role of empathy in raising doubts about positivistic or formalistic accounts that both deny one's transferential implication in the problems one treats and

---

51. I find this tendency toward surrogate victim status in Claude Lanzmann as interviewer in his film *Shoah*. See my discussion in "Lanzmann's *Shoah*: 'Here There Is No Why,'" *Critical Inquiry* 23 (1997): 231–69; reprinted in *History and Memory after Auschwitz*, chap. 4.

attempt to create maximal distance from them—and those involved in them—through extreme objectification.[52] But empathy that resists full identification with, and appropriation of, the experience of the other would depend both on one's own potential for traumatization (related to absence and structural trauma) and on one's recognition that another's loss is not identical to one's own loss.[53]

Everyone is subject to structural trauma. But, with respect to historical trauma and its representation, the distinction between victims, perpetrators, and bystanders is crucial. "Victim" is not a psychological category. It is, in variable ways, a social, political, and ethical category. Victims of certain events will in all likelihood be traumatized by them, and not being traumatized would itself call for explanation. But not everyone traumatized by events is a victim. There is the possibility of perpetrator trauma which must itself be acknowledged and in some sense worked through if perpetrators are to distance themselves from an earlier implication in deadly ideologies and practices. Such trauma does not, however, entail the equation or identification of the perpetrator and the victim. The fact that Himmler suffered from chronic stomach cramps or that his associate Erich von dem Bach-Zelewski experienced nocturnal fits of screaming does not make them victims of the Holocaust. There may, of course, be ambiguous cases in what Primo Levi called the gray zone, but these cases were often caused by the Nazi policy of trying to make accomplices of victims, for example, the Jewish Councils or kapos in the camps. The gray zone serves to raise the question of the existence and extent of problematic—at times more or less dubiously hybridized—cases, but it does not imply the rashly generalized blurring or simple collapse of all distinctions, including that between perpetrator and victim. The more general point is that historical trauma has a differentiated specificity that poses a

---

52. Compare the formulation in Saul Friedlander, *Memory, History, and the Extermination of the Jews of Europe* (Bloomington: University of Indiana Press, 1993), 130–34.

53. As noted in Chapter 1, the type of empathy I am defending is discussed by Kaja Silverman in terms of heteropathic identification. See her *The Threshold of the Visible World* (New York: Routledge, 1996).

barrier to its amalgamation with structural trauma and which poses particular questions for historical understanding and ethicopolitical judgment.[54]

Structural trauma is often figured as deeply ambivalent, as both shattering or painful and the occasion for *jouissance,* ecstatic elation, or the sublime. Although one may contend that structural trauma is in some problematic sense its precondition, I would reiterate the basic point that historical trauma is related to particular events that do indeed involve losses, such as the Shoah or the dropping of the atom bomb on Japanese cities. The strong temptation with respect to such limit events is to collapse the distinction and to arrive at a conception of the event's absolute uniqueness or even epiphanous, sublime, or sacral quality.[55] Perhaps this is the tangled region of thought and affect

54. Here the cases of Blanchot and de Man pose a similar problem in judgment: whether early, direct, dubious, at times vehement writings receive an adequate critical response in later, indirect, allegorical, at times elusive writings that may indiscriminately mingle historical and structural trauma.

55. I discuss this problem from various perspectives both in *Representing the Holocaust* and in *History and Memory after Auschwitz,* esp. chap. 4. Inaugurating a form of what later came to be called "nuclear criticism," Georges Bataille, in an essay first published in 1947, denies the uniqueness of the bombing of Hiroshima in terms that threaten to go to the opposite extreme of leveling or hypostatizing the suffering and losses related to it by maintaining that "horror is everywere the same" and appealing indiscriminately to "misfortune's profound nonsense." For Bataille, "the tens of thousands of victims of the atom bomb are on the same level as the tens of millions whom nature yearly hands over to death. . . . The point that, in principle, the one horror is preventable while the other is not is, in the last analysis, a matter of indifference" ("Residents of Hiroshima," in *Trauma: Explorations in Memory,* ed. Cathy Caruth [Baltimore: Johns Hopkins University Press, 1995], 229). Going beyond even the initiative of Horkheimer and Adorno in *The Dialectic of Enlightenment,* he makes a mind-boggling attempt to show that the bombing of Hiroshima jeopardizes the pursuit of projects (or means-ends rationality) and attests instead to the "sovereignty" of excessive expenditure and "a boundless suffering that is joy, or a joy that is infinite suffering" (232). Comparable to Lyotard's construction of "the jews" and Auschwitz as tropes or Trojan horses for his conception of postmodernism in terms of nomadism, un(re)presentability, and the sublime, Bataille's questionable initiative includes the following assertions (which might most generously be read as an overreaction to his own tangled prewar relation to the charismatic appeal of fascism): "The sensibility that goes to the furthest limits moves away from politics and, as is the case for the suffering animal, the world has at a certain point nothing more to it than an immense absurdity, closed in on itself. But the sensibility that looks for a way out and enters along the path of politics is always of cheap quality. It cheats, and it is clear that *in serving* political ends it is not more than a *servile,* or at least a

where one should situate the founding trauma—the trauma that paradoxically becomes the basis for collective or personal identity, or both. The Holocaust, slavery, or apartheid—even suffering the effects of the atom bomb in Hiroshima or Nagasaki—can become a founding trauma. Such a trauma is typical of myths of origin and may perhaps be located in the more or less mythologized history of every people. But one may both recognize the need for and question the function of the founding trauma that typically plays a tendentious ideological role, for example, in terms of the concept of a chosen people or a belief in one's privileged status as victim. As historical events that are indeed crucial in the history of peoples, traumas might instead be seen as posing the problematic question of identity and as calling for more critical ways of coming to terms with both their legacy and problems such as absence and loss.

A prominent motivation for the conflation of structural and historical trauma is the elusiveness of the traumatic experience in both cases. In historical trauma, it is possible (at least theoretically) to locate traumatizing events. But it may not be possible to locate or localize the experience of trauma that is not dated or, in a sense, punctual.[56] The belated temporality of trauma makes of it an elusive experience related to repetition involving a period of latency. At least in Freud's widely shared view, the trauma as experience is "in" the repetition of an early event in a later event—an early event for which one was not prepared to feel anxiety and a later event that somehow recalls the early one and

---

subordinated[,] sensibility" (228). In addition to note 25 above, see Lyotard's *Heidegger and "the jews,"* trans. Andreas Michel and Mark T. Roberts, foreword by David Carroll (1988; Minneapolis: University of Minnesota Press, 1990), as well as my comments in *History and Reading: Tocqueville, Foucault, French Studies* (Toronto: University of Toronto Press, 2000), 206–9.

56. Bessel A. van der Kolk makes the questionable attempt to localize in a portion of the brain the trace or imprint of the experience of trauma. See Bessel A. van der Kolk and Onno van der Hart, "The Intrusive Past: The Flexibility of Memory and the Engraving of Trauma," in Caruth, *Trauma: Explorations in Memory*, 158–82. Curiously, Caruth, despite her subtle analyses and stress on the elusiveness and belated temporality of the experience of trauma, accepts van der Kolk's literalizing view. Along with her contributions to *Trauma: Explorations in Memory*, see her *Unclaimed Experience: Trauma, Narrative, and History* (Baltimore: Johns Hopkins University Press, 1996).

triggers a traumatic response. The belated temporality of trauma and the elusive nature of the shattering experience related to it render the distinction between structural and historical trauma problematic but do not make it irrelevant. The traumatizing events in historical trauma can be determined (for example, the events of the Shoah), while structural trauma (like absence) is not an event but an anxiety-producing condition of possibility related to the potential for historical traumatization. When structural trauma is reduced to, or figured as, an event, one has the genesis of myth wherein trauma is enacted in a story or narrative from which later traumas seem to derive (as in Freud's primal crime or in the case of original sin attendant upon the Fall from Eden).

One may well argue that the Holocaust represents losses of such magnitude that, while not absolutely unique, it may serve to raise the question of absence, for example, with respect to divinity. Still, despite the extremely strong temptation, one may question the tendency to reduce, or confusingly transfer the qualities of, one dimension of trauma to the other—to generalize structural trauma so that it absorbs or subordinates the significance of historical trauma, thereby rendering all references to the latter merely illustrative, homogeneous, allusive, and perhaps equivocal, or, on the contrary, to explain all posttraumatic, extreme, uncanny phenomena and responses as exclusively caused by particular events or contexts. The latter move, what one might term *reductive contextualism,* is typical of historians and sociologists who attempt to explain, without significant residue, all anxiety or unsettlement—as well as attendant forms of creativity—through specific contexts or events, for example, deriving anxiety in Heidegger's thought exclusively from conditions in interwar Germany or explaining structuralism and the turn to the history of the *longue durée* in France solely in terms of the postwar avoidance of Vichy and the loss of national prestige and power.[57] The former tendency, deriving his-

---

57. The important and influential work of Pierre Bourdieu is sometimes prone to contextual reductionism or at least to a limited understanding of differential responses to contextual (or "field") forces. See, for example, his *L'Ontologie politique de Martin Heidegger* (Paris: Editions de Minuit, 1988) and *The Rules of Art: Genesis and Structure of the Literary Field,* trans. Susan Emanuel (1992; Stanford: Stanford University Press, 1995).

torical from structural trauma, is a great temptation for theoretically inclined analysts who tend to see history simply as illustrating or instantiating more basic processes. It should go without saying that the critique of reductive contextualism and theoreticism does not obviate the importance of specific contexts or of theory that addresses them and both informs and raises questions for research.

In *Telling the Truth about History,* the noted historians Joyce Appleby, Lynn Hunt, and Margaret Jacob write that "once there was a single narrative of national history that most Americans accepted as part of their heritage. Now there is an increasing emphasis on the diversity of ethnic, racial, and gender experience and a deep skepticism about whether the narrative of America's achievements comprises anything more than a self-congratulatory masking the power of elites. History has been shaken down to its scientific and cultural foundations at the very time that those foundations themselves are being contested."[58]

In this passage, one is close to reductive contextualism involving a variant of a golden age mythology, a variant in which the proverbial past-we-have-lost becomes the metanarrative we have lost. The purpose of the authors' own narrative is to explain current forms of multiculturalism and skepticism, and the contrast between past and present serves to frame or even validate that explanation. Yet we are never told precisely when "there was a single narrative of national history that most Americans accepted as part of their heritage." Nor are we told from what perspective that putative narrative was recounted. How, one might well ask, could one ever have fully reconciled narratives from the perspectives of Plymouth Rock, Santa Fe, and the Alamo? What about the perspective of American Indians in relation to the open frontier and manifest destiny? Where does one place the Civil War and the narratives related to it? I think one might argue that there never was a single narrative and that most Americans never accepted only one story about the past. The rhetorical attempt both to get one's

58. Joyce Appleby, Lynn Hunt, and Margaret Jacob, *Telling the Truth about History* (New York: W. W. Norton, 1994), 1.

own narrative off the ground and to account for current conflicts or discontents by means of a questionable opposition between the lost, unified past and the skeptical, conflictual present runs the risk of inviting underspecified, if not distorted, views of the past and over-simplified interpretations of the present.

Specificity is also in jeopardy when Žižek, who tends to be pre-occupied with structural trauma (often construed as constitutive loss or lack), complements his convincing indictment of reductive contextualism with this comparably reductive assertion: "All the different attempts to attach this phenomenon [concentration camps] to a concrete image ('Holocaust,' 'Gulag' . . .), to reduce it to a product of a concrete social order (Fascism, Stalinism . . .)—what are they if not so many attempts to elude the fact that we are dealing here with the 'real' of our civilization which returns as the same traumatic kernel in all social systems?"[59] Here, in an extreme and extremely dubious theoreticist gesture, concentration camps are brought alongside castration anxiety as mere manifestations or instantiations of the Lacanian "real" or "traumatic kernel."

One way to formulate the problem of specificity in analysis and criticism is in terms of the need to explore the problematic relations between absence and loss (or lack) as well as between structural and historical trauma without simply collapsing the two or reducing one to the other. One may well argue that structural trauma related to absence or a gap in existence—with the anxiety, ambivalence, and elation it evokes—may not be cured but only lived with in various ways. Nor may it be reduced to a dated historical event or derived from one; its status is more like that of a condition of possibility of historicity (without being identical to history, some of whose processes—for example, certain ritual and institutional processes—may mitigate or counteract it). One may even argue that it is ethically and politically dubious to believe that one can overcome or transcend structural trauma or constitutive absence to achieve full intactness, wholeness, or communal identity and that attempts at transcendence or salvation

59. Slavoj Žižek, *The Sublime Object of Ideology* (London: Verso, 1989), 50.

may lead to the demonization and scapegoating of those on whom unavoidable anxiety is projected. But historical traumas and losses may conceivably be avoided and their legacies to some viable extent worked through both in order to allow a less self-deceptive confrontation with transhistorical, structural trauma and in order to further historical, social, and political specificity, including the elaboration of more desirable social and political institutions and practices.

3 ■ *Holocaust Testimonies*

Attending to the Victim's Voice

The interest in testimonies has been on the rise in the course of the last twenty years or so. Claude Lanzmann's *Shoah* of 1985 was not only a significant film; it also heralded the turn to survivor videos, a turn that helps to place Lanzmann's film in a broader context and enables a more informed and critical response to it, notably with reference to problems of interviewing and representation.[1]

The interviewer in survivor testimonies is in a position comparable to that of the oral historian, and one important role for testimonies is to serve as a supplement to more standard documentary sources in history. But they may at times be of limited value when used narrowly to derive facts about events in the past. Historians who see testimonies as sources of facts or information about the past are justifiably concerned about their reliability. Less justifiably, they are at times prone to dismiss an interest in them. The importance of testimonies becomes more apparent when they are related to the way they provide something other than purely documentary knowledge. Testimonies are significant in the attempt to understand experience and its aftermath,

---

1. On this problem, see my *History and Memory after Auschwitz* (Ithaca: Cornell University Press, 1998), chap. 4.

including the role of memory and its lapses, in coming to terms with— or denying and repressing—the past. Moreover, the interviewer in an exchange with the survivor or witness generally does not seek purely documentary knowledge of the past. His or her manifest implication in an affectively charged relationship to the survivor or witness and the special, stressful demands this relationship places on inquiry may have more general implications for historical research, especially with respect to highly sensitive, emotionally laden, and evaluatively significant issues—issues quite prominent in (but of course not confined to) Holocaust studies. One issue that is raised in accentuated form by the study of survivor videos is how to represent and, more generally, come to terms with affect in those who have been victimized and traumatized by their experiences, a problem that involves the tense relation between procedures of objective reconstruction of the past and empathic response, especially in the case of victims and survivors.

The psychoanalyst and interviewer for the Yale Fortunoff collection of survivor videos, Dori Laub, tells the following story:

> A woman in her late sixties was narrating her Auschwitz experience to interviewers from the Video Archive for Holocaust Testimonies at Yale. . . . She was relating her memories as an eyewitness of the Auschwitz uprising; a sudden intensity, passion and color were infused into the narrative. She was fully there. "All of a sudden," she said, "we saw four chimneys going up in flames, exploding. The flames shot into the sky, people were running. It was unbelievable." There was a silence in the room, a fixed silence against which the woman's words reverberated loudly, as though carrying along an echo of the jubilant sounds exploding from behind barbed wires, a stampede of people breaking loose, screams, shots, battle cries, explosions.[2]

Laub continues:

> Many months later, a conference of historians, psychoanalysts, and artists, gathered to reflect on the relation of education to the Holo-

2. Shoshana Felman and Dori Laub, M.D., *Testimony: Crises of Witnessing in Literature, Psychoanalysis, and History* (New York: Routledge, 1992), 59.

caust, watched the videotaped testimony of the woman, in an attempt to better understand the era. A lively debate ensued. The testimony was not accurate, historians claimed. The number of chimneys was misrepresented. Historically, only one chimney was blown up, not all four. Since the memory of the testifying woman turned out to be, in this way, fallible, one could not accept—nor give credence to—her whole account of events. It was utterly important to remain accurate, lest the revisionists in history discredit everything. (59–60)

Referring to himself, Laub comments that

a psychoanalyst who had been one of the interviewers of this woman, profoundly disagreed. "The woman was testifying," he insisted, "not to the number of chimneys blown up, but to something else, more radical, more crucial: the reality of an unimaginable occurrence. One chimney blown up in Auschwitz was as incredible as four. The number mattered less than the fact of the occurrence. The event itself was almost inconceivable. The woman testified to an event that broke the all compelling frame of Auschwitz, where Jewish armed revolts just did not happen, and had no place. She testified to the breakage of a framework. That was historical truth." (60)

Lest one leap immediately to the conclusion that there was a confusion of tongues in this interchange between "the historians" and "a psychoanalyst" or even a différend based on two utterly incompatible visions of the truth, one may offer a different interpretation. The woman testified to and, to some extent, relived her experience of events. At a certain intense point in her narrative, as Laub puts it, "she was there"—or so it seems. In one important sense, her testimony is not open to criticism as evidence of her experience as she now recalls and relives it. How that testimony relates to an accurate empirical reconstruction of events involved in her account, such as the number of chimneys exploded or set aflame at Auschwitz, is a distinguishable question. What she relives of the past, as if it were happening now in the present, may, to a greater or lesser extent, be (or not be) an accurate enactment, reconstruction, or representation of what actually occurred in the past. It may involve distortion, disguise, and other permutations relating to processes of imaginative transformation and narrative shaping, as well as perhaps repression, denial, dissociation, and foreclosure. But these issues have a bearing only on certain aspects of her account and could not invalidate it in its entirety. Moreover, one may well argue that the woman testifies not only to her personal experience but to something larger having social significance: the breaking of what Laub terms an "all compelling frame." The ability to break this compelling frame, if only retrospectively by talking about it in a certain way, is an indication that the woman is not simply reliving or compulsively acting out the past but to some extent working it over and possibly working it through. The performativity of her narration is complex insofar as it extends over analytically distinguishable but existentially intertwined processes of acting out, working over, and working through—processes that of course have many subtle intermediaries and combined or hybridized forms.

The response of the woman in Laub's story prompts one to raise the question of traumatic memory and its relation to memory both in the ordinary sense of the word and in its more critical sense insofar as it is tested and, within limits, controlled by historical research. In traumatic memory the event somehow registers and may actually be relived in the present, at times in a compulsively repetitive manner. It may not be subject to controlled, conscious recall. But it returns in nightmares, flashbacks, anxiety attacks, and other forms of intrusively repetitive behavior characteristic of an all-compelling frame. Traumatic memory (at least in Freud's account) may involve belated temporality and a period of latency between a real or fantasized early event and a later one that somehow recalls it and triggers renewed repression or foreclosure and intrusive behavior. But when the past is uncontrollably relived, it is as if there were no difference between it and the present. Whether or not the past is reenacted or repeated in its precise literality, one feels as if one were back there reliving the event, and distance between here and there, then and now, collapses. To use Heidegger's term, one might perhaps refer to traumatic *Dasein* as experientially being back there, anxiously reliving in its immediacy something that was a shattering experience for which one was not prepared—for which one did not have, in Freud's term, *Angstbereit-schaft* (the readiness to feel anxiety). Traumatic *Dasein* haunts or possesses the self, is acted out or compulsively repeated, and may not be adequately symbolized or accessible in language, at least in any critically mediated, controlled, self-reflexive manner. Words may be uttered but seem to repeat what was said then and function as speech acts wherein speech itself is possessed or haunted by the past and acts as a reenactment or an acting out. When the past becomes accessible to recall in memory, and when language functions to provide some measure of conscious control, critical distance, and perspective, one has begun the arduous process of working over and through the trauma in a fashion that may never bring full transcendence of acting out (or being haunted by revenants and reliving the past in its shattering intensity) but which may enable processes of judgment and at least limited liability and ethically responsible agency. These processes are crucial for laying ghosts to rest, distancing oneself from haunting revenants, renewing an interest in life, and being able to engage memory in more critically tested senses.

In memory as an aspect of working through the past, one is both back there and here at the same time, and one is able to distinguish between (not dichotomize) the two. In other words, one remembers—perhaps to some extent still compulsively reliving or being possessed by—what happened then without losing a sense of existing and acting now. This duality (or double inscription) of being is essential for memory as a component of working over and through problems. At least in one operative dimension of the self, one can say to oneself or to others: "I remember what it was like back then, but I am here now, and there is a difference between the two." This is not moralistically to blame someone tragically possessed by the past and reliving its suffering to such an extent that present life and the assumption of its responsibilities become impossible. Nor is it to assert the possibility of total mastery or full dialectical overcoming of the past in a redemptive narrative or a speculative *Aufhebung* and *Versöhnung*—a stereotypically Hegelian overcoming and reconciliation—wherein all wounds are healed without leaving scars and full ego identity is achieved. Indeed, severely traumatized people may have different dimensions of the self engaged in acting out, working over, and working through which may not, to a greater or lesser extent, effectively communicate with one another. The process of working over and through the past is itself repeated and subject to remission, but it counteracts the compulsively repetitive, full reliving of the traumatizing past and the feeling that one is simply back there in which "there" involves an experiential identity between here and there, now and then. It also enables ethically responsible behavior, including consideration for others, which may not be available to someone insofar as he or she is in an impossible situation (as were certain inmates of concentration and death camps) or compulsively reliving a traumatic past. Moreover, it is conceivable that in working through problems, memory may assimilate the results of critical testing and integrate accurate information as a validated component of the way the past is recalled, especially as memory is disseminated in the public sphere. Indeed, one of the ways history is not merely professional or a matter of research is that it undertakes to create a critically tested, accurate memory as its contribution to a cognitively and ethically responsible public sphere. Memory of this sort is important for an attempt to acknowledge and relate to the past in a manner that helps to make possible a legitimate democratic polity in the present and future.

I have broached the perplexing question of how to represent and relate to limit events. Traumatic limit events pose challenges to both reconstruction or representation and dialogic exchange. Jean-François Lyotard and others (Saul Friedlander, for example) have theorized this problem in terms of the unrepresentable excess of extreme events that call for discursive and affective responses that are never adequate to them.[3] This is, I think, an important point even if one would want to signal its dangers and qualify it in certain ways. In videos one has the embodied voices of witnesses and survivors who typically have been overwhelmed by the excess of traumatizing events and the experience

---

3. See Lyotard, *The Differend: Phrases in Dispute*, trans. George Van Den Abbeele (1983; Minneapolis: University of Minnesota Press, 1988), and Saul Friedlander, *Memory, History, and the Extermination of the Jews of Europe* (Bloomington: Indiana University Press, 1993).

of them. Those interviewed are both living archives and more or other than living archives. Viewing these videos has effects on people. The sound of the voices, the often agonized looks on the faces have a powerful, at times an overwhelming, effect, and the impression may remain with the viewer long after the actual event. Different people are able to view these videos for variable but limited periods before they shut down and are unable to take more. (In using videos in teaching, I have found that about one hour is a general limit for students.) There is, moreover, the ethically induced feeling that one may not be responding with sufficient empathy, a reaction that increases the anxiety one feels both because of the evident, often overwhelming pain of the survivor recalling and even returning to the position of helpless victim and because of one's own helplessness in doing anything about what is being recounted or relived.[4]

Despite its significance, the notion that traumatic limit events involve and convey an unrepresentable, anxiety-producing excess may have two questionable consequences, even if one does not go to the hyperbolic point of identifying that excess with the "real" or with the idea that, in traumatic memory, the event is repeated in its incomprehensible, unreadable literality. First, an exclusive emphasis or fixation on unrepresentable excess may divert attention from what may indeed be represented or reconstructed with respect to traumatizing limit events, and should be, as accurately as possible. The latter includes the daily life of victims, a problem to which Saul Friedlander's *Nazi Germany and the Jews* is dedicated. As Friedlander says in his introduction:

> At each stage in the description of the evolving Nazi policies and the attitudes of German and European societies as they impinge on the evolution of those policies, the fate, the attitudes, and sometimes the initiatives of the victims are given major importance. Indeed, their voices are essential if we are to attain an understand-

---

4. It is important to note that the person being interviewed was not *simply* a victim in the past but that victimage may well have been an especially difficult, disempowering, and incapacitating aspect of the past which may at times be relived or acted out in the present. Testifying itself, in its dialogic relation to attentive, empathic listeners, is a way of effecting, at least in part, a passage from the position of victim compulsively reliving the past to that of survivor and agent in the present.

ing of this past. For it is their voices that reveal what was known and what *could* be known; theirs were the only voices that conveyed both the clarity of insight and the total blindness of human beings confronted with an entirely new and utterly horrifying reality. The constant presence of the victims in this book, while historically essential in itself, is also meant to put the Nazis' actions into full perspective.[5]

A second dubious consequence of the notion of an unrepresentable excess in traumatic limit events is that it may lead to a construction of these events in terms of an insufficiently differentiated, rashly generalized, hyperbolic aesthetic of the sublime or even a (positive or negative) sacralization of the event which may prompt a foreclosure, denigration, or inadequate account not only of representation but of the difficult issue of ethically responsible agency both then and now. One may perhaps detect such a hyperbolic appeal to the sublime and the unrepresentable in Lyotard himself.[6] I have speculated that the sublime may itself be construed as a secular displacement of the sacred in the form of a radically transcendent, inaccessible, unrepresentable other (including the alterity of radical evil). The typical response it evokes is silent awe. I have also argued that one important tendency in modern thought and practice has been the attempt to link the traumatic to—or even convert it into—the sublime by transvaluing it and making it the basis for an elevating, supraethical, even elated or quasi-transcendental test of the self or the group. Such an attempt took a particular form in certain Nazis themselves, involving the ability to perpetrate and endure scenes of unheard-of devastation and horror. Here one may briefly recall Himmler's 1943 Posen speech to upper-level SS officers—in important ways a proof text of Nazi ideology and of an important dimension of modern thought more generally, par-

---

5. Saul Friedlander, *Nazi Germany and the Jews*, vol. 1, *The Years of Persecution, 1933–1939* (New York: Harper Collins, 1997), 2.

6. See his *Differend: Phrases in Dispute* and *Heidegger and "the jews,"* trans. Andreas Michel and Mark S. Roberts, foreword by David Carroll (1988; Minneapolis: University of Minnesota Press, 1990). One may also find a hyperbolic appeal to a "thematic" of the traumatic and the sublime, in different ways, in Shoshana Felman, Lawrence Langer, Claude Lanzmann, Hayden White, and Elie Wiesel.

ticularly with respect to the fascination with excess and unheard-of transgression. In that speech, Himmler asserted that Nazis remained decent in the face of a geometically increasing expanse of corpses and that their ability to combine these antinomic features—decency (in Kantian terms, the morally beautiful and uncontaminated), on the one hand, and an obscene, seeming mathematical sublime, on the other—is what made them hard.

Moreover, I have suggested that the notion of a negative sublime, one in which the negativity perhaps always involved in sublimity becomes particularly accentuated, is applicable to dimensions of the Shoah, notably to the Nazi quest for redemption or regeneration through an extremely violent, distorted sacrificial process involving quasi-ritual anxiety about contamination and the quest for purification of the *Volksgemeinschaft* from putatively contaminating presences.[7] The possible role of a Nazi sublime should be understood as one factor (not a total explanation) of Nazi ideology and practice, especially with respect to fanatically committed Nazis such as Hitler, Himmler, and Goebbels as well as many upper-level SS officers who were prime movers of the Holocaust. (It probably did not apply, at least typically, to middle- and lower-level functionaries or to such groups as police battalions of "ordinary" men motivated by "ordinary" forces such as obedience to orders, peer pressure, and the desire to conform.) Its possible role nonetheless attests to the importance of distinguishing between the different modalities of the sublime and of being as careful as possible about its invocation, especially with respect to a dubiously homogenizing and possibly evasive use of it in one's own voice to apply to the Holocaust as an undifferentiated scene of excess and unimaginable horror.

Despite its clear and present dangers, the value of the notion of an unrepresentable excess is to foreground the problem of the possibilities and limits of both representation and dialogic exchange in responding to, or coming to terms with, events of the Shoah (as well as

---

7. See my *Representing the Holocaust: History, Theory, Trauma* (Ithaca: Cornell University Press, 1994), esp. 100–110. See also *History and Memory after Auschwitz*, 27–30.

other limit events in history). And it simultaneously raises the question of the relations between research, memory, and what limits them.

A goal of historical understanding is, as I have intimated, to develop not only a professionally validated public record of past events but also a critically tested, empirically accurate, accessible memory of significant events which becomes part of the public sphere. A related, problematic, even impossible goal is to assist in the effort to restore to victims (at least symbolically or even posthumously) the dignity perpetrators took from them—a restorative effort in which historical discourse is itself engaged to some extent in processes of mourning and attempts at proper burial (important forms of working through the past). This process of memory work is related to, but not identical with, research, and it is bound up with the problem of trauma and the challenges it poses to memory in the sense of critically tested recall or recollection. Research is, of course, crucial, and, in an important sense, it is broader than memory; it involves elements that are not committed to memory either by the collectivity or by the individual, including the historian. But one may contend that the past is significant in its bearing on the present and future to the extent that it makes contact with problems of memory. It is what is allowed or made to enter into publicly accessible memory—not historical research in general—which enables the past to be available for both uses and abuses, and the precise manner in which it becomes available (or is suppressed, distorted, or blocked) is of the utmost importance.[8] Accurate memory of the past may or may not be necessary for an individual "cure" (if one can indeed provide an acceptable definition of this medicalized notion which it may be best to avoid, at least in historical and critical-theoretical work). But one may argue that such memory, including memory that confronts the traumatic dimensions of history, is ethically desirable in coming to terms with the past both for the individual and for the collectivity. It is bound up with one's self-understanding and with the nature of a public sphere, including the

8. How one remembers the Shoah is of obvious importance in Israel, Germany, and the United States, as well as elsewhere, and memory will, of course, have different personal, collective, cultural, and political functions in its different modes and sites.

way a collectivity comes to represent its past in its relation to its present and future. One may also argue that accurate memory concerning events that play a crucial part in a collective past is an important component of a legitimate polity.[9] Moreover, accurate, critically tested memory work is related to the kind of active forgetting of the past, or letting bygones be bygones, which (to the extent it is possible) is both earned through collective effort and desirable in group relations—not simply a matter of political expediency. (In this sense, active forgetting is, of course, a complement of, not an alternative to, remembering and memory work.) In this context, an extremely difficult problem is how to respond to, and give an account of, traumatic limit events and their effects in peoples' lives in different genres and areas of study.

Any answer to this question is problematic and contains—in the dual sense of "includes" and "holds or hems in"—paradoxes because trauma invites distortion, disrupts genres or bounded areas, and threatens to collapse distinctions. The problem here is how one tries to inscribe and bind trauma and attendant anxiety in different genres or disciplinary areas in spite of the fact that no genre or discipline "owns" trauma as a problem or can provide definitive boundaries for it. I think

9. This is the kind of point Habermas made concerning Germany during the 1986 *Historikerstreit*. One may ask whether the point is slighted in Habermas's defense, ten years later, of Daniel Jonah Goldhagen's *Hitler's Willing Executioners: Ordinary Germans and the Holocaust* (New York: Alfred A. Knopf, 1996). On this question, see Chapter 4. The problem of a collectivity's relation to its past is also at issue in contemporary Israel in the debate over post-Zionist historiography in the work of Benny Morris and others. For Habermas's contributions to the Historians' Debate, see his *New Conservatism: Cultural Criticism and the Historians' Debate*, ed. and trans. Shierry Weber Nicholsen, intro. Richard Wolin (Cambridge: MIT Press, 1989). For a comparison of the German Historians' Debate and the debate in Israel over post-Zionist historiography, see José Brunner, "Pride and Memory: Nationalism, Narcissism, and the Historians' Debates in Germany and Israel," *History and Memory* 9 (1997): 256–300. Brunner does not note that the stage that may well follow the post-Zionist debate in Israel may bring out elements shared by (but concealed by the heated debate over) so-called Zionist and post-Zionist historiography, notably a focus (if not a fixation) on Israel, a very restricted interest in comparative history, a limitation of research on the Holocaust largely to Israeli responses, and the absence of any rereading or reinterpreting of the Diaspora (which tended to be presented negatively in Zionist historiography and is marginalized in post-Zionist historiography, which focuses, understandably enough, on Israeli-Arab relations).

the anxiety attendant on trauma and related to a questioning of clear-cut definitions of genres or disciplines should in important ways remain active and not be denied or repressed. It is, for example, what motivates a certain hesitancy (what in Thomas Mann's *Doctor Faustus* is expressed in terms of the narrator's or writer's trembling hand) in putting forth a general method or even a limited interpretation of a problem, and it also inhibits unqualified rejection or avoidance of analyses or interpretations with which one does not agree. But all distinctions, while being subjected to pressure and recognized as more or less problematic in their relation to phenomena, should not be conflated with binary oppositions and blurred or collapsed. Nor should the notion of trauma be rashly generalized or the difference between trauma victim and historian or secondary witness—or, for that matter, between traumatization and victimhood—be elided.[10]

In testimonies the survivor as witness often relives traumatic events and is possessed by the past. These are the most difficult parts of testimony for the survivor, the interviewer, and the viewer of testimonies. Response is a pressing issue, and one may feel inadequate or be confused about how to respond and how to put that response into

10. One may also contest the idea that one of the roles played by the historian is that of secondary witness. One may argue that the historian is limited to objective modes of understanding involving only empirical inquiry, observation, analysis, and commentary. It is probably less contestable to argue that the interviewer is a secondary witness in bearing witness both to the witness and to the object of testimony conveyed by the witness. This status implies an affective bond with the witness which Dori Laub desribes as follows: "Bearing witness to a trauma is, in fact, a process that includes the listener. For the testimonial process to take place, there needs to be a bonding, the intimate and total presence of an *other*—in the position of one who hears" (*Testimony,* 70). This statement is dubious even for the interviewer, indeed for the interviewer-cum-therapist, whose presence, however intimate, is never total and who may not undergo secondary traumatization. In any event, it is implausible for the historian or other commentator. At most one may argue that the historian is a secondary witness through empathy that nonetheless respects the otherness of the other and does not pretend to full and intimate presence of either self or other, much less to bonding (mis)understood as fusion or identification. To the extent that one denies the role of transference and rejects an affective component in understanding, notably in the form of empathy (or what I term empathic unsettlement), one will also resist the notion that one role played by the historian is that of secondary witness, even when that witnessing is situated at a respectful distance from the experience of the victim, not necessarily tantamount to secondary traumatization, and correlated with knowledge (analogous to that of the expert witness in court).

words. One question is whether one can and should develop what might be called an ethics of response for secondary witnesses—interviewers, oral historians, and commentators. Such an ethics would at least become a force or consideration in a larger force field. Here it is important to recognize that a historian or other academic, however attentive and empathetic a listener he or she may be, may not assume the voice of the victim. In addition, the academic (as academic) is not—and is not entitled simply to identify with—a therapist working in intimate contact with survivors or other traumatized people. Reading texts, working on archival material, or viewing videos is not tantamount to such contact. Moreover, with respect to the interviewer or oral historian, one may argue that it is dubious to try to induce the survivor to relive trauma and in a sense be revictimized before the camera even if one's motive is to empathize or even to identify fully with the victim and transmit the experience to the viewer. (Such an attempt to take the survivor back—figuratively and at times even literally—to the scene of victimization and traumatization is evident in Claude Lanzmann as interviewer in *Shoah,* and at times it leads to intrusive questioning.) More generally, one may question the desire to identify fully with, and relive the experience of, the victim in however vicarious a fashion. The force of this desire may both occlude the problem of agency in one's own life and desensitize one to the problem and process of attempting to move, however incompletely, from victim to survivor and agent in survivors themselves. This arduous process, which bears on the afterlife of victims as survivors, warrants extensive study. It is not a concern in Lanzmann's *Shoah* or even in Lawrence Langer's *Holocaust Testimonies,* both of which are concerned with victims as victims, not as survivors or agents.[11] Also dubious is a response to which Lanzmann and Langer are decidedly (I think justifiably) opposed—one that circumvents, denies, or represses the trauma that called it into existence, for example, through unqualified objectification, formal analysis, or harmonizing, indeed redemptive

11. Claude Lanzmann, *Shoah: The Complete Text of the Acclaimed Holocaust Film* (New York: Da Capo Press, 1995); Lawrence Langer: *Holocaust Testimonies: The Ruins of Memory* (New Haven: Yale University Press, 1991).

narrative through which one derives from the suffering of others something career-enhancing, "spiritually" uplifting, or identity-forming for oneself or one's group.[12]

Unqualified objectification and narrative harmonization as well as unmediated identification are particularly questionable when they occur in areas of political and social life, including the classroom. Without positing a simple binary opposition, I would suggest that excessive objectification, purely formal analysis, and narrative harmonization (including what Eric Santner has termed *narrative fetishism*) may be more likely when one uses printed sources or does archival research.[13] In partial contrast, videos may present in an especially powerful form the temptation of extreme identification.[14]

Objectivity is a goal of professional historiography related to the attempt to represent the past as accurately as possible. One may reformulate and defend this goal in postpositivistic terms by both questioning the idea of a fully transparent, unproblematic representation of the way things in the past "really were" and recognizing the need to come to terms with one's transferential implication in the object of study by critically mediating projective inclinations, undertaking meticulous research, and being open to the way one's findings may bring into question or even contradict one's initial hypotheses or assumptions. One may also distinguish objectivity from excessive objectification that restricts historiography to narrowly empirical and analytic techniques and denies or downplays the significance of the problems of subject position and voice in coming to terms with the implication

12. This is a temptation both in professional historiography and in the media, for example, in a film such as *Schindler's List*. It may, of course, also be a feature of political uses of the Holocaust as symbolic capital or in identity-building group formation and nationalism.

13. For Santner's incisive analysis of narrative fetishism, see his "History beyond the Pleasure Principle: Some Thoughts on the Representation of Trauma," in *Probing the Limits of Representation: Nazism and the "Final Solution,"* ed. Saul Friedlander (Cambridge: Harvard University Press, 1992), 143–54.

14. Of course, the opposite tendencies are also possible, for example, simply shutting down emotionally when viewing testimonies. But I think the dangers I stress occur in some important, influential works, for example, Lawrence Langer's *Holocaust Testimonies*, Lanzmann's *Shoah*, and Shoshana Felman's and Dori Laub's *Testimony*. Moreover, shutting down may be a defense against the threat of identification.

and response of the historian with respect to the object of study (including the voices of others). Simultaneously, one may recognize the need for objectification within limits both for research and for the protection of the researcher, especially in areas in which traumatic suffering is marked and the tendency to identify fully with the victim may be compelling.

Pronounced, if not excessive, objectification is at times present in even so unquestionably important and groundbreaking a work as Raul Hilberg's *The Destruction of the European Jews,* and it is exacerbated by the fact that Hilberg, in his painstaking analysis of the Nazi "machinery of destruction," tended not to employ the testimony of victims and based his study largely on documents left by perpetrators. In Hilberg an objectifying methodology induces (or at least is conjoined with) what may be an insensitivity to the plight of members of Jewish Councils, whom Hilberg discusses in a distanced and harshly critical way, largely oblivious to the double binds or impossible situations in which Nazi policy placed these councils.[15] In marked contrast, Daniel Jonah Goldhagen, while relying on printed sources, has instantiated the possibility of extreme identification with Jewish victims (as Goldhagen understands—or rather imagines—them in their relation to perpetrators) accompanied by an inability to employ evidence to test rather than simply illustrate extremely questionable hypotheses and assumptions. (One such assumption is the idea that "the long-incubating, pervasive, virulent, racist, eliminationist antisemitism of German culture," indeed "the ubiquity of eliminationist antisemitism" in Germany, was the sole significant motivational factor for perpetrators in the Holocaust.)[16]

15. Raul Hilberg, *The Destruction of the European Jews* (New York: Holmes & Meier, 1985). On Jewish Councils and the double binds in which Nazi policy placed their members, see Isaiah Trunk, *Judenrat: The Jewish Councils in Eastern Europe under Nazi Occupation,* intro. by Jacob Robinson; new intro. by Steven T. Katz (1972; Lincoln: University of Nebraska Press, 1996).

16. Goldhagen, *Hitler's Willing Executioners,* 419, 435. See the responses in *Unwilling Germans?: The Goldhagen Debate,* ed. Robert R. Shandley (Minneapolis: University of Minnesota Press, 1998), and Norman G. Finkelstein and Ruth Bettina Birn, *A Nation on Trial: The Goldhagen Thesis and Historical Truth* (New York: Henry Holt and Co., 1998). See

Still, even when one resists going to Goldhagen's extreme, videos may present in an especially forceful manner the temptation of a primarily participatory, identificatory response. In the first of her chapters in *Testimony,* Shoshana Felman recounts how her class at Yale faced radical disorientation and the threat of breakdown, both socially and as individuals, after viewing Holocaust videos. She tells of how she became "a witness to the shock communicated by the subject-matter; the narrative of how the subject-matter was unwittingly *en-acted,* set in motion in the class, and how testimony turned out to be at once more critically surprising and more critically important than anyone could have foreseen" (7). Coupled with reading literary texts, the viewing of testimonies "carried the class beyond a limit that [she] could foresee"—something that took her "completely by surprise. The class itself broke out into a crisis" (47). After consulting with Dori Laub, they "concluded that what was called for was for [her] to reassume authority as the teacher of the class, and bring the students back into significance" (48). One may question whether taking up an authoritative role that brings students "back into significance" is tantamount to working through problems. As I have intimated, one may also raise doubts about an academic's tendency to identify with a

---

also my comments in *History and Memory after Auschwitz.* Finkelstein provides an often convincing, detailed refutation of Goldhagen. But one of Finkelstein's own more dubious tendencies is to postulate a tendentious "disciplinary division between holocaust scholarship—primarily a branch of European history—and Holocaust literature—primarily a branch of Jewish studies"—a division that presumably was "mutually respected" before the publication of Goldhagen's book (which represents the extreme of a "Holocaust literature" or "Jewish studies" approach for Finkelstein). Finkelstein tends to associate objectivity with Holocaust scholarship (the epitome of which is Raul Hilberg's *Destruction of the European Jews*) and sentimentalizing empathy with Holocaust literature, a category that includes not only Elie Wiesel but (along with Lucy Dawidowicz) Yehuda Bauer and Dan Diner (88 n). Finkelstein also ironically states: "Arno Mayer's main blasphemy was emphasizing the salience of anti-Bolshevism alongside anti-Semitism in Nazi ideology" (90 n). By contrast Mayer subordinated anti-Semitism to anti-Bolshevism in Nazi ideology and practice, even going to the extreme of terming "the war against the Jews . . . a graft or parasite upon the eastern campaign, which always remained its host, even or especially when it became mired in Russia." See *Why Did the Heavens Not Darken?: The "Final Solution" in History* (New York: Pantheon, 1988), 270, and my discussion of this book in *Representing the Holocaust,* chap. 2.

therapist in intimate contact with traumatized people as well as about the identification of a class with trauma victims and survivors—tendencies that may induce the reader's identification with one or the other subject position. In any case, the extreme traumatization of a class through a process of unchecked identification with victims would obviously not be a criterion of success in the use of survivor videos. And it would be preferable to avoid or at least counteract such traumatization—or its histrionic simulacrum—rather than to seek means of assuaging it once it had been set in motion.

The broader question is the role of empathy in understanding, including historical understanding, and its complex relations to objectification and dialogic exchange. Empathy is an affective component of understanding, and it is difficult to control. Certain professional identifications or research strategies may attempt to marginalize or even eliminate (perhaps blind one to) its role along with affective response in general. But empathy is bound up with a transferential relation to the past, and it is arguably an affective aspect of understanding which both limits objectification and exposes the self to involvement or implication in the past, its actors, and victims. As I have already tried to argue, desirable empathy involves not full identification but what might be termed empathic unsettlement in the face of traumatic limit events, their perpetrators, and their victims. Empathic unsettlement may, of course, take different forms, and it may at times result in secondary or muted trauma as well as objectionable self-dramatization in someone responding to the experience of victims. It is plausible to think secondary trauma is likely in the case of those who treat traumatized victims or even in the case of interviewers who work closely with victims and survivors. But it may be hyperbolic to argue that all those who come into contact with certain material, such as Holocaust videos, undergo at some level secondary or muted trauma. And one may justifiably be wary of the overextension of the concept of trauma, even though any idea of strictly mastering its use and defining its range may be self-defeating. But it is blatantly obvious that there is a major difference between the experience of camp inmates or Holocaust survivors and that of the viewer of testimony videos. Still, even the viewing of videos may have different subjective effects on different people, including recurrent nightmares, and the possibility of secondary trauma cannot be discounted.

Without implying a rash generalization of trauma, empathic unsettlement should, in my judgment, affect the mode of representation in different, nonlegislated ways, but still in a fashion that inhibits or prevents extreme objectification and harmonizing narratives. Indeed, it is related to the performative dimension of an account, and, despite the ways performativity may lend itself to abuse, the problem of performative engagement with unsettling phenomena is important in an exchange with the past. One's own unsettled response to another's unsettlement can never be entirely under control, but it may be affected by one's active awareness of, and need to come to terms with, certain problems related to one's implication in, or transferential relation to, charged, value-related events and those involved in them. In addition, the attempt to give an account of traumatic limit events should have nonformulaic effects on one's mode of representation even independent of all considerations concerning one's actual experience or degree of empathy. In other words, one may maintain that there is something inappropriate about modes of representation which in their very style or manner of address tend to overly objectify, smooth over, or obliterate the nature and impact of the events they treat.[17] Still, one need not go to the extreme of dissociating affect or empathy from intellectual, cognitive, and stylistic or rhetorical con-

17. The so-called normalization of the Holocaust would presumably entail stylistic normalization in its representation as well. While one may argue that historiography of the Holocaust requires the use of professional techniques in authenticating documents, providing footnotes, validating empirical assertions, and so forth, one may still object to the full normalization of Holocaust historiography if it involves a simple reliance on conventional style and standard operating procedures. But, as I have intimated, it would also be questionable to use an undifferentiated "experimental" style (often associated with the sublime) for all aspects of the Shoah. For pertinent discussions of problems of representation, see Ernst van Alphen, *Caught by History: Holocaust Effects in Contemporary Art, Literature, and Theory* (Stanford: Stanford University Press, 1997); Geoffrey Hartman, *The Longest Shadow: In the Aftermath of the Holocaust* (Bloomington: Indiana University Press, 1996); Michael Roth, *The Ironist's Cage* (New York: Columbia University Press, 1995); and James E. Young, *The Texture of Memory: Holocaust Memorials and Meaning* (New Haven: Yale University Press, 1993).

cerns, and one may ask whether empathy is on some level necessary for understanding (however limited or self-questioning that understanding may be). With respect to perpetrators, one may justifiably resist empathy in the sense of feeling or understanding that may serve to validate or excuse certain acts. In fact, one may feel antipathy or hatred. But one may nonetheless argue that one should recognize and imaginatively apprehend that certain forms of behavior (that of the *Einsatzgruppen* or of camp guards, for example) may be possible for oneself in certain circumstances, however much the events in question beggar the imagination. One may even suggest that recognition is necessary for being better able to resist even reduced analogues of such behavior as they present themselves as possibilities in one's own life.[18]

The foregoing argument does not mean that one can provide a how-to book that stipulates formulaically the manner in which historians or others should respond with "proper" empathy and enable that response to affect their writing or mode of representation. In fact, a primary commitment to objectification and empirical-analytic methods in historiography may confront anyone trying to create a problematic space for empathic response (a space that in no sense excludes careful research and critical, contextual analysis) with a double bind or dilemma. On the one hand, one may be asked for concrete procedures, analogous to those employed in empirical-analytic research, which could be taught and followed as rules of historical method. But how could one, with respect to empathy, provide anything analogous to procedures for footnoting references or authenticating sources? On the other hand, any such procedures or rules—more plausibly, any

18. These points are, of course, contestable and difficult to demonstrate with any degree of adequacy. The minimal desirable function they serve is to inhibit demonization of the other and facile self-certainty or self-righteousness. Moreover, the idea that one should recognize and imaginatively apprehend that certain extreme forms of behavior may be possible for oneself in certain circumstances does not mean that one is prone to, or even capable of, such behavior, although one can never tell how one would respond in a certain situation until one is indeed in that situation. Still, speculations about what one can or cannot imaginatively apprehend do not imply the desirability of trying to run various scenarios of atrocity by one's mind, and such speculations may be particularly pointless in view of the way limit events, such as those of the Holocaust, may disempower the imagination or exceed its ability to conjure up situations.

suggestions one put forward—might bring the charge that they could readily be mechanized and abused. The double bind is a reason why it is difficult to acknowledge affective response within a disciplinary framework that, in any case, may be constitutively informed by an attempt to exclude or marginalize affectivity and attendant anxiety. It may also be taken to indicate that one cannot—and should not even attempt to—provide procedures or rules concerning the proper use or correct "dosage" of affect or empathy. Rather, the problem is how an attentiveness to certain issues may lead to better self-understanding and to a sensitivity or openness to responses that generate necessary tensions in one's account. This attentiveness creates, in Nietzsche's term, a *Schwergewicht*, or stressful weight in inquiry, and it indicates how history in its own way poses problems of writing or signification which cannot be reduced to writing up the results of research.

In literature and art (of course including film), one may observe the role of a practice that has perhaps been especially pronounced since the Shoah but may also be found earlier, notably in testimonial art: experimental, gripping, and risky symbolic emulation of trauma in what might be called traumatized or post-traumatic writing ("writing" in the broad sense that extends to all signification or inscription). This markedly performative kind of writing may be risky—at least insofar as it is not automatized and assimilated in mimetic fashion as an all-purpose methodology that predictably privileges excess, incalculability, the transgression of limits, (self-)shattering, unbound or associative play, and so forth. But, even in its riskier and less predictable forms, it is a *relatively* safe haven compared with actual traumatization. It may even be a means of bearing witness to, enacting, and, to some extent, working over and through trauma whether personally experienced, transmitted from intimates, or sensed in one's larger social and cultural setting. Indeed, such writing, with significant variations, has been prevalent since the end of the nineteenth century in figures as different as Nietzsche, Mallarmé, Flaubert, Woolf, Blanchot, Kafka, Celan, Beckett, Foucault, and Derrida. One crucial form it takes—notably in figures such as Blanchot, Kafka, Celan, and Beckett—is what might perhaps be seen as a writing of terrorized disempowerment as close as possible to the experience of traumatized victims without presuming to be identical to it.

It is debatable whether such writing has a place in literary criticism and the kind of philosophy which is close to it and to literature itself.[19] I would defend its role in criticism that emulates its object, but I would not see it as the only or even the preferred path for literary criticism or for its interaction with philosophy and literature. It is an extremely demanding and easily mishandled limit form of the attempt to bring criticism into close proximity or dialogue with art and prevent it from aspiring to the status of a masterful metalanguage, but the active attempt to distance oneself from this pretension to full mastery may take other forms that include a role for historical analysis and the elucidation, not only the emulation, of experimental literary texts or other artworks. Emulative writing becomes especially open to question when it takes an unmodulated orphic, cryptic, indirect, allusive form that may render or transmit the disorientation of trauma but provide too little a basis for attempts to work it through even in symbolic terms. Still, some of the most powerful and thought-provoking recent criticism is that which opens itself to the reinscription or emulation of disorienting, disruptive, post-traumatic movements in the most powerful and engaging literary texts or works of art. One may at times sense such movements in Cathy Caruth's writing. One remarkable use of the term *precisely,* along with *paradoxically,* in her writing comes precisely when the thought is least precise and most perplexing, perhaps at times disoriented—but in thought-provoking ways that give a "feel" for traumatic experience. In this sense, *precisely* may be invoked more or less unconsciously as a compellingly repeated marker or trace of post-traumatic effects that may not be sufficiently worked through. Shoshana Felman uses the terms *paradoxically* and *paradoxically enough* so repeatedly that their meaning and force are almost

19. Jürgen Habermas, in his hostile reaction to Derrida's way of effecting an interaction between philosophy and literature, does not address this problem in writing, although it would seem germane to his concerns. See *The Philosophical Discourse of Modernity,* trans. Frederick Lawrence (1985; Cambridge: MIT Press, 1987), 161–210.

evacuated—or perhaps they come to function as apotropaic devices that both conjure up and conjure away the unsettling effects of paradox. Still, her last chapter in *Testimony,* in which she discusses Lanzmann's *Shoah,* is quite different from her first chapter, in which she somewhat self-dramatizingly is anxious about the effects of trauma in a class. In her discussion of *Shoah* she writes in a fragmented, lyrical, participatory style that helps to evoke the movement and almost compulsive power of the film, although her approach may entail certain sacrifices in the critical analysis of Lanzmann's masterpiece.[20]

20. Bessell A. van der Kolk's neurophysiological theory of trauma has been especially important for Cathy Caruth. Van der Kolk argues that there is a registration of the traumatic event in its literality as a neural pathway—what in his later work becomes an imprint, engraving, icon, or image in the amygdala of the right side of the brain which is not accessible to symbolization or verbalization. Hence the traumatic event as experience would be inscribed as a literal pathway or image that is in itself incomprehensible or unreadable—one that is read belatedly (*nachträglich*) not because of repression or disavowal but because of literal dissociation from language centers in the left side of the brain. This view is not limited to neuroscientific claims, however. Quoting van der Kolk and Onno van der Hart, Caruth asks whether "the possibility of integration into memory and the consciousness of history thus raises the question 'whether it is not a sacrilege of the traumatic experience to play with the reality of the past' " (Caruth, *Trauma: Explorations in Memory* [Baltimore: Johns Hopkins University Press, 1995], 154). For van der Kolk, the initially inaccessible traumatic imprint may in time be addressed or represented in language as the "translation" between the right and left sides of the brain is achieved. The verbalization of the traumatic imprint and the perhaps "sacrilegious" variations played on it may be necessary for a traumatized person's recovery or "cure." (One example van der Kolk gives of variation or flexibility is imagining "a flower growing in the assignment place in Auschwitz" [Caruth, *Trauma: Explorations in Memory,* 178]. Roberto Benigni's film *Life Is Beautiful* might be seen as a dubious analogue of this idea in that it is an event in the public sphere which both presents a questionable image of concentration camps and, especially in its "magical realist" or even fairy-tale treatment of camp life, may well prove offensive to survivors.) Caruth builds on and extends van der Kolk's argument, often combining it with Freudian views. Indeed, her version of trauma theory, as well as Shoshana Felman's, may itself be interpreted as an intricate displacement and disguise of the de Manian variant of deconstruction. (See also Cathy Caruth, *Unclaimed Experience: Trauma, Narrative, and History* [Baltimore: Johns Hopkins University Press, 1996].) In this view (close to Lacan's), the real or the literal is traumatic, inaccessible, and inherently incomprehensible or unrepresentable; it can only be represented or addressed indirectly in figurative or allegorical terms that necessarily distort and betray it. I would speculate that the further displacement (as well as distortion and disguise) involved here may be with respect to a variant of religion in which the Hidden God is radically transcendent, inscrutable (or unreadable), and, in a

In historiography the attempt at, or effect of, bearing witness to, or even "emulating," trauma (if that is the right term) in an extremely exposed and experimental style would be questionable to the extent that it overwhelmed the demands of accurate reconstruction and critical analysis instead of tensely interacting with and, to some extent,

---

secular context, dead, unavailable, lost, or barred. All representations of such an absolute are sacrilegious or prohibited. In this context, trauma may itself be sacralized as a catastrophic revelation or, in more secular terms, be transvalued as the radical other or the sublime. This compelling frame of reference is also at play in other figures, including Claude Lanzmann in his commentaries on, and role in, *Shoah*. The difficulty is that this frame of reference may either foreclose any attempt to work through problems or immediately conflate the latter with a necessarily Pollyanna or redemptive dialectical *Aufhebung*. By contrast, one may conceive of working through as a limited *process* of integration or introjection of the past which may never fully transcend the acting-out of trauma or achieve full integration and closure.

Van der Kolk himself seems at times to allow for a very optimistic idea of "complete recovery" through full integration of traumatic memory in a "life history" and the "whole" of a personality (*Trauma: Explorations in Memory*, 176), a view perhaps facilitated by his resistance to the notion of a dynamic unconscious that exerts pressure and creates conflict in the self. Van der Kolk also tends to believe that "traumatic memories cannot be both dissociated and repressed" (169). He associates dissociation (which he accepts) with "a horizontally layered model of mind" in which the dissociated forms "an alternate stream of consciousness," while he links repression (which he rejects in cases of trauma) to "a vertically layered model of the mind" in which "what is repressed is pushed downward, into the unconscious" (168). Van der Kolk nonetheless refers to the dissociated as subconscious and as not accessible to consciousness but maintains that it is not repressed or subject to conflictual forces related to forbidden wishes or desires. One might, of course, object that a dissociated "memory" may indeed be associated with or attached to repressed and forbidden desires (for example, the desire for the death of a parent), and such an association would make even more traumatic and conflict-ridden an actual occurrence (for example, the death of the mother in a case van der Kolk discusses—that of Janet's patient Irène, in which the mother's death was associated with abusive behavior toward Irène on the part of her father).

Van der Kolk might himself be seen as transferentially repeating or acting out the processes he studies in that he splits or dissociates repression from dissociation and resists any notion of their connection. Moreover, his notion of the lodging of the traumatic memory in one half of the brain which is inaccessible to the other half could be seen as a questionable yet convenient literalization of the lateral model of dissociation which "explains" why there is dissociation without repression or other unconscious forces. Distortion would arise not from repression but by the very attempt to "translate" what is literally incomprehensible (or unreadable) into language. In any case, it should be evident that what is experienced as the exact repetition of the traumatic "memory" (or scene) does not entail that the repetition is the exact or literal replication of the empirical event itself. Moreover, it should be stressed that van der Kolk's notion of the exact literality of the imprint or icon of trauma is related to his rejection of unconscious processes such as repression with the

raising questions for those demands. One important text in which such a style at times seems to undercut the historical nature of the analysis is Foucault's *Folie et déraison: Histoire de la folie à l'âge classique*.[21] In it Foucault does not quote or even summarize the voices of radical disorientation or unreason but rather allows them to—or is open to the manner in which they—agitate or infiltrate his own tortured, evocative discourse, a discourse that may exhilarate the reader or threaten to make him or her mad (in both senses of the word).[22] I would in general argue that in history there is a crucial role for empathic unsettlement as an aspect of understanding which stylistically upsets the narrative voice and counteracts harmonizing narration or unqualified objectification yet allows for a tense interplay between critical, necessarily objectifying reconstruction and affective response to the voices of victims. I would even entertain the possibility of carefully framed movements in which the historian attempts more risk-laden, experimental overtures in an attempt to come to terms with limit events.

A larger question here is the complex relation of acting out, reliving, or emulatively enacting (or exposing oneself to) trauma and working it over as well as possibly working it through in a manner that never fully transcends or masters it but allows for survival, a measure

---

distortion and disguises it brings about. Whatever one makes of his neuroscientific claims (that may rely on an overly functionally specific model of the brain in which the amygdala becomes something like a neurophysiological analogue of the Kantian noumenal sphere), one may find many of van der Kolk's observations concerning trauma and memory to be insightful, and both Caruth and Felman are amenable to a sympathetic, if still partly symptomatic, reading wherein one may try to bring out how, despite—perhaps at times because of—their critical shortfalls, they each, in their affectively charged modes of writing, convey something of the "feel" and pathos of the experience of trauma.

21. Michel Foucault, *Folie et déraison: Histoire de la folie à l'âge classique* (Paris: Gallimard, 1961). See my analysis in *History and Reading*.

22. Another way of making this point is to say that, at his most disorienting, Foucault in *Folie et déraison* does not so much speak about (or even for) the mad as to—and at times with—the voices of unreason in something close to a free indirect style. I would further note that the operationalized adaptation of Foucault in historiography that provides genealogies of concepts or an objectifying account of disciplines, as in the important work of Jan Goldstein or Ruth Leys, tends to downplay severely, eliminate, or deny this dimension of Foucault's writing.

of agency, and ethical responsibility—a question that bears in significantly different ways on people occupying significantly different and internally differentiated subject positions, such as victim, witness, therapist, "imaginative" writer or artist, and secondary witness or historian. In an attempt to address this extremely complex and difficult question, there may be limited justifications for various responses short of full identification and unqualified objectification. The problem that clearly deserves further reflection is the nature of actual and desirable responses in different genres, practices, and disciplines, including the status of mixed or hybridized genres and the possibility of playing different roles or exploring different approaches in a given text or "performance."

Survivor testimony, including the interviewing process, is in certain ways a new, necessarily problematic genre-in-the-making with implications for oral history, particularly in especially sensitive areas of research. Historians have not yet worked out altogether acceptable ways of "using" testimonies, and their task is further complicated by the at times marked differences between the conditions and experiences of victims as well as their responses to them. As one limited but significant instance of the diversity of responses to limit events within the group of Jewish victims and survivors alone, one may briefly mention the cases of Helen K. and Leon S. in the Yale Fortunoff collection.[23]

23. Fortunoff Video Archive Tape A-35 and Fortunoff Video Archive Tape A-25. Any further discussion of survivor videos would have to include an analysis of problems in interviewing and filming, including the role of seemingly insensitive or dubious questions and the reliance on techniques such as zoom shots or close-ups apparently to intensify emotion that is already overwhelming—hence in a manner that is unnecessary at best and offensively intrusive at worst. Still, the power of testimonies is that they often transcend such stumbling blocks or inadequacies.

The differences in experiences and responses multiply when one adds other groups of victims such as political prisoners, Jehovah's Witnesses, Slavs, homosexuals, and "Gypsies." A related point is that it can be misleading to study victims in isolation from other—at times intricately related or even partially overlapping—subject positions and groups such as perpetrators, collaborators, bystanders, and resisters. In my judgment, the historian should not simply identify with any single participant subject position or group but try to work out varying modes of proximity and distance in the effort to understand each one as well as the

Helen K. seems to see the world in secular terms. She stresses the role of resistance and the manner in which her desire to defeat Hitler in his will to kill her was a force in her survival. Discussing her father's disappearance in the Warsaw ghetto, she speculates on the basis of little evidence that he was picked up by a German patrol. She never allows herself to entertain the possibility that he abandoned the family: this disturbing thought—which can only be suggested by the viewer— is not allowed to enter her mind. Her mother was captured (first thought killed) during the Warsaw ghetto uprising when Germans invaded the house in which they were hiding (a house that also contained the bunker of Resistance leader Mordechai Anielewicz). She later is surprised to find her mother in Majdanek and spends six or eight impossible weeks with the weak and debilitated woman until the mother is "selected" for death. In the tightly packed cattle car in which Helen K. and her thirteen-year-old brother are deported after the fall of the Warsaw ghetto, the brother, suffering from lack of oxygen, dies in her arms. At this point, she tells us, she said to herself: "I'm going to live. I must be the only one survivor from my family. I'm going to live. I made up my mind I'm going to defy Hitler. I'm not going to give in. Because he wants me to die, I'm going to live. I was going to just be very, very strong." She recounts other difficult experiences in Majdanek and Auschwitz and concludes by saying: "I don't know. I don't know if it was worth it. I don't know if it was worth it—because, you know, when I was in concentration camp and even after I said: 'You know, after the war people will learn, they will know. They will . . . they will see. We, we'll learn.' But did we really learn anything? I don't know."

In contrast to Helen K., Leon S. is a gaunt, spectral presence and often speaks in an excruciating, halting manner in which each word, like a fragile monument, is separated by a gap from the following word. He saw his grandmother, upon asking for help from a German, shot before his eyes. His closest friend, who helped him through the

---

relations among them. The historian might even attempt to work out ways of getting beyond the grid that locks participant positions or groups together in theory and practice.

camp experience, later committed suicide. Leon S. becomes religious after his harrowing experiences and says of his belief: "There is God. Despite the terrible things that happened to us, I couldn't deny the existence. I would never." Of his behavior and attitude toward Germans, he observes: "I could say I didn't raise my hand. I didn't hit a single German. And this may come as a surprise to you. I don't hate them." He adds: "You cannot blame the whole people for something that was done by a group of people." Helen K. and Leon S. may share certain sentiments and both undergo moments of breakdown or extreme disempowerment in which they seem to relive in anguish the past that haunts and at times possesses them. But they are very different people with different ways of coming to terms with that past.

Even when one comes to question the inclination of some historians to exclude or marginalize survivor testimonies as unreliable sources of history, one may still be at sea with respect to the proper use of testimonies.[24] The questions I have raised do not settle this issue.

24. I noted Raul Hilberg's tendency not to employ survivor testimonies. Although he continues to emphasize, at times excessively, the role of a machinery of destruction in all aspects of the Shoah, Hilberg's later approach to testimonies and, more generally, to the problem of interpreting the behavior of victims (notably that of members of Jewish Councils) is somewhat more nuanced than in *The Destruction of the European Jews*. See especially his *Perpetrators Victims Bystanders: The Jewish Catastrophe, 1933–1945* (New York: Harper, Collins, 1992); his contributions to *Writing and the Holocaust*, ed. Berel Lang (New York: Holmes & Meier, 1988), esp. 274; and his "The Ghetto as a Form of Government: An Analysis of Isaiah Trunk's *Judenrat*," in *The Holocaust as Historical Experience*, ed. Yehuda Bauer and Nathan Rotenstreich (New York: Holmes & Meier, 1981), 155–71. See also the important discussion and the comments of Isaiah Trunk at the end of the last book. Trunk asserts: "I agree with most of what [Hilberg] said about the Jewish Councils; I disagree only with his characterization of the ghettos and the Councils as a 'self-destructive machinery.' Here he comes close to Hannah Arendt's absurd supposition that without the Councils annihilation would not have been so total" (268).

Despite her proximity to the perspective of victims (as she understands it), Lucy Dawidowicz stresses the importance of corroborating eyewitness accounts through other documentary sources and gives survivor testimonies a rather limited supplementary importance "to fill out, augment, and enrich the substantive sources for the history of the Holocaust" (*The Holocaust and the Historians* [Cambridge: Harvard University Press, 1981], 128). Yehuda Bauer quotes and integrates into his narrative, without comment, limited selections from survivor written narratives and testimonies, both restricting their role and lending them a distinctive authority (*A History of the Holocaust* [New York: Franklin Watts, 1982], chap. 9). Lawrence Langer (not a professional historian) goes to the opposite, comparably

At most they explore options and possibilities, especially with respect to the relation between objectifying reconstruction or representation and what escapes it or is not encompassed by it, including the historian's own implication in, or transferential relation to, the past, having strongly affective and evaluative dimensions, and his or her conscious and unconscious exchange with that past and those living through it. The attempt to come to terms with survivor videos poses an important challenge to history in that it forces a question to which we may at best provide essentially contested answers: how to represent trauma and to give a place in historiography to the voices of victims and survivors.

---

questionable extreme from the early Hilberg in explicitly and emphatically privileging survivor oral testimonies as a locus of authenticity while downplaying the significance of survivor writings (*Holocaust Testimonies: The Ruins of Memory* [New Haven: Yale University Press, 1991]). "Beyond dispute in oral testimony is that every word spoken falls direct from the lips of the witness" (210 n). Indeed, for Langer "oral testimony is distinguished by the absence of literary mediation" (57). Langer, however, also makes this thought-provoking comment: "Though we have the option of rejecting such testimony as a form of history, we also face the challenge of enlarging our notion of what history may be, what the Holocaust has made of it, and how it urges us to reconsider the relation of past to present (in a less hopeful way, to be sure), and of both to the tentative future" (109). (Langer returns to these and related questions in his *Preempting the Holocaust* [New Haven: Yale University Press, 1998].)

See also the insightful analysis of Marianne Hirsch (a literary critic), who extends the investigation of testimonies and witnessing into the study of photographs and their relation to narrative (*Family Frames: Photography, Narrative, and Postmemory* [Cambridge: Harvard University Press, 1997]). She proposes the notion of postmemory for the memory of later generations not directly implicated in events: "Postmemory characterizes the experience of those who grow up dominated by narratives that preceded their birth, whose own belated stories are evacuated by the stories of the previous generation shaped by traumatic events that can be neither understood nor recreated. I have developed this notion in relation to children of Holocaust survivors, but I believe it may usefully describe other second generation memories of cultural or collective traumatic events and experiences" (22).

4 ∎ *Perpetrators and Victims*
The Goldhagen Debate and Beyond

The debate around Daniel Jonah Goldhagen's recent book has crested, and there seems little more to say about it. In fact, too much attention may have already been paid to it and its reception.[1] But, as in the case of a recurrent dream, concern with the book has the tendency not to be laid to rest but to reappear. To the extent this is the case, it may indicate that there are aspects of the book and the debate it provoked with which we have still not come sufficiently to terms. Hence the circumstances attendant on the book's reception may to some extent be reminiscent of the way Goldhagen's book itself tends to act out or return to problems in a compulsively repetitive manner rather than provide ways of working at least partially through them.

Goldhagen's thesis is widely known even beyond the field of Holocaust studies. Put in the simplest terms, Goldhagen argues that the principal perpetrators of the Holocaust were Germans and that the sole motivation for genocide was "the long-incubating, pervasive,

---

1. Daniel Jonah Goldhagen, *Hitler's Willing Executioners: Ordinary Germans and the Holocaust* (New York: Alfred A. Knopf, 1996). See the responses in Robert R. Shandley, ed., *Unwilling Germans?: The Goldhagen Debate* (Minneapolis: University of Minnesota Press, 1998). See also the comments on Goldhagen in my *History and Memory after Auschwitz* (Ithaca: Cornell University Press, 1998).

virulent, racist, eliminationist antisemitism of German culture," indeed "the ubiquity of eliminationist antisemitism" in Germany (419, 435). Goldhagen sees this "eliminationist" anti-Semitism as mutating readily into what he calls "exterminationist" anti-Semitism without providing any explanation for the mutation other than by positing a putative tendency for metastasis because of the cancerous virulence of the phenomenon. For generations, this extreme, fanatical anti-Semitism presumably pervaded the German population in a distinctive, if not unique, manner and made ordinary Germans Hitler's willing executioners. In brief, Germans wanted to do what they did to the Jews because their culture had made them almost Hitleresque in their anti-Semitism, but they nonetheless bore full responsibility for what they did because they wanted—and were not forced—to do it. (Any tension between seeming cultural determinism and a moralistic ascription of full responsibility is not addressed in Goldhagen's account.) *Eliminationist anti-Semitism* is a term almost compulsively repeated in Goldhagen's account, but its workings and bases receive little or no explanation. Instead, one has the assertion that it refers to a generations-old phenomenon of German culture which created a direct path to the Holocaust. Goldhagen simply describes "eliminationist," followed by "exterminationist," anti-Semitism in graphic (at times voyeuristic) psychological terms related to sadism, brutality, gratuitous cruelty, and glee in punishment and torture. This cultural anti-Semitism, which in Goldhagen's account becomes indistinguishable from national character and seems to imply collective guilt, is for him politically and institutionally based; the change of political regime and related institutions (especially the introduction of democracy), including the reeducation of Germans by their Western allies, has presumably brought about a large-scale transcendence of earlier anti-Semitism in Germany.

The overwhelming majority of professional historians who work on the Nazi genocide have been placed in a double bind by what might almost be called the Goldhagen phenomenon. They think that, at least for the most part, Goldhagen's book is not worth serious scholarly attention, and yet they cannot avoid devoting attention to it because of its fantastic popular success and its favorable reception by some noted intellectuals and scholars who for the most part are not professional historians, or at least not experts on the Nazi genocide, but are opinion makers. Moreover, professional procedures of authentication are themselves placed in jeopardy by the fact that the dissertation from which the book derived was not only the basis of Goldhagen's Harvard doctorate but also the object of the highest praise by some world-famous Harvard faculty.[2] Goldhagen was granted an assistant professorship at Harvard and was even one of the five finalists for a prestigious appointment in Harvard's History Department—a department that prides itself on the pronounced, indeed punctilious, care it takes in considering faculty for appointment. How could this bizarre series of events possibly have happened?[3]

Historians and other analysts will ponder this question for some time to come, and there is no easy answer to it. Ruth Bettina Birn writes: "So far, all of the experts in the area of the Holocaust, regardless of their personal background, have been unanimous in severely criticizing Goldhagen's book."[4] One particular aspect of the book to which

---

2. On the dust jacket of the original 1996 edition, Simon Schama (then a member of Harvard's history department) writes: "Daniel Goldhagen's astonishing, disturbing, and riveting book, the fruit of phenomenal scholarship and absolute integrity, will permanently change the debate on the Holocaust. By telling terrible, unavoidable truths, it banishes forever the simple pieties about guilt and innocence that have settled over the mass graves and ashes of the murdered. For anyone wanting to come to terms with the enormity of the genocide, *Hitler's Willling Executioners* will be obligatory reading." Stanley Hoffmann, of Harvard's government department, concurs: "This study of the perpetrators of the Holocaust is a truly revolutionary work because of its scope and because of its argument. Impeccable scholarship, a profound understanding of modern German history, and a fiery blend of moral passion and rigorous analysis lead to a starkly original demonstration of the pervasiveness of antisemitism in German society before and under Hitler, of the way in which strong prejudices can push ordinary citizens into undertaking gruesome policies of extermination, and of the importance of political culture in shaping a society's behavior."

3. I would, however, add that, in my judgment, Goldhagen is an extremely intelligent and informed young scholar—a view of him supported by both his book and his interviews. One's objections to the book or, more generally, to certain arguments or trains of thought Goldhagen employs should not lead to a desire to exclude him from the academy.

4. Norman G. Finkelstein and Ruth Bettina Birn, *A Nation on Trial: The Goldhagen Thesis and Historical Truth* (New York: Henry Holt and Co., 1998), 148. Finkelstein asserts: "*Hitler's Willing Executioners* adds nothing to our current understanding of the Nazi holo-

she objects is described by Goldhagen himself in these terms—terms at times paradoxical or even internally contradictory with respect to his seeming focus on perpetrators:

> I eschew the clinical approach and try to convey the horror, the gruesomeness, of the events *for the perpetrators* (which, of course, does not mean that they were always horrified). Blood, bone, and brains were flying about, often landing on the killers, smirching their faces and staining their clothes. Cries and wails of people awaiting their imminent slaughter or consumed in death throes reverberated in German ears. Such scenes—not the antiseptic descriptions that mere reportage of a killing operation presents— constituted the reality for many perpetrators. For us to comprehend the perpetrators' phenomenological world, we should describe for ourselves every gruesome image that they beheld, and every cry of anguish and pain that they heard. (22)

Here is an example of how Goldhagen tries "to convey the horror, the gruesomeness, of the events *for the perpetrators*"—in a sense, how he tries to represent trauma presumably from the perpetrators' point of view:

> The walk into the woods afforded each perpetrator an opportunity for reflection. Walking side by side with his victim, he was able to imbue the human form beside him with the projections of his mind. Some of the Germans, of course, had children walking beside them. It is highly likely that, back in Germany, these men had previously walked through woods with their own children by their sides, marching gaily and inquisitively along. With what thoughts and emotions did each of these men march, gazing sidelong at the form of, say, an eight- or twelve-year-old girl, who to the unideologized mind would have looked like any other girl? In these moments, each killer had a personalized, face-to-face relationship to

---

caust" (87). *A Nation on Trial* receives strong endorsements from Volker R. Berghahn, István Deák, Raul Hilberg, and Pierre Vidal-Naquet. Finkelstein provides a detailed refutation of Goldhagen's points, and Birn focuses on certain crucial arguments. While agreeing with much of it, I delineate in Chapter 3, note 16, aspects of Finkelstein's account which I find problematic. I also find insufficient Birn's argument that progressive brutalization is a possible explanation for the more carnivalesque sides of the killing of Jews and euthanasia victims.

his victim, to his little girl. Did he see a little girl, and ask himself why he was about to kill this little, delicate human being who, if seen as a little girl by him, would normally have received his compassion, protection, and nurturance? Or did he see a Jew, a young one, but a Jew nonetheless? Did he wonder incredulously what could possibly justify his blowing a vulnerable little girl's brains out? Or did he understand the reasonableness of the order, the necessity of nipping the believed-in Jewish blight in the bud? The "Jew-child," after all, was mother to the Jew.

Goldhagen continues:

> The killing itself was a gruesome affair. After the walk through the woods, each of the Germans had to raise his gun to the back of the head, now face down on the ground, that had bobbed along beside him, pull the trigger, and watch the person, sometimes a little girl, twitch and then move no more. The Germans had to remain hardened to the crying of the victims, to the crying of women, to the whimpering of children. At such close range, the Germans often became splattered with human gore. In the words of one man, "the supplementary shot struck the skull with such force that the entire back of the skull was torn off and blood, bone splinters, and brain matter soiled the marksmen." Sergeant Anton Bentheim indicates that this was not an isolated episode, but rather the general condition: "The executioners were gruesomely soiled with blood, brain matter, and bone splinters. It stuck to their clothes." Although this is obviously viscerally unsettling, capable of disturbing even the most hardened of executioners, these German initiates returned to fetch new victims, new little girls, and to begin the journey back into the woods. They sought unstained locations in the woods for each new batch of Jews. (218)

In this passage as elsewhere in the book, Goldhagen employs a rather uncontrolled narrative in which he mingles free indirect style (or *Erlebte Rede*), direct quotation, rhetorical questions, emotionally manipulative and stereotypical focusing on certain victims (little girls around the age of puberty play a prominent role), and interpolated speculations or projections about feelings seemingly ascribed to perpetrators but coming from a voice or perspective that is not simply their own—indeed, a voice or perspective that equivocates and involves an imputation from some other perspective of what perpetrators must have felt or at times should have felt but perhaps did not feel. Germans are monstrous and beyond the human pale in Goldhagen's account, and their monstrosity is related to the implicit exclamation or rhetorical question conveyed in Goldhagen's prose: How could humans possibly have done this to others, particularly to little girls? (All Germans seem to be figured on the model of the protagonist in Fritz Lang's classic film *M,* against whom even fellow criminals turn.) How could "we" possibly recognize ourselves in any sense in those Germans to whom Goldhagen paradoxically attributes an empathy for victims which he also denies, an empathy that perpetrators, for Goldhagen, in fact did not feel or apparently felt only in the most contained, equivocal, or hardened ways?[5]

In a critical reflection on Goldhagen's approach, Birn observes drily that "the reason for the paucity of scholarly writing on the 'thick lives' of perpetrators is not due to the lack of interest on the part of historians. Rather, it results from the lack of available material on which to base a study" (143). Of Goldhagen's graphic, often imaginative efforts to provide a thick description or phenomenological account of what he rather equivocally or contradictorily asserts to be the experience of perpetrators during their extreme acts (perpetrators who did not only commit horrible acts but somehow experienced horror without always

5. Rather than engage in an equivocal use of a free indirect style in rendering the purported feelings of perpetrators, Goldhagen might have done better to analyze Himmler's 1943 Posen speech to upper-level SS officers, which I discuss later. One may also refer to Himmler's viewing of an *Einsatzgruppe* action in Minsk as described by his associate Karl Wolff. Wolff reported that Himmler jerked convulsively, passed his hand across his face, and staggered. Himmler presumably turned green, wiped a piece of splattered brain from his cheek, and fainted. Peter Padfield comments: "The dynamics of the situation are against Wolff's flying piece of brain, and it is unlikely that Himmler so far lost control as to stagger and vomit. Otherwise he would hardly have stayed while the next truck loads were despatched, then have had the face to give the squad a talk on the sacred necessity of their task— hard as it was—which according to other participants strengthened the men in their resolve to do their duty. That he was shocked, and blanched, is probable. It may even be that this demonstration decided him that another method had to be found. Yet it is more likely, as suggested earlier, that gas had been decided on long since, and he had already ordered Höss to extend Auschwitz for extermination" (*Himmler: Reichsführer-SS* [London: Macmillan, 1990], 343).

being horrified), she states: "Whether this is really the role of a scholar is doubtful. After all, there is an extensive collection of survivors' memoirs and testimonies, in which we can hear the voices of the victims themselves. In the approach Goldhagen advocates, the historian takes on the position of an intermediary who is not interpreting sources but retelling the events in the light of his own imagination. It's his voice we hear!" (147).

Without remarking the shift, Birn turns attention from the experience of perpetrators to the voices of victims and survivors, and she does not pose the question of options in treating those voices besides having survivor testimonies speak for themselves, on the one hand, and Goldhagen's approach, on the other. Indeed, Goldhagen touches confusingly on the problem of perpetrator trauma without explicitly formulating the problem and addressing it in sufficiently cogent and differentiated terms. I would argue that Goldhagen's approach is ostensibly to provide a thick description of the world of perpetrators, but in fact he often "describes" or reconstructs their experiences in good part through his own identification with certain victims as he imagines them and their perception of perpetrators. Perpetrator history in Goldhagen becomes the putative history of perpetrators as seen through the eyes of victims—especially certain victims—with whom Goldhagen identifies and whose experience of events he imaginatively or phantasmatically recounts.

In trying to account for its success, Birn asserts that "this book only caters to those who want simplistic answers to difficult questions, to those who seek the security of prejudices." Like some others, she points to the role of marketing strategies on the part of the book's publisher and states that "its marketing presents a challenge to the scholarly community" (148).[6] One must, of course, recognize that there are complex, overdetermined reasons for the success of Gold-

6. István Deák notes: "To be sure, the publisher's aggressive marketing played a major role in popularizing the work. But that alone does not explain its public appeal in the United States, Germany, and other countries, in all of which it became a bestseller." "Holocaust Views: The Goldhagen Controvesy in Retrospect," *Central European History* 30 (1997): 295.

hagen's book, just as there are complex, overdetermined reasons for the Nazi genocide. It would be self-defeating to account for Goldhagen's success through simplistic, one-dimensional explanations of the sort to which one objects in the argument of his book itself. The reasons Birn gives may play some part in the success of Goldhagen's book, but they cannot, for example, account for Habermas's praise of it.[7] Habermas is hardly someone who looks for "simplistic answers to difficult questions" or seeks "the security of prejudices." Indeed, Habermas pointed to the book's reception, which Birn criticizes, as a primary reason for his laudatory remarks, while he was considerably more reserved about the scholarly qualities of the book's argument, which he largely left to professional historians to evaluate. Of course, one may object to Habermas on Habermassian grounds by pointing out that a book (or other artifact such as a film) cannot be adequately defended on the basis of the mere fact that it keeps an issue alive in the public sphere and somehow forces a people to confront its past. A great deal depends on precisely how a book (or any other artifact) accomplishes this feat and what it contributes to public discussion of sensitive, indeed volatile, issues—issues that bear forcefully on contemporary politics and self-understanding.[8]

Before turning to what I see as some limitations in many otherwise cogent critical responses to Goldhagen's book, I would like to speculate about its popular success and the tendency of some intellectuals to endorse that success. I have already suggested that, while Goldhagen's book is ostensibly a contribution to perpetrator history, the basis of its argument is an excessive, unchecked identification with certain victims as Goldhagen understands them or imagines them to be.[9] In

7. Jürgen Habermas, "Goldhagen and the Public Use of History: Why a Democracy Prize for Daniel Goldhagen?" in Shandley, *Unwilling Germans?*, 263–73.

8. These observations would also apply to the 1979 miniseries *Holocaust*, which has often been praised for its ability to bring the past to the attention of a very large popular audience without sufficient critical attention being paid to the precise manner in which the docudrama managed to achieve this feat.

9. Identification is facilitated by Goldhagen's avowed relation to his father, with whom he discussed his book as work in progress: a survivor, a teacher at Harvard, and the one person who is an exception to the putative consensus Goldhagen sees himself as challenging—

"describing" the experiences of perpetrators, notably in terms of gratuitous cruelty and pleasure in others' pain, he is speaking for certain victims with whom he identifies, whose experience of events he vicariously re-creates, whose voice he ventriloquizes, and whose image of perpetrators he often imaginatively renders. For Goldhagen, the victims in question are Jews. Despite a schematic appendix on Slavs and the "mentally ill," he does little to compare the treatment of Jews with that of other victims of racial purification such as "Gypsies" and the handicapped (classified by Nazis as mentally ill). Goldhagen may formulate and give what seems to be scholarly legitimation to the visceral response or "gut reaction" of some (certainly not all) Jewish victims and of those who identify with them in unmediated form. He may also make identification more available for younger Germans who may now dissociate themselves from the perpetrators of the past, cathartically identify with the victims, and find their identity solidified by Goldhagen's argument that the seeming leopard of "eliminationist" anti-Semitism has changed its spots with a change in institutions and political culture. Postwar Germany has for Goldhagen metamorphosed into a "normal" bastion of democracy just like "us."

If one shares Goldhagen's view, the intricate process of confronting both the past and one's relation to one's forebears as well as attempting to disengage oneself from questionable traditions (such as anti-Semitism and victimization) may become much more easily accomplished and self-celebratory in nature than they would otherwise be.[10]

---

the person to whom he owes his "greatest debt" and to whom his "understanding of Nazism and of the Holocaust is firmly indebted" (604; see also 479–80). In offering an interpretation that goes against a professional consensus and is indistinguishable close to his father's (at least as the son presents things), Goldhagen, in defending his own views, is at one and the same time vindicating his father as victim, survivor, and historian. Although the concept of transference I employ stresses the broad-ranged significance of the tendency to repeat— notably to repeat in one's own discourse or practice the processes active in, or projected onto, one's object of inquiry—this is no reason to slight the role of transference in a more restricted oedipal sense given the still significant role of the nuclear family and the parent-child relation in contemporary society.

10. Habermas refers to this type of explanation only to dismiss it as one of the "agitated reactions" he cannot understand: "With a retrospective identification with the victims, so it is said, the descendants of the perpetrators have gotten themselves a free and self-justifying

They may also become more subject to self-deception and ideological distortion, especially insofar as one is dispensed from a careful and self-critical examination of one's own implication in dubious ideas and practices. Anti-Semitism transformed into philo-Semitism may still trade in stereotypes (typically with the negative evaluation of supposed traits of the other—for example, nomadism and diasporic dissemination—converted into positive values), and it may remain within a quasi-sacrificial scapegoat mechanism whereby the victim of the past becomes the redeeming figure of the present with whom one identifies. Hence one may respond to Habermas that Goldhagen's book may have kept certain issues alive in public memory and the public sphere, but it may not have contributed to the attempt to come to terms with and work through the past in the manner Habermas advocated during the 1986 Historians' Debate, that is, a manner that accurately and critically engages a traumatic past, assists understanding while simultaneously counteracting prejudice and victimization, and helps lay the basis for a legitimate, self-scrutinizing, and self-critical democratic polity.

I nonetheless think that Goldhagen raises a question that deserves to be addressed, although he does relatively little to formulate or

---

kind of satisfaction, or have again seized the opportunity to reject their own tradition and to flee into the chimerical dream of a postnational nation" (264). Habermas's response should at least inhibit one from putting forth an explanation of this type in too self-certain a form. However, I think one may in significant ways contest Habermas's belief that "Goldhagen's case histories are well suited for an ethical-political process of self-understanding free from moralistic misunderstandings" (266). This is especially the case to the extent that the case histories are informed by Goldhagen's general thesis and propensity for identification. In addition, I think Habermas drives too sharp a wedge between professional historians and ordinary readers or intellectuals "of a current generation [who] seek to secure for themselves a historical heritage that, as citizens and members of a collective political life[,] they must inherit in one way or another" (267)—a wedge so sharp that it seems to undercut the dialogic dimension of professional history and the significance of historiography in the public sphere. On the other hand, Habermas also seems to ignore the degree to which Goldhagen himself identifies with victims in a manner that goes well beyond a carefully controlled, empirically and analytically tested dialogue with the past and tends to collapse any distinction between the historian and a group of (real or imagined) participants in events. Here it is possible to agree with certain of Habermas's goals concerning the attempt to come to terms with the past but respectfully disagree with his defense of Goldhagen's book as a useful or valid medium for that attempt.

provide the bases for addressing it in the right way. In any event, one should not respond to his hyperbole and one-sidedness with a comparable hyperbole or one-sidedness in framing issues. The question Goldhagen raises in an inadequate manner is that of victimization—particularly victimization linked to racial ideology—in its relation to genocide. He focuses on a dimension of victimization undertaken by perpetrators, perpetrators whom he understands in ways both too general (equating them with virtually all Germans) and too narrow (he lacks a comparative perspective and shows little concern for "willing" or complicitous actors in other countries). He also treats victimization in ways that are excessively general (through the use of under-specified psychological categories) and excessively narrow (a focus on anti-Semitism and Jews with insufficient investigation of broader racial ideology and other groups of victims).

The excessively general psychological terms include the (German) perpetrators' sadism, enjoyment of cruelty, and glee in the punishment and suffering of victims. Christopher Browning, of course, preceded Goldhagen in bringing out the extent to which members of Police Battalion 101 participated willingly in the killings and did not face punishment of an overt or severe sort if they did not participate.[11] It is no derogation of Browning's remarkable book to note that Goldhagen is, at least in one sense, not far from Browning, who (unlike Goldhagen) is multivariate in his approach to motivation but still stresses general psychological effects of sociocultural factors such as response to peer pressure, the felt need to be hard or macho and appear as "one of the guys," progressive brutalization in given circumstances, and the role of careerism. The effects may not be those Goldhagen emphasizes, but they are still situated on the level of general psychology with a more or less sociocultural inflection. The key difference, which Goldhagen polemically accentuates, is, of course, that Browning refers to ordinary men and implies that anyone in a certain situation might well be motivated to behave in a certain way while Gold-

---

11. Christopher Browning, *Ordinary Men: Reserve Police Battalion 101 and the Final Solution in Poland* (New York: Harper Collins, 1992).

hagen restricts his general psychological categories to Germans and argues that no explanation of a deviation from putative normality is required because of the long-term conditioning of Germans in "eliminationist" anti-Semitism.

The limitation that is at times apparent in the responses to Goldhagen lies in the tendency to restrict explanations to two broad, binaristically opposed options: (1) the role of industrialized mass murder, bureaucracy, the machinery of destruction, "desk murder," the banality of evil, and the behavior of ordinary men in extraordinary circumstances and (2) the role of perpetrators as anti-Semitic, cruel, sadistic, gleeful monsters. Moreover, the second option may be criticized solely or predominantly in terms of the first: for example, Norman G. Finkelstein writes:

> For what is the essence of Goldhagen's thesis if not that only deranged perverts could perpetrate a crime so heinous as the Final Solution? Lurid as Goldhagen's account is, the lesson it finally teaches is thus remarkably complacent: normal people—and most people, after all, *are* normal—wouldn't do such things. Yet the overwhelming majority of SS guards, Auschwitz survivor Dr. Ella Lingens-Reiner testified after the war, were "perfectly normal men who knew the difference between right and wrong." "We must remember," Auschwitz survivor Primo Levi wrote, that "the diligent executors of inhuman orders were not born torturers, were not (with a few exceptions) monsters: they were ordinary men." Not deranged perverts but "perfectly normal men," "ordinary men": *that* is the really sensational truth about the perpetrators of the Final Solution. (98)

Finkelstein also quotes Hannah Arendt: "The trouble with Eichmann was precisely that so many were like him, and that the many were neither perverted nor sadistic, that they were, and still are, terribly and terrifyingly normal" (99). The correlative stress is on the cold, efficient, dutiful bureaucrat who is (really or psychologically) distant from the victim, is prone to suspend ethical questions and compartmentalize tasks or aspects of existence, and forms part (often a cog in the wheels) of the "machinery of destruction." In line with this approach, the point is often made that the uniqueness of the Holocaust, its disconcerting modernity, lies in its conformity to standard operating procedures that typify the modern world. This stress is found in such important figures as Raul Hilberg, Zygmunt Bauman, and Tzvetan Todorov, among many others (including Heidegger and Philippe Lacoue-Labarthe, with their emphasis on modern technological enframing [*Gestell*]). The crux of this perspective is well formulated by Omer Bartov: "What was—and remains—unprecedented about the Holocaust is a wholly different matter, which Goldhagen avoids treating: the industrial killing of millions of human beings in factories of death, ordered by a modern state, organized by a conscientious bureaucracy, and supported by a law-abiding, patriotic, 'civilized' society."[12]

Bartov and others are certainly right to emphasize the importance of certain factors and to criticize Goldhagen for ignoring or downplaying them. Moreover, Goldhagen's belief in an emphatic, monocausal interpretation of perpetrator motivation is dogmatic and misleading; at times it amounts to little more than the compulsively repetitive illustration or imaginative, at times novelistically embellished, enactment of a preconception. Here it is important to realize that, whatever set of factors one treats, or even emphasizes, because of one's feeling that they are not being given due weight, one must insist on the point that the Nazi genocide was indeed overdetermined and complex in its causation and its motivation. This insistence is not simply evasive, as Goldhagen believes.[13] It is required by the complexity of the problems one is attempting, however inadequately, to address. Indeed, it is related to the critical and self-critical need to be open to a careful examination of different interpretations or explanations and not foreclose issues in a premature manner. But it is also the case that the stress on industrialized mass murder, the machinery of destruction, technology, (pseudo-)science, and bureaucracy (as well as peer pressure or careerism) do not fully account for the forces Goldhagen obsessively

12. Omer Bartov, "Ordinary Monsters," *New Republic* (April 29, 1996): 38.

13. Daniel Jonah Goldhagen, "Motives, Causes, and Alibis: A Reply to My Critics," *New Republic* (December 23, 1996): 39.

and graphically depicts and at times imaginatively projects or enhances. Nor are these forces accounted for by Goldhagen's appeal to a putatively generations-old German political culture of "eliminationist" anti-Semitism in its relation to general psychological traits such as cruelty, sadism, and *Schadenfreude.*

What the theses concerning both bureaucratic modernization and culturally induced sadistic cruelty tend to downplay are more specific responses and practices related to such tendencies as victimization, anxiety about contamination or pollution by outsiders who are—or threaten to be—within the *Volksgemeinschaft,* the desire to get rid of (*entfernen*) these unsettling others, and regeneration or even redemption through violence against relatively powerless or disempowered victims experienced (often in contradictory terms)—indeed, in some equivocal but predominantly negative fashion valorized—as powerful, conspiratorial, world-historical, erotically charged threats to the community and the self. The theses concerning bureaucratic modernization and gratuitous sadistic cruelty also downplay the specific role of Nazi ideology as both a cause and an enabler of these tendencies. I would also argue that appeals to "brutalization" (for example, through the experience of war) or to a regression to "barbarism" are of insufficient explanatory value and may even be misleading. So are notions of normality or ordinary behavior, for they tend (as Hannah Arendt seems to intimate) to prejudge what normal or ordinary people— "we"—are capable of doing and hence to stereotype and demonize so-called perversity. In other words, they assume too complacently that "we" know who "we" are and what "we" are capable of doing. They also engender a false sense of surprise about certain forms of belief, feeling, or behavior. Even more basically, they deflect attention from the need for more cogent categories of understanding and explanation—including self-understanding.[14]

14. Giorgio Agamben in *Homo Sacer: Sovereign Power and Bare Life,* trans. Daniel Heller-Roazen (1995; Stanford: Stanford University Press, 1998), discusses the "sacred man" as one who is a victim or outsider subject to murder by anyone but not to sacrifice or homicide. Agamben bases his elaborate intepretation on a relatively obscure Latin text of Pompeius Festus, whose import, as he understands it, is generalized and even applied to

I would also note that the focus on the motivation and behavior of "lower-level" and "middle-range" perpetrators, such as members of police battalions or, for that matter, functionaries in bureaucratic positions or even camp guards, is important but of restricted explanatory value. It is important to try to understand how seemingly "ordinary" people react in certain situations and to define those situations as carefully and accurately as possible. It is also important not to restrict responsibility for the Nazi genocide to Hitler and a small group of henchmen and instead to raise the larger question of the role and responsibility of people in other positions. But what may explain the behavior of "ordinary" people who went along with genocidal initiatives may not explain that of "movers and shakers" who put them in those positions or situations. Without excluding other factors or restricting responsibility to a handful of powerful figures, one thus returns to the question of the role of Hitler and other elite and often fanatically committed Nazis (a group not coterminous with the German people but also not restricted to Hitler and a few henchmen) and to the question of the relations between anti-Semitism, racism, and "bonding" with the leader (*Führerbindung*). Here one has a spec-

---

victims in the Holocaust. This procedure is, I think, dubious. The result is an overly reduced, analytic idea of the (impure) sacred divorced from ambivalence (which Agamben explicitly rejects and sees as a "mythologeme"). This one-sided conception of the sacred in its application to the Holocaust inserts the latter into one more variant of modernization theory in which the Holocaust becomes the culmination and paradigm of modernity. It also coincides with an often exaggerated emphasis on confined, positivistic, relatively antiseptic notions of biology, medicalization, and eugenics, which in Agamben are coordinated with a Foucauldian notion of biopower and biopolitics. Agamben gives little indication of how his interpretation fits into one current of historiography on the Shoah. Given the complexity of the phenomena, I do not think one can simply reject the dimension on which Agamben insists, but I find it too narrow. It does not account for Nazi quasi-ritual horror at contamination, elation in victimization, regeneration or redemption through violence, fascination with extreme transgression, and equivocation or even at times ambivalence with respect to the Jew (who was seen as abject—even as a germ or vermin—but to whom erotic energies and incredible powers of world conspiracy were also imputed). Moreover, Agamben does not account for the possible role of "cynical reason" whereby one may (at least in one part of the self) see through the baselessness of an ideology or practice—here the sacrifice of the presumably abject or verminlike Jew to the supreme leader as a means of redemption—but affirm or enact it anyway.

trum of possibilities applicable to the prime movers or perpetrators of the Nazi genocide (notably to upper-level SS and other extremely committed Nazis), including (1) fanatical racism (including anti-Semitism) and commitment to the leader along with affirmation of other aspects of the party program; (2) fanatical racism leading (or helping to lead) to commitment to the leader; (3) commitment to the leader leading (or helping to lead) to fanatical racism; and (4) commitment to the leader with the acceptance or at least the nonrejection of racism.[15] Few would doubt Hitler's fanatical racism and anti-Semitism, but different elite or relatively elite Nazis (including members of the SS at least above a certain rank) would fall on different points of this spectrum—a spectrum that, of course, could be further refined, especially in terms of possible combinations and changes in view or position over time. There is also the question of the relation of racism and anti-Semitism to the broader yet differentiated issue of victimization.

Jews were indeed victims of Nazi ideology and practice, and their victimization was legitimated and exacerbated by anti-Semitism. But there were other victims, and behavior, perhaps even motivation, with respect to them could be more or less similar to that directed at Jews. Without denying the distinctiveness of the history of anti-Semitism, the problem is to analyze the precise fashion in which it is related to other forms of racism and victimization in terms of similarities and differences. In these respects one needs more finely tuned and theoretically informed studies of victims and processes of victimization as well as a more complex understanding of (racist) ideology. To what extent may ideology mingle biological with murkier ideas, even with secular displacements of religion, and in what manner is it internalized and enacted by people? A simplistic idea of the relation between political culture and personality or a primary focus on the question of whether a perpetrator is willing or unwilling provides too restricted a basis for an approach to ideology and attendant phenomena, includ-

---

15. In significant ways, one might situate Martin Borman or Joseph Goebbels in the first category, Julius Streicher in the second, Heinrich Himmler in the third, and Albert Speer or Martin Heidegger in the fourth.

ing the problems of subject formation, ambivalence, equivocation, dissociation, evasion, and the role of more or less unconscious forces (notably the compulsive repetition of traumatic scenes).

There is also a point at which interpretation and explanation become more or less speculative and should be explicitly framed as such. Of course, any evidence confirming or discrediting speculation should be adduced, but certain speculations may open up areas of investigation and help lead to the discovery or reinterpretation of evidence (for example, the role of quasi-ritual anxiety about contamination or of carnivalesque glee and "gratuitous" cruelty in killing or punishing victims).[16] The difficulties with Goldhagen's speculations concerning the near ubiquity of longstanding "eliminationist" anti-Semitism in Germany and its effects in the Holocaust are at least fourfold: (1) they are not carefully framed as speculations but both asserted as factually confirmed hypotheses and adhered to dogmatically even in the face of strong counterevidence; (2) they are discredited by significant empirical considerations such as the widespread opposition to anti-Semitism of Social Democrats, the largest German political party in the late nineteenth and early twentieth centuries;[17] (3) they are confusingly

16. Commenting on a point I made concerning Nazi quasi-ritual or phobic anxiety about contamination, Gavriel Bach, a prosecutor at the Eichmann trial, told the audience at the May 28, 1998, session of the "Ideology and Historiography" conference in Jerusalem (the Second Leo Baeck Institute Summer Seminar of German and Israeli Historians) of a document that crossed his desk during the trial. It was a vitriolic letter complaining that milk taken from a woman one-quarter Jewish might contaminate pure German infants to whom it might be fed.

17. István Deák in "Holocaust Views" shows how Goldhagen traduces or fails to mention aspects of his own evidence which go against his thesis. Deák also succinctly adds the following points that counter Goldhagen's idea that the Germans embraced "eliminationist" anti-Semitism since the early nineteenth century: (1) "While there were laws against Catholics, Socialists, and Poles in the Second Reich, the Jews were gaining more rights. There was no shortage of anti-Semitic Germans at that time, some of them in important positions, but there were just as many, if not more[,] Germans, again some of them in important positions, who, for one reason or another, felt that the Jews should be made legally equal to the other Germans. Jews rose to much greater prominence in Germany than, for instance, in the United States." (2) "If 'racial antisemitism, pregnant with murder,' was as widespread in Germany as Goldhagen argues, then why did hundreds of thousands of Jews flee from Russia and Eastern Europe to Germany, and why were they allowed to settle there and even to thrive?" (3) "Anti-Semitism was more pronounced in pre–World

embedded in and made to color a narrative of events rather than situated clearly on an interpretive and explanatory level, where they may be critically examined and debated; (4) they warrant greater critical control, especially because they apply to highly sensitive material with at times pressing social and political implications in the present.

I would suggest that what is extremely difficult to understand in the Shoah is the combination of "modern" phenomena of the sort stressed by Hilberg and others and those that seem to be utterly out of place and even uncanny in a "modern" context—what Goldhagen alludes to in insufficiently nuanced or interpretively convincing terms, for example, scenes of beard burning, strip-searching, beating, and elation or carnival-type celebration during or after mass killings. I think this unexpected, indeed uncanny combination of the new and the (seemingly) old is oversimplified or even mistakenly understood in terms of regression to barbarism or even brutalization. (This kind of behavior is not typical of other animals but is distinctive of humans in certain contexts or situations. And, as Norbert Elias notes in terms still too beholden to theories of progress and regress bound up with notions of barbarism, the "progressive" movement of civilizing processes is not one-directional.)[18] In my own work I have directed attention, at least in a tentative and carefully framed fashion, to such phenomena as a deranged sacrificialism and even a returning repressed insofar as both a quasi-sacrificial ritual anxiety involving a perceived threat of contamination and a regenerative or even redemptive quest for purification, despite their importance in the modern world as well as in earlier times, often seem to find little place in conceptions of "modernity" or "modernization" and may at times be explicitly apparent only in relatively restricted ways in Nazi ideology itself.[19] Such phenomena are

War I France than in Germany. Tensions between Protestants and Catholics were actually more important to the Germany of Bismarck than the 'Jewish question'" (302).

18. Norbert Elias, *The Germans: Power Struggles and the Development of Habitus in the Nineteenth and Twentieth Centuries*, ed. Michael Schröter, trans. with a preface by Eric Dunning and Stephen Mennell (1989; New York: Columbia University Press, 1996).

19. They are, however, fairly evident in this statement from Hitler's *Mein Kampf:* "With satanic joy in his face, the black-haired Jewish youth lurks in wait for the unsuspecting girl

not unique to the Holocaust or to Germans, but there may be a distinctiveness in their correlation with, or imbrication in, more "modern" processes—a distinctiveness related to their uncanny side. Moreover, these phenomena have an equivocal relation to scientific or pseudoscientific racism and social Darwinism even in its extreme Nazi form. The putative struggle for survival of a superior race required war against peers and an elimination of "inferior" races, but this elimination of the putatively inferior could be formulated (often at one and the same time) both in seemingly neutral, bureaucratized, or sanitized terms (for example, pest control) and in quasi-ritualistic, phobic ones involving anxiety about contamination and degradation and a desire for liberation, regeneration, or even redemption.

Anti-Semitism was a crucial form of a discourse and practice which was at least in part quasi-sacrificial, but the latter could extend beyond anti-Semitism to encompass other more or less disempowered and debased (or abjected) victims such as the handicapped and "Gypsies," at times even Bolsheviks, Slavs, and homosexuals. The historically shaped (contingent but not simply arbitrary) scapegoating side of sacrificialism might, moreover, help to explain how the movement from the elimination to the extermination of victims could be, at least in one respect, made quickly or facilitated ideologically, for the basic problem is to get rid of (*entfernen*) the polluting other or constitutive "outsider" (the paradoxical insider/outsider or the outsider threatening to be within the *Volksgemeinschaft*), and the means of doing so

---

whom he defiles with his blood, thus stealing her from her people. With every means he tries to destroy the racial foundations of the people he has set out to subjugate. Just as he himself systematically ruins women and girls, he does not shrink back from pulling down the blood barriers of others, even on a large scale. It was and it is Jews who bring the Negroes into the Rhineland, always with the same secret thought and clear aim of ruining the hated white race by the necessarily resulting bastardization, throwing it down from its cultural and political height, and himself rising to be its master." *Mein Kampf,* trans. Ralph Manheim (1925; Boston: Houghton Mifflin, 1971), 325. The notion of race in such a passage functions in a number of inextricably intertwined or confused registers: pseudoscientific, magical, ritual, and phantasmatic. The anxiety about contamination in such a passage cannot be seen as purely scientific or hygienic.

may well be an instrumental matter. (Of course, this is not to deny that in other respects the move from expulsion or exclusion to genocide is of crucial significance for victims and may pose problems for perpetrators.) In any case, it might be fruitful to expand (without simply shifting or blurring) the focus of Saul Friedlander's notion of redemptive anti-Semitism in order to address the broader problem of (quasi-sacrificial) redemptive victimization and regeneration through violence—with anti-Semitism as one crucial, in certain ways distinctive, component of a larger range of more or less racialized perpetrator reactions to victims which should be investigated in further detail and in the light of certain theoretical issues.[20]

I would also note that the response to extreme, traumatizing events or limit cases, notably those involving victimization, tends to be ambivalent and often combines attraction and repulsion. One crucial role of certain moral norms is to help resolve this ambivalence in the direction of empathy with the victim and repulsion toward the perpetrator, including inhibitory repulsion with respect to the tendency toward perpetration or victimization in oneself. Sacrifice maintains the ambivalence of victimization and is in this sense extramoral or "beyond good and evil." Indeed, it compounds ambivalence insofar as it identifies the victim with a gift to a divinity or divinelike being (a status Hitler held for his committed followers). Moreover, in Nazi ideology and practice certain victims were abusively debased or abjected such that the ambivalent reaction toward them, which in other contexts might even involve identification with the victim, might be resolved in a predominantly, if not exclusively, negative direction with attraction or identification being foreclosed or repressed. This largely one-sided resolution of ambivalence, abetted by Nazi "transvalued" norms and propaganda, facilitated extreme hos-

20. Saul Friedlander, *Nazi Germany and the Jews* (New York: Harper Collins, 1997). For Friedlander, redemptive anti-Semitism "was born from the fear of racial degeneration and the religious belief in redemption" (87). Moreover, "Nazism was not mere ideological discourse; it was a political religion commanding the total commitment owed to a religious faith" (72).

tility and violence toward these victims whether taking bureaucratically distant or direct forms.[21] In contrast, to the extent ambivalence was sustained or resolved in the direction of empathy with victims, particularly when empathy was corroborated by normative principles (or when prejudice-induced, even visceral, repulsion was superseded by normative considerations enjoining help for victims), the response to victims could be different and even involve assistance or at least the desire to assist.[22]

To a significant extent, the type of participation in killing was different in bureaucratic contexts or, at least to some extent, in death camps, on the one hand, and in the earlier operations of *Einsatz-*

---

21. Still, the crucial role of Jews in German culture and the bonds formed over time implied that, in eliminating Jews, Germans were also tearing out and rejecting an important part of themselves. The extreme negativity of Nazi thought and practice with respect to Jews, as well as the anxiety (including Hitler's) over whether one had some Jewish "blood," attests to the internal force and significance of that which one had to repress, deny, and try to extirpate—in some confused and equivocal sense even to sacrifice. Moreover, as I noted in *History and Memory after Auschwitz* (36 n), Nietzsche was a figure appropriated by Nazis, and certain dimensions of his thought—reinforced by a hyperbolic, elated, at times oracular style—are open to interpretation in terms of Dionysian ecstasy or intoxication, radically transgressive and cruelly festive experimentalism, tradition-shattering transvaluation, equivocal anti–anti-Semitism allowing for anti-Semitic barbs, and this-worldly regeneration as well as the role of eugenics and breeding to create a race of superior beings. Yet there are also countercurrents in Nietzsche, including often self-directed irony and parody in addition to important tendencies critical of scapegoating and victimization. For an attempt to trace the uses and abuses of Nietzsche by Nazis, see Steven E. Aschheim, *The Nietzsche Legacy in Germany, 1890–1990* (Berkeley: University of California Press, 1992), chap. 8, and *Culture and Catastrophe: German and Jewish Confrontations with National Socialism and Other Crises* (New York: New York University Press, 1996), chap. 4.

22. Some combination of these factors seemed active in members of the Polish Zegota group, which helped Jews despite the Nazi penalty of death if they were caught. Various "righteous Gentiles" from different countries are, of course, honored at Yad Vashem in Jerusalem, and Steven Spielberg's *Schindler's List* has helped to focus perhaps excessive attention on the role of "rescuers"—a recent category in the cast of roles in the Holocaust. One may also note that even Major Trapp, the commander of Police Battalion 101, discussed by both Goldhagen and Christopher Browning, was emotionally as well as ethically upset by orders to kill Jews, and he delivered those orders in a tearful voice, at times continuing to weep throughout the day. He also offered to excuse any older men who felt unable to execute the killings, and a dozen or so men accepted his offer despite the fact that some of them elicited the disapproval of their comrades. Most men obeyed and continued obeying the orders for whatever combination of motives (the issue, of course, divides Browning and Goldhagen).

gruppen and related groups such as police battalions, on the other. The "machinery-of-destruction" approach emphasizes the former, and Goldhagen stresses the latter with the added proviso that more direct, cruel, and sadistic behavior also occurred in camps or on death marches. As Hilberg himself fully realized, the earlier operations resulted in the death of some million and a half victims, and this is a far from negligible aspect of the Nazi genocide. And, as Steven Aschheim, despite his generally critical appraisal of Goldhagen, remarks: "Goldhagen's shift of focus, although not entirely original, is important. He correctly reminds us that millions of people were murdered outside of the death camps, and that the dominant image of depersonalized, bureaucratic industrial murder tends to underplay the importance of the perpetrators themselves."[23] One obvious question is the extent to which the same forces set both the bureaucratic machinery and direct killing squads in motion and even whether key perpetrators, especially at relatively upper levels, shared important features. Despite its undoubted importance, even fanatical anti-Semitism may not be the only consideration in this regard, and the broader (but often overlapping) issue may be the complicity or investment in victimization, a quasi-sacrificial quest for purification from putatively contaminating others, regeneration or even redemption through violence, and the role of a negative sublime related to a fascination with excess or extreme transgression. In these respects figures such as Hitler or Himmler and Eichmann or Höss—despite their differences—might have shared important characteristics.

I have intimated that a negative sublime should be added to the complex mixture or combination of elements I have been discussing. By it is meant a tendency to accentuate the negativity that is perhaps always an important element of the sublime, for example, with respect to elation or exhilaration in extreme, traumatizing circumstances involving the risk of death or breakdown. Indeed, a function of certain ideologies is to transvalue the traumatic into a figure of the sublime, and Nazi ideology and practice achieved this feat in a particular, invid-

23. Steven Aschheim, "Reconceiving the Holocaust?" *Tikkun* 11 (1996): 64.

iously harmful, and extremely destructive way. One might also see the sublime as a secularization of the sacred and of the desire for radical transcendence of ordinary conditions and banality, including ordinary moral limits. In this respect, the sublime both converts trauma into an ecstatic source of elation and correlates—even conflates— transcendence with extreme transgression that breaks or goes beyond normative limits. (From certain perspectives this conflation would be blasphemous or, in secular terms, radically misguided.) Moreover, the quest for sublimity for the self or the in-group may require the abjection of the other.[24]

At least an aspect of Nazi ideology and practice involved a negative sublime and a fascination with unheard-of extremes of transgression. This aspect is prominent in one crucial dimension of Heinrich Himmler's 1943 Posen speech to upper-level SS officers, in which he, in this select public, transgressively discloses, this one time, the secret of extreme transgression that constitutes, for insiders, the glory of the Nazi genocide. In this speech, the prized quality of Nazi hardness is grounded in a seemingly paradoxical combination of (1) the ability to bring about and behold a geometrically increasing expanse of corpses (what might be seen as a sinister version of the Kantian mathematical sublime) and (2) ordinary moral decency or integrity (*Anständigkeit*) in other spheres of life (a notion of decency which might be related to the Kantian idea of beauty requiring form and limits). Conviction or even fanatical commitment, required for this hardness involving an antinomic linkage of the sublime and the morally beautiful, is seen by

24. This relation between the abject and the sublime may covertly be at play in certain sado-masochistic scenes that encrypt a quasi-sacrificial scenario. It may also be active in conversion experiences wherein the one reborn presumably goes from a former abject self to a transfigured and sublime new being. For Hitler the Germans (as well as Hitler himself) went from abjection after the Treaty of Versailles (and Hitler's own period of being down and out in Vienna) to sublime Aryan status, a status that required the abjection of the Jews and other victims. This dynamic of the sublime and the abject undermines or even excludes the beautiful, which depends on normative limits counteracting the role of extremes. Still, the complex and contradictory ideology of the Nazis allowed for an ideological conception of beauty as applied not only to conventional art but to the nation as a putatively well-ordered whole, indeed a totality.

Himmler as an initiatory quality of his audience in contrast to the more compromising or reasonable attitude of "ordinary" Germans, who, for Himmler, are prone to make an exception, benefiting at least one "decent" or "A-1" Jew, to the policy of evacuation and annihilation or extermination (which are in very close, indeed labile, proximity in this speech). Since (as noted in the last chapter) I take Himmler's speech to be in certain important respects a proof text of Nazi ideology and of an important current in modern thought more generally (especially with respect to an aesthetic of the sublime and the fascination with excess), I shall quote a portion of it which is still worth pondering:

> I also want to make reference before you here, in complete frankness, to a really grave matter. Among ourselves, this once, it shall be uttered quite frankly; but in public we will never speak of it. Just as we did not hesitate on June 30, 1934, to do our duty as ordered, to stand up against the wall comrades who had transgressed, and shoot them, also we have never talked about this and never will. It was the tact which I am glad to say is a matter of course to us that made us never discuss it among ourselves, never talk about it. Each of us shuddered, and yet each one knew that he would do it again if it were ordered and if it were necessary.
>
> I am referring to the evacuation of the Jews, the annihilation of the Jewish people. This is one of those things that are easily said. "The Jewish people is going to be annihilated" says every party member. "Sure, it's in our program, elimination of the Jews, annihilation—we'll take care of it." And then they all come trudging, 80 million worthy Germans, and each of them has his one decent Jew [*seinen anständigen Juden*]. Sure, the others are swine, but this one is an A-1 Jew [*ein prima Jude*]. Of all those who talk this way, not one has seen it happen, not one has been through it [*keiner hat es durchgestanden*]. Most of you know what it means to see a hundred corpses lie side by side, or five hundred, or a thousand. To have stuck this out, and—excepting cases of human weakness [*abgesehen von Ausnahmen menschlicher Schwächen*]—to have kept our integrity [*anständig geblieben zu sein*], that is what has made us hard. In our history this is an unwritten, never-to-be-written page of glory, for we know how difficult we would have made it for

ourselves if today—amid the bombing raids, the hardships and the deprivations of war—we still had the Jews in every city as secret saboteurs, agitators, and demagogues. If the Jews were still ensconced in the body of the German nation, we probably would have reached the 1916–17 stage by now.[25]

One may also quote in this respect a statement from Saul Friedlander, commenting on a segment of this passage—a statement in which Eichmann seems very close to Himmler at Posen with respect to a penchant for negative sublimity and radical transgression:

> Could one of the components of "Rausch" [elation or intoxication] be the effect of a growing elation stemming from repetition, from the ever-larger numbers of the killed others: "Most of you know what it means when 100 corpses are lying side by side, when 500 lie there or 1000." This repetition (and here indeed we are back, in part, at Freud's interpretation) adds to the sense of *Unheimlichkeit* [uncanniness], at least for the outside observer; there, the perpetrators do not appear anymore as bureaucratic automata, but rather as beings seized by a compelling lust for killing on an immense scale, driven by some kind of extraordinary elation in repeating the killing of ever-huger masses of people (notwithstanding Himmler's words about the difficulty of this duty). Suffice it to remember the pride of numbers sensed in the Einsatzgruppen reports, the pride of numbers in Rudolf Höss's autobiography; suffice it to remember Eichmann's interview with Sassen: he would jump with glee into his grave knowing that over five million Jews had been exterminated; elation created by the staggering dimension of the killing, by the endless rows of victims. The elation created by the staggering number of victims ties in with the mystical Führer-Bond: the greater the number of the Jews exterminated, the better the Führer's will has been fulfilled.[26]

25. In Lucy Dawidowicz, ed., *A Holocaust Reader* (West Orange, N.J.: Behrman House, 1976), 132–33. See my discussions of related issues in *Representing the Holocaust*, 105–10, and *History and Memory after Auschwitz*, 27–42.

26. Saul Friedlander, *Memory, History, and the Extermination of the Jews of Europe* (Bloomington: Indiana University Press, 1993), 110–11. One may compare my approach to victims and victimization with the more theoretically restricted but informative and thought-provoking account in Omer Bartov, "Defining Enemies, Making Victims: Germans, Jews, and the Holocaust," *American Historical Review* 103 (1998): 771–816.

These quotations from Himmler and Friedlander indicate that there may be certain often ignored or underplayed issues, however indirectly related to the Goldhagen debate, which are still worth considering and discussing in an attempt to understand better the Nazi genocide. A sensitivity to such issues might also alert researchers to otherwise ignored aspects of archival material that might further test the credibility of the considerations I have tried to bring forth.[27]

27. After finishing this book, I read Inga Clendinnen's *Reading the Holocaust* (New York: Cambridge University Press, 1999). Although written by an "outsider" and not based on original archival research, it is one of the reflective books on the Holocaust that raises consistently significant questions of interpretation and deserves to be widely read. Despite my appreciation of the book, it might be useful to mark some important differences from the approach I have taken. Clendinnen takes Clifford Geertz as guide to reading and interpretation, and she gives pride of place to Christopher Browning and Gitta Sereny in the specific area of Holocaust studies. The limitation of this perspective is that the often stylized semiotic focus on cognitively satisfying "meaning" avoids both the issue of excess that disorients or limits meaning and the problem of affect in general as well as empathy in particular, which Clendinnen identifies with intuition and dismisses (90). Moreover, the valorization of narrative tends to downplay the significance of theory and the explicit formulation of arguments or hypotheses in a manner that allows their critical testing. Hence, for example, Clendinnen does not indicate the perhaps necessary limitations of Sereny's biographical or Browning's largely narrative approach. Nor does she ask whether Geertz's highly stylized and choreographed "reading" of the Balinese cockfight, which she takes as paradigmatic for the reading of culture, is in important ways inadequate for the Holocaust—indeed, might lead to the type of "fetishized" narrative which tends stylistically to deny or smooth over the trauma that evoked it.

Clendinnen is critical of Saul Friedlander's emphasis on the role of excess, *Rausch* (intoxication, elation at excess), and the bond with the *Führer* (*Führerbindung*) (131), and although she sees some merit in Goldhagen's approach, she does not stress the elements that I find important. She also sees value in Hayden White's idea of the middle voice in historiography, indeed "would argue that we already hear something like this 'middle voice' in good historical writing today," for example, in Peter Brown, Robert Darnton, William Taylor, and E. P. Thompson. But Clendinnen provides no analysis of the nature and working of the middle voice, which remains vague in her account (179–80). Instead, her reliance on Browning and Sereny helps to induce a relatively atheoretical approach that remains on the level of common sense in stressing the more "ordinary" dimensions of the Holocaust, notably in terms of commonsensical interpretations of the extreme behavior of seemingly ordinary people such as those in police battalions. Clendinnen does recognize the nonutilitarian, ritualistic, and theatrical dimensions of Nazi behavior. But, despite her earlier work on Aztec sacrifice (and perhaps because of her restricted, rather humanistic understanding of sacrifice as requiring a markedly positive valorization of the other), she does not even raise the question (even though she touches on some of the elements) of deranged quasi-sacrificial behavior in at least certain Nazis, involving ritual anxiety at contamination, at times carnivalesque glee or even a theater of cruelty and absurdity, and a quest for regeneration, if not redemption, through violence against victims.

On the latter issues, in addition to my *Representing the Holocaust* and *History and Memory after Auschwitz*, see James M. Glass's ambitious study, *"Life Unworthy of Life"* (New York: Basic Books, 1997), esp. chap. 8. Glass provides abundant documentation concerning the role of the professions—notably physicians, administrators, and scientists—in developing and disseminating medicalized notions of racial hygiene based on purity of blood. But his argument that such groups "created the ideology and values of the regime" (60) goes too far in downplaying the role of political leaders and committed Nazis in other areas. Moreover, his idea of a group consciousness enthusiastically supporting the elimination of "life unworthy of life" and encompassing, with almost negligible exceptions during Hitler's reign, the entire German population does not go as far as Goldhagen in seeing a generations-long orientation, but it still constitutes a dubious exaggeration without sufficient evidence to back up the hyperbole. Yet, whereas Goldhagen is content to invoke—without adequately explicating the nature of—"eliminationist antisemitism," Glass does attempt to provide an extensive account of motivation. In my judgment, he does not pose with sufficient acuity the problem of the relation between medicalized, hygienic concerns and phobic or quasi-ritual reactions. At one point, he even makes the question-begging assertion that "racial hatred elaborated itself as a set of scientific principles obsessed with blood cleanliness, genetic purity, and a phobic reactivity to the potential of race contamination" (33). He may also rely overmuch on the contestable idea that Germany was beset with a collective pathology, indeed psychosis, that became normalized. Still, he does provide valuable material and partial analyses that may be integrated into a somewhat different overall understanding of the Nazi genocide.

5 ▌ *Interview for Yad Vashem (June 9, 1998)*

"Acting Out" and "Working through" Trauma

QUESTION: In all your writings on the Holocaust, you distinguish between two forms of remembering trauma (and historical writings on it). The first, which you consider the desirable one, results in the process of "working through"; the other is based on denial and results in "acting out." Can you characterize these two different kinds of memory?

LA CAPRA: I'm obviously trying to take the concepts of "acting out" and "working through" from Freud and from psychoanalysis and then developing them in a way that makes them especially interesting for use in historical studies. This means that I don't try to be orthodox as a psychoanalyst but really aim to develop the concepts in a manner that engages significant historical problems—and for me, the Holocaust is one of the most important of these problems.

This kind of approach has applications elsewhere, but it's especially important with respect to events (or series of events)—often traumatic events that are heavily charged with emotion and value and that always bring out the implication of the observer in the observed. This is what I discuss as transference—trying to understand it in a very broad sense, but in a way that is also faithful to Freud. The basic sense of transference in Freud is a process of repetition: specifically, the repetition of the oedipal scene in later life, the relationship between parent and child in situations such as that of teacher/student, or analyst/patient, in ways that may be inappropriate. Although oedipal relations have an obvious importance in a society in which the nuclear family becomes the typically overcharged locus of emotion and often a more or less mystified "haven in a heartless world," I think that transference extends beyond the oedipal relationship and that its confinement within that scenario amounts to a domestication that may well divert attention from one's implication in institutions and social relations that extend beyond but of course include and help to shape the family.

Hence, for me, transference basically means implication in the problems one treats, implication that involves repetition, in one's own approach or discourse, of forces or movements active in those problems. Transference takes place in relations between people (for example, students, notably graduate students, and professors) and perhaps more interestingly—because less developed—in one's relationship to the object of study itself. When you study something, at some level you always have a tendency to repeat the problems you are studying. Something like transference (or one's implication in the material along with a tendency to repeat) always occurs. This transferential relation helps one to understand the so-called contagiousness of trauma—the way it can spread even to the interviewer or commentator—and it provides a possibly thought-provoking way to rethink the problem of observer participation.

There are two very broad ways of coming to terms with transference, or with one's transferential implication in the object of study: acting out and working through. Acting out is related to repetition, and even the repetition compulsion—the tendency to repeat something compulsively. This is very clear in the case of people who undergo a trauma. They have a tendency to relive the past, to be haunted by ghosts or even to exist in the present as if one were still fully in the past, with no distance from it. Victims of trauma tend to relive occurrences, or at least find that those occurrences intrude on their present existence, for example, in flashbacks or in nightmares or in words that are compulsively repeated and that don't seem to have their ordinary meaning, because they're taking on different connotations from another situation, another place. The interviewer or even the commentator or observer may also tend to repeat the traumas of the victim, particularly when identification proceeds in an uncritical manner and is even valorized. Such repetition may in some sense be necessary, but it may also be mitigated through empathy that recognizes and respects the alterity or "otherness" of the other.

I think that, in Freud, if there's any broad meaning of the death drive that is not altogether mystifying or implicated in biological fantasies, it's the death drive as the tendency compulsively to repeat traumatic scenes—often violent scenes—in a way that is destructive and self-destructive. Yet I also believe that for people who have been severely traumatized, it may be impossible to fully transcend acting out the past. In any case, acting out (or "traumatic memory") should not be disparaged or seen as an utterly different kind of memory than working through—they are intimately related parts of a process. Acting out, on some level, may very well be necessary or inevitable, even for secondary witnesses or historians. On a certain level, there's that tendency to repeat which, if not confronted, tends to take place in a blind and unchecked manner— to return as the repressed or to recur as the dissociated.

I see working through as a kind of countervailing force (not a totally different process, not even something leading to a cure), and I tend to take my distance from therapeutic conceptions of psychoanalysis. Instead, I try to take psychoanalysis in more ethical and political directions. This, of course, does not mean blaming the victim, but it does mean that I see working through as a desirable process. In working through, the person tries to gain critical distance on a problem and to distinguish between past, present, and future. To put the point in drastically oversimplified terms: for the victim, this means the ability to say to oneself: "Yes, that happened to me back then. It was distressing, overwhelming, perhaps I can't entirely disengage myself from it, but I'm existing here and now, and this is different from back then." There may be other possibilities, but it's via the working through that one acquires the possibility of being an ethical and political agent.

Moreover, especially in an ethical sense, working through does not mean avoidance, harmonization, simply forgetting the past, or submerging oneself in the present. It means coming to terms with the trauma, including its details, and critically engaging the tendency to act out the past and even to recognize why it may be necessary and even in certain respects desirable or at least compelling. (The latter is especially the case with respect to a fidelity to trauma and its victims, the feeling, especially pronounced in certain victims, that there is something in the repetition of the past—say, in a nightmare—that amounts to dedication or fidelilty to lost loved ones and is a kind of memorial that is not based on suppression or oblivion.)

In any case certain wounds, both personal and historical, cannot simply heal without leaving scars or residues in the present; there may even be a sense in which they have to remain as open wounds even if one strives to counteract their tendency to swallow all of existence and incapacitate one as an agent in the present. One of the most difficult aspects of working through is the ability to undertake it in a manner that is not tantamount to betraying the trust or love that binds one to lost others—that does not imply simply forgetting the dead or being swept away by current preoccupations. The feeling of trust betrayed or fidelity broken (however unjustified the feeling may in fact be) is one of the greatest impediments to working through problems.

The other general thing I would add is this: it's interesting that the acting-out/working-through distinction—and it's a distinction, not a dichotomy or a separation into different kinds or totally different categories, but a distinction between interacting processes—is one way of trying to get back to the problem of the relationship between theory and practice. This is a problem we have almost tended to leave behind or leave in abeyance. And this is perhaps something we can get back to—at least we ought to make the attempt along with the effort to connect psychoanalytic categories to ethical, political, and historical issues.

In recent criticism (with which I agree in part), there has perhaps been too much of a tendency to become fixated on acting out, on the repetition compulsion, to see it as a way of preventing closure, harmonization, any facile notion of cure—but also, by the same token, to eliminate or obscure any other possible response, or simply to identify all working through as closure, totalization, full cure, full mastery. The result is a paralyzing kind of all-or-nothing logic in which one is in a double bind: either totalization and the closure you resist, or acting out the repetition compulsion, with almost no other possibilities. Within this constricted frame of reference, politics often becomes a question of blank hope in the future, an openness toward a vacuous utopia about which you can say nothing. And this view very often links up with an apocalyptic politics or perhaps a politics of utopian hope in the form of indefinite deferral of institutional change or even of substantive recommendations.

The tendency to valorize trauma, along with what is a fidelity to it or to its victims that brings a resistance to working through, is most understandable in the case of victims for whom leaving an unsettling bond with the past may be experienced as tantamount to betraying intimates who died or were destroyed by it. But, even in the case of severely traumatized victims, you may also find other tendencies in the self, including the ability to rebuild a life. For certain victims, for example, for certain Holocaust survivors, the ability to put together a personal life and sustain certain relationships may be all one can or should realistically expect. But in the case of others, this is not all that one can or should expect. One danger of identification with the victim is that it seems to make one a surrogate victim and a survivor, hence to justify an approach to life, including politics, that is not justified for someone who has in fact not undergone truly incapacitating experiences in relation to which survival may itself be more than enough. In any case, I don't think a resistance to working through or a fidelity to trauma should be generalized or emulated, however unconsciously through identification, by those who have the good fortune to be "born later" and are in a position to have different demands placed on them, notably in terms of forms of thought related to social and political action.

QUESTION: Where do acting out and working through affect the historian?

LA CAPRA: They affect the historian in secondary ways: As the historian studies certain processes, there are tendencies toward identification—or toward negative identification, total denial. In a sense, there are at least two extreme identificatory possibilities for the historian: the first is the extreme of full identification with participants. In a case such as that of the Holocaust, the figures with whom the historian has at least implicitly identified have often been bystanders, because the identification with the bystander is at least superficially closest to the other possibility for the historian— that is, the idea of full objectivity, neutrality, not being a player, not being a participant. There's also the possibility that the historian (or any other observer) might go to the extreme of full identification with the victim. There is something in the experience of the victim that has an almost compulsive power and should elicit our empathy. This empathy may go to the point of fascination or extreme identification, wherein one becomes a kind of surrogate victim oneself and assumes the victim's voice.

I've written that I think this happens to some extent to Claude Lanzmann in his film *Shoah*. There is in Lanzmann a fascination with the victim (in an older sense of *fascinatio*) and almost the desire to identify with the experience of the victim because Lanzmann himself was *not* a victim of the Shoah yet somehow feels that he *should* have been a victim, that he *should* have been part of this process. On one level, this is very moving, but it can also lead to a very intrusive kind of questioning in the actual encounter with the victim. It may even lead to an identification with the aggressor or perpetrator that manifests itself in aggressive, at times inquisitorial, questioning and in the ability flagrantly to transgress norms, as when Lanzmann says in an interview that he lied to Suchomel—a guard at Treblinka with a rank (*Unterscharführer*) analogous to that of sergeant—with "absolute arrogance."[1] One may justify lying in the circumstances Lanzmann found himself in, but not with absolute arrogance. So the way that the question of acting out and working through applies to the historian is in terms of this process of, at some level, being transferentially implicated in the problems you study and having to have some kind of response to them—a response that may, of course, include denial that anything like a transferential relation to the material exists.

I agree with very important conventional dimensions of historical research: gathering information and making sure that it is accurate as possible; checking facts; providing footnotes when necessary; and trying to arrive at a reconstruction of the past that is as validated and as substantiated as possible. This is absolutely necessary to historical understanding, but it's not *all* of it. There are other dimensions, including one's implication in the object of study, affective or emotional response, and how one comes to terms with that response. Again, the extremes in trying to come to terms with emotional response are full identification, whereby you try to relive the experience of the other, or find yourself unintentionally reliving it; and pure objectification, which is the denial of transference, the blockage of affect as it influences research, and the attempt to be as objectifying and neutral an observer as possible—whether as empirical fact gatherer or as structural, formal analyst.

The alternative to these complementary, mutually reinforcing extremes is trying to work out some very delicate, at times tense, relationship between empathy and critical distance. This is very much the problem of trying to relate acting out to working through

1. As Lanzmann puts it, "to lack human respect is to promise a Nazi that one will not disclose his name while it has already been given. And I did that with an absolute arrogance." "Les non-lieux de mémoire," in *Au sujet de Shoah: Le Film de Claude Lanzmann,* ed. Michel Deguy (Paris: Belin, 1990), 287.

itself. In acting out, one relives the past as if one *were* the other, including oneself as another in the past—one is fully possessed by the other or the other's ghost; and in working through, one tries to acquire some critical distance that allows one to engage in life in the present, to assume responsibility—but that doesn't mean that you utterly transcend the past. It means that you come to terms with it in a different way related to what you judge to be desirable possibilities that may now be created, including possibilities that lost out in the past but may still be recaptured and reactivated, with significant differences, in the present and future.

QUESTION: You said that acting out and working through are not opposites but a distinction. But you also stress the process. Now, isn't the word *process* already taken from the sphere of working through, and not from that of acting out? That means that you actually see acting out through the eyes of working through, and they're not balanced in your theory?

LA CAPRA: Acting out is a process but a repetitive one. It's a process whereby the past, or the experience of the other, is repeated as if it were fully enacted, fully literalized.

QUESTION: Correct me if I'm mistaken, but that's not the original, or the accepted, meaning of the word *process*—to proceed from one place to another.

LA CAPRA: Not all processes are teleological or developmental. Processes may be complex and involve various modalities of repetition. Acting out is compulsively repetitive. Working through involves repetition with significant difference—difference that may be desirable when compared with compulsive repetition. In any event, working through is not a linear, teleological, or straightforward developmental (or stereotypically dialectical) process either for the individual or for the collectivity. It requires going back to problems, working them over, and perhaps transforming the understanding of them. Even when they are worked through, this does not mean that they may not recur and require renewed and perhaps changed ways of working through them again. In this sense, working through is itself a process that may never entirely transcend acting out and that, even in the best of circumstances, is never achieved once and for all. If the process is dialectical, it is in terms of an open or unfinished dialectic that engages the complex prob-lem of repetition and may even lead to a rethinking of historic-ity and temporality in terms of various modes of repetition with change. For example, secularization is best understood neither as the identity of a present phenomenon or problem (for example, an ideology) with past religions nor as the total difference (or episte-mological break) between a present phenomenon or problem (ra-tionality, discipline, or punishment) and a past religious form. It is best understood as posing the question of the various forms of repetition and change over (or as) time, including repetitions that come with traumatic breaks but should not be understood in iso-lated terms as involving only discontinuities or breaks.[2]

Though I think that binary oppositions *are* very important in thinking, one of the fruitful contributions of deconstruction (the work of Jacques Derrida, for example) has been to show the in-stability of binary oppositions and the way in which binary opposi-tions (including the crucial opposition between identity and differ-ence) may be dubious. I think the binary opposition is very closely related to the scapegoat mechanism and that part of the process of scapegoating is trying to generate pure binary oppositions between (self-identical) self and (totally different) other, so that the other (let's say in the context of the Holocaust, the Jew) becomes totally different from the Nazi, and everything that causes anxiety in the Nazi is projected onto the other, so you have a pure divide: Aryan/Jew—absolutely nothing in common. You can show that this ex-treme binarization is actually a way of concealing anxiety and the ways in which the seemingly pure opposites also mark each other and may share certain things.

2. On these issues, see especially my "Temporality of Rhetoric," in *Soundings in Critical Theory* (Ithaca: Cornell University Press, 1989), chap. 4; "The Return of the Historically Repressed," in *Representing the Holocaust: History, Theory, Trauma* (Ithaca: Cornell Univer-sity Press, 1994), chap. 6; and "Rereading Foucault's History of Madness," in *History and Reading: Tocqueville, Foucault, French Studies* (Toronto: University of Toronto Press, 2000), chap. 3.

A distinction, I would argue, is different. It is *not* a pure binary opposition but rather involves a notion of difference, but a difference that's not a pure or total difference. The problem that deconstruction leaves us with in the wake of the undoing of pure binaries, with which I agree, is: How do we then elaborate desirable distinctions? From my point of view, deconstruction does not blur or undermine all distinctions; it leaves you with a problem of distinctions that are, if anything, more difficult and more necessary to elaborate, given the fact that you cannot rely on simple binaries. One also has to insist on the point—a point at times obscured in work that addresses texts in the literal sense—that deconstructing a binary opposition does not automatically cause it to go away or to lose its often constraining role in social and political reality: analyzing that role and its force is also crucial both for historical understanding and for social or political action. Acting out and working through, in this sense, constitute a distinction, in that one may never be totally separate from the other, and the two may always mark or be implicated in each other.[3] But it's very important to see them as countervailing forces and to recognize that there *are* possibilities of working through that do not simply loop endlessly back into the repetition compulsion or go to the (illusory) extreme of total transcendence of acting out, or total transcendence (or annihilation) of the past.

One of the important tendencies in recent thinking has been to eliminate possibilities of working through, or at least not to provide much insight into them. Rather, one remains within a double bind or even within a notion of acting out, almost collapsing—or blurring entirely—the distinction between acting out and working through. In other words, one remains within, or identified with, the traumatized victim for whom the distinction between acting

3. One may even argue that deconstruction underscores the propensity to act out binaries as if they were pure oppositions, and the challenge is not simply to blur or undo them but to work (and play) through them toward viable distinctions that may, at least provisionally, be articulated in desirable ways.

out and working through may indeed be unavailable or utterly blurred. At times one has a newer, even a psychoanalytically based, fatalism.

With reference to certain problems, such as mourning—which can be seen in Freud as one important mode of working through—one may never entirely transcend an attachment to a lost other, or even some kind of melancholic identification with a lost other. But one may generate countervailing forces so that the person can re-engage an interest in life. One sign of this in the process of mourning is the ability to find a new partner, to marry, to have children, and not to be so enmeshed in grieving that the present doesn't seem to exist for you, and there is no future.

In certain forms of contemporary theorizing, whereby working through is simply seen in a kind of extreme Pollyanna redemptive mode, mourning itself may always seem fatalistically to come back to an endless melancholy. There may be very little, if any, distinction between mourning and melancholy: the mourning that is criticized is that which utterly transcends the past, and the mourning that's affirmed is virtually indistinguishable from endless melancholy and a kind of repetition compulsion.

At times, I wonder whether in someone like Derrida the notion of impossible mourning, as endless grieving, is virtually indistinguishable from endless melancholy. The reason is that mourning itself seems to become an almost metaphysical or metametaphysical, quasi-transcendental process, and the distinction between the metametaphysical and the historical may itself be evanescent or very difficult to perceive. Moreover, there may be little, if any, attention paid to mourning as a *social* process or ritual and not simply an individual or quasi-transcendental state of bereavement or compulsively endless grieving, often related to a putative loss of absolute foundations or origins.

In the case of someone like Walter Benjamin (at least in the early Benjamin, for example, in the *Origin of German Tragic Drama*), what you seem to have is the notion of the mourning play as a play of endless melancholy. Melancholy cannot be transcended, and Benjamin himself is in some sense against a redemptive notion of mourning. Now again, what I want to argue is this: that I, too, would want to criticize any kind of fully redemptive notion of mourning and that, especially for the victim, it may be impossible fully to transcend acting out.

Especially with respect to an event of such incredible dimensions as the Holocaust, it may also be impossible for those born later ever to transcend this event fully and to put it in the past, simply as the past. And it may be important to stress that impossibility, especially in cultural settings that valorize pragmatism, often in relatively superficial forms, and are immersed in the vapid triumphalism and self-congratulatory histrionics of Reaganism or a simplistic therapeutic, "feel-good" ethos in general. But it may be possible, and in some sense it has to be possible, if you believe in anything like a viable democratic politics, to enable and try to bring about processes of working through that are not simply therapeutic for the individual but have political and ethical implications.

The one thing that's a mystery to me is this: if you have an analysis in which mourning is always impossible mourning, that is, in the very closest proximity to melancholy, if not fatalistic or identical with interminable melancholy, how, then, do you affirm a democratic politics with a viable and desirable conception of a possible future? What are the mechanisms for bringing about agency that would enable people to engage in civil society, in political activity? Doesn't that always remain somehow beyond one's grasp, beneath one's dignity, or beneath one's level of metametaphysical interest?

This is why I think that what very often happens in Walter Benjamin, and in Derrida's rather sympathetic analysis of Benjamin (when he discusses the "Critique of Violence" with some caveats), or even at times in someone like Fredric Jameson, or in Hayden White, is that you have an analysis that doesn't seem to enable other forms of working through—an analysis that somehow wants to affirm the necessity of being implicated in trauma and yet also wants politics.[4] But the politics that comes out is often a blind messianism or what Derrida terms a "messianicity without a messiah," even at times apocalyptic politics or what I call the "hope in a blank utopia"—a utopia that is utterly blank because you can say nothing about it, and it has virtually nothing to do with processes in the present. It is important to stress that an ideal of justice or goodness can never be fully realized and that an existing institution is always open to criticism, but this emphasis does not entail a conflation of responsibility with decisionism, absolute risk taking and a leap of faith, or the hope in a blank utopia—or even creation *ex nihilo*.

This is a kind of paradox: How do you affirm a democratic politics if you don't have some notion of working through that is not identical to full transcendence (or a leap of faith) and yet is distinguishable from, and acts as a countervailing force to, endless repetition of the past or being compulsively implicated in trauma, or continually acting out and validating trauma?

Redemptive Narratives

QUESTION: What do you really mean by redemptive narrative, and why do you criticize it so much? Can you give examples from the United States, from Germany, or from Israel?

LA CAPRA: I agree with something like the necessity for what Benjamin calls "weak messianic values," and I would see them in terms of ethics, its relation to politics, and the need to develop a notion of ethics, both in the broader sense and in more specific senses. One of the crucial problems of ethics is the relationship of normative limits and that which transgresses or exceeds limits. You also have to try to

4. See Jacques Derrida, "The Force of Law: The 'Mystical' Foundation of Authority," *Cardozo Law Review* 11 (1990): 920–1045, and my response to it in the same volume, "Violence, Justice, and the Force of Law," 1065–78, which was written before Derrida added the footnote on 977–78 and the "Post-scriptum" on 1040–45. See also my "Reconfiguring French Studies," in *History and Reading,* chap. 4, which includes a discussion of Derrida's addenda.

see the ways in which that relationship really can be worked out in different areas of life: the relationship between normative limits that you want to affirm and the possibility of transgressing those limits, which is the only way in which you get a newer normativity. There are some forms of normativity you might want to place in question, some you may want to reform, and others you may want to test critically and perhaps validate. But the relationship between limits and excess is a crucial problem. Again, one of the difficulties in certain forms of contemporary, postmodern, poststructural thinking is the focus on or even the affirmation of excess without sufficient attention to the problem of the actual and desirable relationship between excess and limits (or hyperbole and framing).

Even someone like Saul Friedlander, in his partial affinity with postmodernism, would accept the idea that in the Holocaust there is excess, which is unrepresentable and difficult to conceptualize. On a certain level, I agree. But one of the techniques of certain forms of poststructural thinking has been to try to counteract excess through excess. This is, in a way, a homeopathic response. You take the "illness" and you counteract it through a proper dosage of the illness itself. I think that may be necessary. The modern context is, in some sense, excessive. Eric Hobsbawm refers to the modern period as an "age of extremes."[5] The so-called postmodern context may be even more excessive—what Lyotard sees as an intensification of the modern. The recent past is also a post-Holocaust context, and this has had, usually in subterranean ways, until the present, an effect on thinking—it tends to contribute to the destabilization of thinking and to render less feasible certain kinds of redemptive thinking, for example.

This is one reason why traditional religions, Hegelianism (seen in stereotypical ways), and any form of thinking that seems to redeem the past and make it wholly meaningful through present

5. Eric Hobsbawm, *Age of Extremes: A History of the World, 1914–1991* (New York: Pantheon, 1994).

uses no longer seem plausible. The extent of the crisis, the extent of the unsettlement, are simply too great to make that feasible to people; it just doesn't seem to hang together. It's what Lyotard calls the incredulity or the disbelief about grand narratives: we no longer seem to take seriously these grand narratives that make sense of everything in the past—narratives that at certain points seem to appeal to people very much.

If you believe in the biblical story, you do, in a sense, believe in a grand narrative of history, so that everything, even the most disastrous catastrophes, will ultimately make sense to you—maybe not now, but at some point of illumination in the future. This no longer seems to be feasible to many, or at least a significant number of, people.

So I agree that there is something like an excess with which one has to come to terms. And that at certain levels one has to realize that one, oneself, participates in this excess; that there may be certain excessive, hyperbolic features in oneself; and that one has to undergo the temptation of excess. Then, though, the question is how one comes to terms with it. One of the things I've written is that in certain thinkers there is, at times, the tendency to overdose on the antidote or simply go with the flow—of excess, of desire, of symptomatic behavior. This is to say, to participate too fully in excess and to affirm excess, with almost an oblivion of the problem of how to relate excess to legitimate limits (or desire to desirability), which is the ethical problem. If you affirm excess only, I think that's a transcendence or an undercutting of ethics toward, often, an aesthetic of the sublime.

There's a relationship between excess and the sublime. The sublime is, in some sense, an excess, an excess that overwhelms the self, almost brings it to the point of death, but then leads to elation when the self escapes the threat of death. In recent thinking, there's an incredible fascination with an aesthetic of the sublime. Again, this is in some sense necessary, but one should also try to situate it. The one way in which one tries to situate it is to try to distinguish among possibilities of the sublime, not simply, for example, to see the Holocaust as sublime in its excess. There is a tendency at times to envision the Holocaust homogeneously as some overwhelming, sublime event. This can perhaps be found at times in Lyotard, in Hayden White, and it's somewhat questionable. There you really need to have a much more modulated, self-critical response. But what this emphasis on the excess of the Holocaust does is to insist upon a certain unsettlement in its aftermath and to place in radical jeopardy any facile notion of redemption or harmonization—and I agree with this.

On the question of examples of redemptive narratives, if you take the conventional narrative structure itself—with a beginning, a middle, and an end, whereby the end recapitulates the beginning after the trials of the middle and gives you (at least on the level of insight) some realization of what it was all about—there's a sense in which the conventional narrative is redemptive. Various people, including Northrop Frye and M. H. Abrams, have argued (perhaps too much in terms of secularization as the basic identity of, or continuity between, past and present) that conventional narratives are displacements of the biblical structure of Paradise, Fall, History—history as a period of trial and tribulation—and then redemption. So, in the conventional narrative itself, there is a kind of displacement of a biblical structure that is redemptive.

Frank Kermode is another scholar who has also written about this in his book *The Sense of an Ending*.[6] He calls the conventional narrative "apocalyptic," in that the end resonates with the beginning on a higher level of meaning and significance. Through the more or less catastrophic events of the middle, the beginning is riven or split apart and gives way to a progressive or revelatory insight at the end. Kermode has a rather amusing, low-keyed example of the way we listen to, and perceive the ticking of, a clock: "tick-tock, tick-tock." He sees the "tick" as a humble genesis, and

6. Frank Kermode, *The Sense of an Ending: Studies in the Theory of Fiction* (New York: Oxford University Press, 1967).

the "tock" as a feeble apocalypse, so that all of time is coded in terms of "tick-tock" that's developmental and progressive.

A specific example of a redemptive narrative is *Schindler's List*. This is a very interesting film for the first three-quarters or so, where you have the ambiguities of the Schindler character brought out. The fact that he is a Nazi trying to help Jews is retained in its tension, for you have a Nazi who is also an impresario, self-interested, self-indulgent, but nonetheless trying to help other people—in that, you have a certain interesting tension. Toward the end, you have the resolution of all the tensions as Schindler emerges as a martyr and a hero. His associate becomes a sort of Gandhi figure, leading the people across the horizon toward some unimaginable new beginning—you don't know where they're going; you think they may be going to a land of redemption. And then there is also the final ritual, which is really a kind of redemptive ritual, rather than a form of mourning that is tensely bound up with the problems of the past. Instead you almost have a "Yellow Brick Road" along which the survivors come and in some sense redeem their past.

Another example of redemptive narrative is a certain kind of Zionist narrative. Here it's rather curious that a certain kind of Zionist narrative has almost a biblical model of some past Eden, when there was a state and a people, then Diaspora related to a fall. The Holocaust is in some sense the necessary culmination of Diaspora, showing the error of stateless wandering, during the Diaspora, and then the foundation of the state of Israel as the redemptive moment. This is a very simplistic Zionist narrative, and not all people who call themselves Zionists affirm this narrative. But it had a certain force in Israeli history—related to why, for such a long time, survivors were not understood in terms of their experiences, might not even be listened to. The demand on the survivor was to undergo transformation into a new Israeli citizen—that demand has problematic implications for people in the way they relate to one another. In Israel itself, it is only relatively recently that people have been willing to listen to survivors.

There are many reasons for survivor videos: first, the obvious sense that soon people will no longer be alive and they'll no longer be available to listen to; second, the role of an audience. As many people have pointed out, right after the events there was a rush of memoirs and diaries, and then it all sort of died down for a fairly long period of time—what is tempting to interpret as a period of latency after a traumatic series of events. One of the reasons is that survivors found—in different countries, for different reasons—that they didn't have an audience; they didn't have people who wanted to listen to them.

In Israel, they didn't want to listen to survivors basically because Israelis were trying, for understandable reasons, to construct a different kind of state with a different kind of political agent. So, in a way, the aim was to go from victim to agent, without passing through survival and the process of working through the past. There was a desire to leap from victim to agent without having that intervening process, just transcending the status of victim. This doesn't work; it can only create difficulties, at least in human relations, and often politically.

In the United States, the survivors didn't have an audience in the general public either. To oversimplify, it was almost like going from Auschwitz to Disney World—and in Disney World, people don't want to hear about Auschwitz. It's a very different context.

Different things can also be said about different countries. In France, for example, why was there the notion of the *déporté* that was used as a homogenizing device to amalgamate various victims, notably Jews and political prisoners? It's rather amazing that, for a rather long time, the prototypical survivor account was that of Robert Antelme—very interesting, very important, but the account of a political prisoner. This is the figure about whom Maurice Blanchot and others wrote and took as the prototypical survivor. Again, this tendency worked to mask certain things, such as the specific problems of Jews as survivors and as victims under Vichy and under the Nazis. There are many, many redemptive forms of narrative.

The Uniqueness of the Holocaust and the Proper Name

QUESTION: Vis-à-vis your answer about excess and the sublime, I have a question about the uniqueness of the Holocaust and the proper name for it. Should it be called this, or perhaps the "Judean genocide" or something else?

LA CAPRA: The problem of uniqueness has been a cause of concern to many people, and it bears on the question of what happens when you call the Holocaust unique. There's an obvious sense in which everything is unique, and everything is comparable, but this is not really the sense in which people are trying to address the Holocaust. My feeling is that it's probably best to talk about the distinctiveness of the Holocaust, rather than its absolute uniqueness, and my perspective on the notion of uniqueness is multiple.

There is a *contextual* justification for arguing the uniqueness of the Holocaust, when there are very strong tendencies toward revisionism, denial, and normalization. For this reason, let's say in the context of the German historians' debate (of 1986), there may have been good reasons for someone like Eberhard Jäckel to insist on the uniqueness of the Holocaust and then even try to define how, historically, it was unique to that point in time. The American historian Charles Maier has argued that it's even more forceful and more cogent when a German in that context argues for uniqueness than for a Jew to do it. The German in such a case is not deriving the same kind of benefit but even doing something that may not entirely be in accord with self-interest. The difficulty with the concept of uniqueness is that it *can* easily serve identity politics and a certain kind of self-interest, and it can also become involved in what may be termed a grim competition for first place in victimhood. Whose experience was it that was *really* unique? I think that such an approach is unfortunate. You should try to understand various phenomena, both in their own specificity and in ways whose conceptualization may enable you better to understand, and to come to terms with constructively, other phenomena.

There's another sense of uniqueness, which Saul Friedlander

touches upon in one of his essays: that something is unique when it passes or transgresses a certain limit, when it becomes a limit experience. This is a really interesting notion of uniqueness, a non-numerical notion of uniqueness. It doesn't mean this happened only once, and in all probability *can* happen only once, but that something happened that was so outrageous, so unheard of, that it is . . . unique. And in that way you can have something unique that is indeed repeated in history, but repeated in uniqueness, in a kind of paradoxical way. This is also a valid notion of uniqueness: that something is so excessive in its transgressiveness that it somehow is unique.

The danger of becoming fixated on the concept of uniqueness is that it necessarily has ideological functions, and the question is whether you really want it to have those functions. It may also lead to research about similarities and differences that after a certain point becomes rather pointless as research. It may divulge very interesting historical information (as it has in the work of Steven Katz), but you really wonder, in spite of denials, if there is a very strong ideological motivation when you're directing all of your research around this question of uniqueness.

So, again, my perspective on uniqueness is a qualified one. And the same sorts of considerations are at play in the use of a term. This, for me, brings out the significance of what I mentioned before—the importance of one's implication in one's research—and some kind of transferential process that goes on. With respect to enormously significant events, this process starts on the level of naming: How do you name the event? There is not a single name you might invoke that is entirely devoid of connotations or entirely innocent. In some way, that problem of implication, your own implication, your own response, begins on the level of naming. Whether you call it the Holocaust with a capital *H,* the holocaust with a small *h,* the Shoah, the Nazi genocide, and so forth—all of these exist in different semantic and affective spaces.

For an American to use the term *Shoah* may have a slightly exoticizing potential. And it also owes a great deal to Lanzmann's film. I don't think anywhere in the world it was called *Shoah* in a frequent public way before that film, and it's evidence of the power of the film, or more generally the media, in our culture that this term has been taken up. *Holocaust* apparently came into prominence in the fifties in the United States in the discourse of survivors, and it has raised objections because it exists in a sacrificial context: it means a burnt sacrificial offering. Scholars sometimes point this out and even use it as a reason to avoid the term, but most people who use the term today probably have no idea of, or at least little concern for, its etymology. It's the term they use because it's the one that's in currency in the culture.

There's even a way in which the common use of the term has a perhaps beneficial, banalizing effect, because it counteracts the sacrificial connotations. Again, my feeling is that the problems of implication (ideological implication, emotional implication) begin with naming, and certainly with the question of whether or not the event is unique. Whether the name should be unique is closely related to whether the event is unique, and all of these questions of uniqueness and naming necessarily get pulled up into a kind of theological matrix, because it's a question of negative sacralization. And the problem of uniqueness is related to the extent to which the Holocaust has become part of a civil religion of sorts and has at least a kind of negative sacrality—the way in which it becomes what I've recently been calling a "founding trauma"—a trauma that should, and (in the best of all circumstances) does, raise the question of identity as a very difficult question but that, as a founding trauma, itself becomes the basis of an identity.

This is an extreme and interesting paradox—how something traumatic, disruptive, disorienting in the life of a people can become the basis of identity formation. If you think about it, this probably happens in the lives of all peoples, to a greater or lesser extent. All myths of origin include something like a founding trauma, through which the people pass and emerge strengthened; at least they have stood the test of this founding trauma. The Civil War or, more recently, the war in Vietnam for the United States, the French Revolution in France, the battle of Kosovo in Serbia, and certainly the Holocaust in Israel (and for worldwide Jewry, and perhaps even more broadly at the present time) can be seen as in some way indicating that through a trauma one finds an identity that is both personal and collective at the same time. Again, this is understandable, but it also should be questioned: the trauma should be seen as raising the question of identity, rather than simply founding an identity. So this is a complex of problems: the uniqueness of the Holocaust; how you name the Holocaust; and how the Holocaust is functioning ideologically and politically.

The "Negative Myth of Origin"

QUESTION: Can you be more specific about the dangers of the "negative myth of origin"?

LA CAPRA: This, again, relates to the notion of the redemptive narrative, and the ways in which certain events, which should really pose ethical and political problems as serious problems, are assimilated in a way that is too easily redemptive. There are at least two ways in which the Holocaust, as a founding trauma, becomes somewhat questionable. The first is in providing people with too facile an identification, which is not earned and which becomes a basis of identity that is too readily available. For example, it has often been said, with respect to American Jewry, that identification of oneself through the Holocaust becomes a way of constructing an identity that one is not able to elaborate otherwise, and that identification is somewhat questionable.[7]

The more specific political uses have been documented to some extent by someone like Tom Segev, where you have the argument that at least during significant portions of Israeli history, the Holocaust could be invoked as a way of justifying policies that it would

---

7. As noted in Chapter 1, one finds an extremely forceful, albeit contestable, analysis and critique of this identification in Peter Novick, *The Holocaust in American Life* (New York: Houghton Mifflin, 1999).

be hard to justify fully on other grounds.[8] This is understandable in certain ways: it is true that people who have personally been through a certain experience (or at least have that experience as part of their cultural heritage) are sensitized to specific things and may react to experiences in a way in which someone who has not shared in that past will not even initially understand. But, in addition, becoming more aware of the way in which a phenomenon can serve as a founding trauma and can have political functions may enable one to take a certain distance from those functions and say, "Wait a minute. Am I doing things here that are not entirely justified by the situation, but are being stimulated by a past that is still very active in the present, and that I have not worked through as the past?"

Functionalism, Intentionalism, and the Concept of Scapegoating

QUESTION: There are two large schools of thought in the historiography of the Holocaust and of Nazism: the functionalist versus the intentionalist approach. Can you explain your critique of both of these schools? What is your suggestion vis-à-vis scapegoating, and why is it different in essence (if you can say that) from the above-mentioned two approaches?

LA CAPRA: One would have to argue that there *is* no singular key to the explanation of the Holocaust. There are a number of factors, and often it's very difficult to give the appropriate weight to the different factors. Most people at the present time (for example, Christopher Browning or Saul Friedlander) are neither functionalist nor intentionalist. They see a limited value in both approaches: there are some elements that were planned, at least on some level, even if you cannot go back to 1923 and see an entire schema of the Holocaust laid out. There are those who would also argue that the dynamic of institutions, the functioning of institutions, the activity of bureau-

8. Tom Segev, *The Seventh Million: The Israelis and the Holocaust* (New York: Hill & Wang, 1993).

crats on the middle and lower levels were significant phenomena—these are the things that are generally focused on by functionalists. But most people now would argue that there is not really a debate and that the qualification of something as a debate between two schools is a sign of its professionalization within a discipline. Professionalization in this sense is something that's understandable, and also—insofar as it implies routinization—something about which one might want to raise questions.

One way of questioning it is by seeing what the combatants actually share and what is invisible to them. In this respect the functionalist/intentionalist controversy may be compared to the Zionist/post-Zionist debate in Israeli historiography. The post-Zionists are making the important argument that the Zionist redemptive narrative blinded people to certain aspects of the Israeli past, including the ways in which relations between Israelis and Palestinians were much more complicated than would be implied by the little-Israel-against-the-whole-Arab-world or "David-and-Goliath" narrative. Thus the entire question of relationship to the Palestinians has to be rethought. What is very interesting from the "outside," however, is the way in which both the Zionists and the post-Zionists share a great deal. They share a focus, if not a fixation, on Israel, often in noncomparative ways. Their interest in the Holocaust tends to be limited to the reactions of Zionist leaders to the Holocaust. Not renewed in the entire debate are, for example, the questions of world Jewry, including German Jewry, *Yiddishkeit,* the significance of the reconstruction of *Yiddishkeit,* and the importance of the Diaspora. You might say that within the Zionist narrative, the Diaspora was an erring that somehow showed the necessity of the state of Israel. This is not the message of the post-Zionist narrative, but still the Diaspora is marginalized in it. You don't have a new reading of the Diaspora. From the outside, you can see what these contending schools tend to share, which is extremely important but not very visible to them, because they're so caught up in the debate that its terms define the parameters of the argument.

Something similar happens with the intentionalists versus the functionalists. There, too, you might say that they share a great deal and also don't look carefully enough at certain dimensions of the Shoah. What I've been trying to insist upon is that the dimension they don't look carefully at is a certain aspect of Nazi ideology and practice. This I tend to see in terms of a somewhat crazed sacrificialism and scapegoating, which seems especially uncanny and out of place because it happens within a modernized context, where indeed you do have phenomena such as extensive bureaucratization, industrialization of mass murder, functional imperatives, and so forth. One can see these phenomena and how important they are. But I think there is also scapegoating in a specific sense within contingent historical circumstances, scapegoating related to a horror, an almost ritual and phobic horror, over contamination by "the other." Within a certain Nazi framework, the Jew was a pollutant or a contaminant literally or figuratively in the *Volksgemeinschaft* that had to be eliminated for the Aryan people to reachieve its purity and wholeness. Part of the regenerative, or what Friedlander calls redemptive, violence of the Holocaust was directed at trying to eradicate anxiety localized on the Jew and perhaps at times on other victims in terms of that fear of contamination.

The way in which it was done is related to another dimension of sacrificialism, which in a secular context is very close to the sublime and might be seen as a displacement of the sacred. The sublime is a sort of secular sacred, related to that which goes beyond ordinary experience and is almost, if not altogether, transcendent. Within the Nazi phenomenon you had something like a fascination with unheard-of transgression, bound up with this fear of ritual contamination that led to behavior that is otherwise unintelligible or seen only in terms of general psychological or sociopsychological categories (peer pressure, careerism) and universal traits of human behavior (hatred, sadism). This behavior did include extremely cruel, at times gleeful, pleasure in the suffering of others and scenes that are almost like those out of a carnival, scenes of bloody massacre, where people are elated—clapping, cheering—at what is happening, in ways that may be incomprehensible to them if you were to ask them about it and that they may very well repress or suppress in later life. The question is how this behavior may be understood in historically specific although not altogether unique terms, and I think the notions of victimization, ritual or phobic anxiety, a crazed sacrificialism, and scapegoating—uncanny because inserted within a seemingly inhospitable "modern" context involving bureaucratization, the "machinery of destruction," biologism, and so forth—may be of use in this respect.

So the intentionalists stress conscious policy, but there are aspects of ideology that may not be altogether conscious to the person, at least in terms of the way these aspects operate or are captivating. People may be aware that they are doing something, but they may not entirely know what they are doing (say, enacting a radically transgressive, scapegoating—or quasi-sacrificial, "sublime"—scenario). One of the things I evoke as a proof text is Himmler's 1943 Posen speech. It should be read carefully as an exceptionally lucid document of Nazi ideology. It can be taken rather seriously because it wasn't meant simply as propaganda. It was addressed to upper-level SS—by someone in the know, to people in the know, in terms of an intimacy, the intimacy of the initiated who share radically transgressive, criminal behavior. At the beginning of the speech, Himmler actually says that, on this occasion alone, the Nazi taboo on silence about what they're doing can be broken, and something can be told that otherwise will always be kept secret. Then he goes on to explain what it is that they're involved in. Here one may see how something (for example, the movement from expulsion to extermination) is intelligible in terms of scapegoating that may not be from another perspective.

Many historians have spent years on research trying to trace exactly when one had the move from expulsion to extermination of the Jews. That is an important problem, and in many ways, the movement from expulsion to extermination is a drastic difference, certainly for the people involved. But within the scapegoat mechanism, it can be a minute step, and a step quickly taken, because the basic problem within this frame of reference, where there is a certain horror at contamination by "the other," is getting rid of "the other"—*entfernen,* in German. How this is done is more a secondary issue: it can be expulsion, it can be extermination, but the problem is the "getting rid of." This is very much at play within Himmler's speech, where the expulsion and the extermination are separated only by a slight pause, a comma, in the speech itself. Then Himmler goes on to give his understanding of what it is to be hard within Nazi ideology, what Nazi hardness is. In his own terms, it is a combination of two things that seem to be antithetical— bringing together the extremes of what would seem to be a binary opposition: remaining decent (*anständig geblieben zu sein*), morally beautiful, upright, while at the same time engaging in unheard-of transgression.

The way in which Himmler expresses that is in terms of seeing one hundred, five hundred, one thousand corpses lying side by side. He says that most of you (the SS officers) will understand what that means. This kind of endless expanse of corpses in a repetitive process of killing, repeating traumatic scenes of killing, is, in its own distorted way, the Kantian mathematical sublime, which increases geometrically. So you have the combination of these two seemingly antithetical things: the morally beautiful, remaining decent—and the typical cases given by other people are the German who loves his wife and family, goes home, is a wonderful family man, feeds his canary, loves his dog, and so forth, in a word, remaining morally upright. Himmler himself mentions the neo-Kantian rule—often in fact disobeyed—that the Nazi will eliminate Jews with what might almost be called purity of intention and ethical disinterest, not taking a cigarette or a mark for himself. So: being *Biedermeier* in your private life, presumably suffering no moral damage to the self, and at the same time engaging in these incredibly unheard-of scenes of mass devastation, which constitute a kind of negative sublime, something that goes beyond ordinary experience and that most people would find utterly shocking or unbelievable.

That is the dimension of Nazi ideology in practice. It is significant, again, not to become fixated on but to introduce it because it's probably the most difficult thing to understand. It's *not* difficult to understand how a person has a plan of extermination and tries to carry it out. It's *not* difficult to understand how bureaucracies function and have certain consequences, and how people try to do their job, and how you have little functionally rational technocrats who are trying to arrange demographic schemes or implement biopolitics. What's difficult to understand is *that* combined with other things that really seem out of place.

Most people who've discussed Daniel Goldhagen's book have not seen that complex of problems as something he touches upon himself but doesn't know how to explain. Goldhagen, in his book, gives many examples of almost carnivalesque glee in doing things that were *not* required by the situation, that were not functional. He himself cannot really explain this and simply invokes, time and time again, the phrase "eliminationist antisemitism." This phrase becomes a kind of mantra that's never fully explicated, and it's also involved in a very rash generalization concerning all the German people for generations back, a view that almost amounts to a stereotype of national character.

But what's significant in Goldhagen's enterprise is that there is a small, good book struggling to get out of the very big, dubious book. And that very small, good book provides documentation for an involvement in outlandish transgression and even in taking a carnivalesque glee in the suffering of others that doesn't seem to be intelligible from any "rational" point of view. One has to try to approximate an understanding of why this was happening (to the extent it was happening), because I don't think this was unique to the Germans but was something that had happened elsewhere (although it should not be seen simply in universal psychological terms). What was distinctive to the Nazi genocide was the extent to which it went and the way in which it was bound up with other things, such as more "rational" dimensions of behavior. But it is a possibility for virtually anyone, and one has to recognize it as a possibility for oneself. I would be tempted to suggest that it's only with that recognition that one has some chance of resisting even reduced analogues of certain kinds of behavior, including victimization, in one's own experience.

QUESTION: You mentioned that scapegoating is ubiquitous and not unique to the Holocaust. One still has to question, though, how a total mass murder such as the Shoah could take place.

LA CAPRA: That's right. What's different about the Nazis is the extent to which they went in their attempt to eliminate difference—that extent is paradoxically what made them different. And how can you possibly explain it? One can agree that it is distinctive, that with respect to the Jews (in contradistinction to the other groups of victims), the goal was the elimination, down to the last child, of this people anywhere in the world. You would persecute them anywhere in the world; you would follow them anywhere in the world. This is obviously where Nazi policy became irrational with respect to its own goals: the extermination of the Jews might preempt economic or military considerations, so that, at least at times, when either a bureaucrat or a military leader in a certain area said, "Look, you want us to kill these people. These are skilled craftspeople, and we absolutely need them for the war effort," the answer they received in effect was, "You don't understand what's going on. You have to do this, even if it counters economic or military policy."

How do you understand, or try to understand, that? I try to do so in part in terms of this problem of enemy brothers—there were so many ways in which German Jewry and Germans were extremely close culturally, many different ways. German Jews did not believe that their German culture, their German quality, could be denied them. The unpreparedness of German Jews, at least at first, was very much linked with the extent to which they felt German, culturally. They could not believe what was happening to them.

One recent, and almost fantastic, example of this is the diary of Victor Klemperer, who managed to survive the war and who always believed that he was a good German. He even believed that the Germans were a chosen people and that the Nazis were un-German; that he himself as a German Jew (who converted to Christianity) *was* German, and even part of the chosen people, whereas the Nazis were the un-Germans. That may well be the extreme limit of the sense of German Jewry, especially more assimilated German Jewry, that German *Bildung* was their *Bildung*. The apprehension on the part of the Nazis, including Hitler, was that indeed this was true. That's why it was so hard to bring about not only a distinction but this utter and total difference—this unbreachable divide—between the German and the Jew, because that difference was so unbelievably implausible, given the cultural formation of the peoples. They did indeed owe so much to each other and were utterly hybridized as a people. The need to extirpate from oneself what is indeed a very intimate part of oneself leads to incredibly rash behavior. This is one aspect of it: in a sense, the problem of enemy brothers, where the animosity came from the Germans (not initially from the Jews, obviously) but was flowing overwhelmingly in one direction, an extreme hostility—that kind of crazy desire to get rid of something that is very much part of yourself is like ripping organs from yourself.

QUESTION: Most of the Holocaust took place in eastern Europe, where Jews were very removed from German culture. What is your explanation?

LA CAPRA: The big problem, from the Nazi point of view, was that of the Jew who could pass, and who in that sense was a kind of invisible presence that was presumably totally different but whose difference could not be perceived. In the case of eastern European Jewry, the differences could be perceived, and there you could have the stereotype acting as a kind of sledgehammer. How do you explain this? What happens in certain forms of extremist ideology based on scapegoating and a kind of sacrificialism is that you oppose "the other" for contradictory reasons, so that there can be no counterevidence to the ideology. The Jews were to be eliminated, both because they could pass and because they were so utterly different that they could be immediately identified, just as they should be eliminated because they were the bearers of both capitalism and communism simultaneously; both the bearers of modernity (just like the Germans) and the bearers of antimodernity and reaction, which the Germans in certain ways exemplified and wanted to overcome in themselves as well. There were elements of German society that were not altogether modern, that somehow had to be reconstructed in the German image. And there were "premodern" phenomena that the Nazis wanted to recover or regenerate— Nordic mythology or pagan beliefs and practices more generally.

The Holocaust as a Denial of Other Traumas?

QUESTION: Don't you think that the overemphasis on the Holocaust in the popular culture, the politics, and the economics of America is some kind of denial of the traumas with which America is directly involved? These traumas (such as that of the African Americans and the Native Americans) are still relevant there, and America may be blinded to its present by emphasizing the traumas of others in the past.

LA CAPRA: I think that that's altogether possible. We can come back to America, but it's not altogether unique to Americans. I think that generally what happens (both in personal and in collective life) is that one comes to focus on a given trauma when there may be other traumas that are more pressing. This often happens: that you look at an earlier trauma as a way of not looking too closely at contemporary traumas, or it could be to avoid or mitigate other past traumas that are just coming to a fully articulate voice in the present.

This happens in France. The French concern with Vichy is a way of displacing anxiety about Algeria and its aftermath. In Israel, the problem of Israeli/Palestinian relations can be displaced by a focus on the Holocaust. And in the United States, contemporary problems related to the heritage of slavery and the treatment of American Indians can also be obscured by a focus on the Holocaust. Charles Maier has raised the question, somewhat rhetorically, of why, on the Mall in Washington, we have a Holocaust museum but no museum dedicated to slavery or to the American Indians. After all, they were our victims, and we were part of the forces that tried to combat those who victimized the Jews in Europe. So why are we commemorating the Holocaust, rather than something that points more directly at our own involvement in dubious processes? This is a very good question. The obvious answer is that people do indeed attempt to obscure or displace certain problems by focusing on other problems. This can happen; the point is to recognize it and try to resist it. But it doesn't mean that the Holocaust is not a significant problem, even in the United States.

It is interesting that throughout the world, with various timing, the direct interest in the Holocaust has been somewhat belated. Again, there was that initial rush of memoirs and diaries right after the war, and then, for varying periods of time, a great deal of suppression, repression, avoidance, and denial. And even today, what is also surprising to me in the United States is the number of historians of Germany (even of modern Germany, twentieth-century Germany) who don't focus on the Holocaust, who don't work on the Holocaust as at least one of their research or teaching areas. I think there is now pressure on people to do the history of the Holocaust. The role of donors creating chairs in Holocaust studies is an important factor. But, on a more general level, one can say that what has happened to the Holocaust as a problem is that it has emerged from being ghettoized within Jewish history, and perhaps as a subsection of German history, to become an important component not only of German history but of European and world history.

At the present time people (certainly historians and other commentators) have recognized that, if you are trying to understand the twentieth century and Western history in general, the Holocaust is a problem with which you, to some extent, have to be concerned in an informed way. This is why things like the Paul de Man and the Heidegger incidents were significant, in that they functioned almost as classical cases of psychoanalytic displacement. In terms of the history of the Holocaust, the de Man incident is worth a footnote—if that. The Heidegger case, if you're interested in philosophy, is important, but in the general history of the Holocaust, Heidegger is one figure—a somewhat significant figure whom you might discuss briefly, but that's about it. What is important is that many commentators (including very important figures, such as Derrida) started to address the Holocaust more directly in the aftermath of these incidents, so that it was these relatively small incidents that brought the larger problems into clearer focus.

When you reread the early Derrida, you can argue (as has been done) that it often reads like an allusive, indirect survivor discourse, where the source of the problem is never mentioned. But somehow you have the inscription of post-traumatic effects in the writing. You can read him in many other ways, but this is one interesting way. Even in the case of other people, earlier in their work there were allusions, analogies, but not sustained interest, and perhaps other smaller things triggered their interest. In my own case, it was not so much the de Man and Heidegger affairs—although they were significant—but the fact that Friedlander invited me to this conference that brought to my attention (not really as a cause but as an occasion) the necessity for greater reflection on something I had mentioned, that had been part of my awareness, but never a focus of attention.

I believe my case is rather typical, but what is important at the present time is that the problem itself has become an important one. Now if you are studying the twentieth century, or even Western history and its broader implications, it would be difficult to justify *not* discussing the Holocaust or at least explaining why you are not discussing it. The challenge is to discuss it in ways that don't allow it to serve diversionary functions, so that you can actually study the Holocaust and raise comparative issues in the right way.

This is a problem that brings up questions of transference. Observer participation is a question of transference, for example, involving such issues as whether the anthropologist remains a scientist or goes native—or tries to work out some approach that is neither remaining a purely objective scientist nor going native.

boundaries break down— 173
self vs. other binary

That's a question of how you work through something like an implication in the object of study, or a transferential relation, and I think that the question of the anthropologist, the non-native anthropologist, in relation to the native population also brings up all of these issues.

I tend to believe that, at the present time, the level of theoretical reflection may be highest in Holocaust studies, because of both the intensity of the thought devoted to it and the array of figures who've taken it as an object of concern. But, to avoid a displacement of competitive victimology onto competitive theory, let's simply say that much attention has been devoted to the Holocaust by people who are well worth reading. In their work, there's a great deal there that *is* significant for research into other areas, including other genocides, or even issues such as slavery. If slavery constitutes a genocide, it's a genocide over an extremely long period of time, with relations between masters and slaves not altogether the same as those between Nazis and victims. For example, it would be difficult to conceive of a practice involving Jewish mothers in Nazi Germany that would be analogous to the role of the black nanny who would nurse a white baby in the American South under slavery. And Jews at times pleaded for work relations not far from slavery in order to avoid slow death through starvation and abominable conditions in ghettoes and work camps or "extermination" in death camps. The fact that slaves at times might seek death for themselves or a loved one rather than endure slavery itself indicates a significant difference in situation. Slavery, like the Holocaust, nonetheless presents, for a people, problems of traumatization, severe oppression, a divided heritage, the question of a founding trauma, the forging of identities in the present, and so forth.

The other thing is that one has to be able to study certain problems, even if one is a member of the population (either oppressed or oppressing) that isn't totally within identity politics but that tries to achieve some perspective on identity politics. One way in which you can define identity politics is in terms of a form of thinking wherein research or thought simply validates your beginning subject position. Through identity politics, your initial subject position remains firm and, if anything, through research or inquiry is further strengthened time and again. Yet the challenge of research and thought is somehow to try to test critically, perhaps in certain ways validate, or perhaps transform one's subject position, so that one doesn't end up where one began. If anything, I think that one of the great problems in research is that there is a grid of subject positions, and through processes of identification or excessive objectification, one remains within that grid.

The grid of the Holocaust is one that you also see elsewhere. It involves the victim, perpetrators, bystanders, collaborators, resisters, those in the gray zone, and those born later—a bit of an elaboration on Raul Hilberg's grid. (Recently one has another role—the rescuer—brought into special and questionable prominence by the success of Spielberg's *Schindler's List.*) This grid is immensely strong. It's very difficult to try to elaborate a position whereby you don't simply find yourself identifying with one of those positions or simply combining certain positions. The challenge of research—that is also an ethical and a philosophical challenge—is trying to elaborate subject positions that don't simply fall within that grid but that allow relations between people that are not beholden to victimization and the consequences of victimization. The question is whether there are possibilities that don't fall within a broadly conceived sacrificial mechanism that involves victimization of the other (including the nonhuman animal) to achieve one's own identity.

Modernism, Postmodernism, and Rationality after the Holocaust

QUESTION: I want to ask you about rationality after Auschwitz. Why is it that the Holocaust has gained such prominence, such a centrality, in Western consciousness? What does it seem to be saying to us, and what lessons can we possibly learn from it?

LA CAPRA: The centrality of the Holocaust in Western consciousness is related to the kind of challenge it poses to certain forms of Western self-understanding. If we really believe that the West is the high point of civilization and that there has been a civilizing process or some development over time in the direction of increased sensitivity to suffering and injustice, and if we really do see the story of the West as that of enlightenment, then it's very difficult to come to terms with the Holocaust within that frame of reference.

Charles Taylor's book *Sources of the Self* has received a great deal of praise from people (including historians), and he *does* try to integrate the Holocaust into a kind of neo-Hegelian developmental account of the West, wherein the West is exceptional in its degree of enactment of justice and in the prevalence of a concern about suffering.[9] In certain ways, you can see that development; but in other ways, it's a story that doesn't have full credibility.

I think that the shock of the Holocaust is its shock to an enlightened self-consciousness. I tend to believe that there are two forms of rationality, as scholars from the Frankfurt school tried to argue. One is instrumental rationality in the adaptation of means to ends. This is a narrow, technical rationality. The other kind of rationality is a more substantive form, which is harder to define and may even include emotional response or affect. Karl Mannheim is someone who tried to struggle with this problem.[10] In his case, in his own

9. Charles Taylor, *Sources of the Self: The Making of the Modern Identity* (Cambridge: Harvard University Press, 1989).

10. See especially Karl Mannheim, *Man and Society in an Age of Reconstruction* (New York: Harcourt, Brace & World, 1940). One passage is especially interesting in light of my preceding argument, although its notion of displacement is associated with a dubious idea of the relation of the "primitive" to the modern as well as a questionable functionalism:

The secret of taboo and the collective formation of symbols in primitive societies is mainly that the free expression of impulses is held in check by the various mechanisms of social control and directed towards certain objects and actions which benefit the group. Only the impulsive energies which have been set free by the disintegration of society and are seeking integration about a new object have those eruptive, destructive qualities which are customarily and vaguely regarded as characteristic of every type of mass behavior. What the dictatorships in certain contemporary mass-societies are striving to do is to co-ordinate through organizations the impulses which the revolutionary period unchained and to direct them towards prescribed objects. The consciously guided fixation of mass impulses upon new objec-

way, with his limitations, he tried to affirm a substantive rationality in a critique of a limited technical rationality. One of the dangers in Western self-consciousness has been to think that technical rationality can solve all problems. We try to define things in terms of a technical solution, and often that simply doesn't work.

I also feel that if one is going to talk about enlightenment, one should include both forms of rationality. The critique of instrumental rationality (especially an instrumental rationality that becomes dominant—the kind of critique that Theodor Adorno and Max Horkheimer try to make, as well as Martin Heidegger, Philippe Lacoue-Labarthe, and many others) is important, but it should not be made to exclude the significance of a more substantive rationality that allows for emotional response as well. One can affirm enlightenment as substantive rationality and see that rationality as one of the best ways to criticize a limited technical rationality. I also feel, however, that one doesn't simply begin with that complex, indeed internally contested concept of rationality that also involves affect, which is never entirely under one's "rational" control. One cannot assume enlightenment as a presupposition or as a basis for all forms of analysis. So there is something very limited when you start understanding the Holocaust only in terms of human dignity and problems related to human dignity, as if human dignity were simply there as a constant, and then you had to understand deviations from it. Perhaps one of the lessons of the Holocaust is that you cannot assume a respect for human dignity as something characteristic of human beings. Within the Holocaust there was such an attempt to deprive victims of human dignity that it shatters the assumption that there's something like a common humanity binding people together.

This is something that Jürgen Habermas said: there was some-

tives takes the place of earlier forms of wish fixation which found their objectives organically, that is to say, through a slow selective process. So, for instance, the attempt is made to create a new religion, the function of which is first to destroy the old emotional setting, and then to make these disintegrated impulses more subservient to one's own aim through the use of new symbols. (62)

thing that happened in the Holocaust that seemed to change the face of humanity; that something emerged that we didn't conceive of before or that we were not able to expect. On the basis of that assertion, I would tend to conclude that there is an argument to be made for enlightenment, not as an assumption but as something you strive for—that you strive for in a way that understands it in terms of its complexity—as a substantive rationality that you cannot simply define in a neat way. You can define technical rationality in a very neat way, in terms of the adjustment of means to ends, cost-benefit analysis, and so forth, and this has become very prevalent, and it still is. Whatever its complexity or the difficulties it poses for neat definitions and circumscribed plans of action, substantive rationality also has to be affirmed, not simply as an assumption but as a goal that is never achieved or won once and for all.

I would also say that part of history and historical understanding that includes research, but is not restricted to it, is related to problems of enlightenment or substantive rationality. One of the goals of historiography (including historiography as working through) is an attempt to restore to victims, insofar as possible, the dignity of which they were deprived by their oppressors. This is a very important component of historical understanding: to try, symbolically, to compensate for certain things that can never be fully compensated for. One should see historical understanding as involving processes of working through in the broadest sense (that is to say, engaging in a discourse that is also a discourse of mourning and that involves critique—critique is another form of working through). One may also mention in this respect the attempt to elaborate narratives that are not simply redemptive narratives but more experimental, self-questioning narratives. I also think that the essay, as an exploratory form of writing, is related to processes of working through that are not simply coded in an entirely predictable way. If you understand these forms or processes as dimensions of historiography—involving an attempt to work through the past without denying our implication in it and without denying the

history//reality

after effects of trauma—then historiography may be argued to be part of a broadly conceived enlightenment project. But it is part of an enlightenment project that includes an understanding of the way the project has been shattered on the level of taken-for-granted assumptions by recent events. It nonetheless requires the postulation of certain goals as desirable goals as well as an attempt to elicit the ways in which research can be related to these goals without undermining the nature of research itself.

This is one dimension of the study of the Holocaust that perhaps not only involves the greatest challenges to the enlightenment project but also poses the question of how to reconstitute this project when it can no longer simply be taken as an assumption.

QUESTION: To what extent would you consider the Holocaust as the turning point between modernism and postmodernism?

LA CAPRA: For some people, the Holocaust can be seen as a kind of divider between modernism and postmodernism. And postmodernism can also be defined as post-Holocaust; there's an intricate relationship between the two. It certainly is fruitful to reread certain figures in the light of problems that have not heretofore been foregrounded in our attempts to understand them. So within limits, this recent view of the Holocaust and its aftermath is significant.

The other way you could formulate this view is to see the post-Holocaust in terms of the post-traumatic and how many forms of activity—such as writing but also painting and even dance, or everything on the level of signification—have, in the postwar context, a kind of a post-traumatic dimension. Many forms of writing—or intellectual and artistic activity in general—seem to be post-traumatic forms that are coming to terms in different ways with the traumas that called them into existence.

But let's get back to the problem of narrative and redemption. Redemptive narrative is a narrative that denies the trauma that brought it into existence. And more experimental, nonredemptive narratives are narratives that are trying to come to terms with trauma in a post-traumatic context, in ways that involve both acting out and working through. This is a perspective through which you can read a great deal of modern literature and art, as a kind of relatively safe haven in which to explore post-traumatic effects.

Once you come to that understanding of figures such as Samuel Beckett and Paul Celan (and, to some extent, Derrida and Lyotard on a more theoretical level), then you can go back to so-called modernist writers and also see the extent to which, in modernism itself, you can find these elements. Take Virginia Woolf, for example. There's a sense in which Virginia Woolf's writings—perhaps more in terms of personal crisis but then also something broader felt as a cultural crisis, her own abuse as a child and her sensitivity to the problematic nature of existence in post–World War I Europe—are also post-traumatic writings. What she writes is in no sense a conventional narrative but one that both traces the effects of trauma and somehow, at least linguistically, tries to come to terms with those effects, so that they will be inscribed and recalled but perhaps reconfigured in ways that make them not entirely disabling. It is very interesting to read a novel such as *To the Lighthouse* within this frame of reference.[11]

QUESTION: Thank you.

11. On this point see my *History, Politics, and the Novel* (Ithaca: Cornell University Press), 1987, chap. 6.

6 ▌ *Conclusion*

Writing (about) Trauma

Cathy Caruth begins her important book *Unclaimed Experience: Trauma, Narrative, and History* with an analysis of the points of intersection between Freud's *Beyond the Pleasure Principle* and Tasso's *Gerusalemme liberata*. She takes the relationship between these texts as paradigmatic of the relation between theory and literature, especially with respect to the problem of trauma. She quotes Freud writing of Tasso's epic:

> Its hero, Tancred, unwittingly kills his beloved Clorinda in a duel while she is disguised in the armour of an enemy knight. After burial he makes his way into a strange magic forest which strikes the Crusaders' army with terror. He slashes with his sword at a tall tree; but blood streams from the cut and the voice of Clorinda, whose soul is imprisoned in the tree, is heard complaining that he has wounded his beloved once again.[1]

Caruth comments:

> The actions of Tancred, wounding his beloved in a battle and then, unknowingly, seemingly by chance, wounding her again, evoca-

1. Cathy Caruth, *Unclaimed Experience: Trauma, Narrative, and History* (Baltimore: Johns Hopkins University Press, 1996), 2.

tively represent in Freud's text the way that the experience of a trauma repeats itself, exactly and unremittingly, through the unknowing acts of the survivor and against his very will. . . . I would like to suggest here . . . that the literary resonance of Freud's example goes beyond this dramatic illustration of repetition compulsion and exceeds, perhaps, the limits of Freud's conceptual or conscious theory of trauma. For what seems to me particularly striking in the example of Tasso is not just the unconscious act of the infliction of the injury and its inadvertent and unwished-for repetition, but the moving and sorrowful *voice* that cries out, a voice that is paradoxically released *through the wound.* Tancred does not only repeat his act but, in repeating it, he for the first time hears a voice that cries out to him to see what he has done. The voice of his beloved addresses him and, in this address, bears witness to the past he has unwittingly repeated.

Caruth thus offers the image of the voice of trauma emerging from the wound itself—a voice testifying to the role of the victim as witness in addressing the "perpetrator" with reference to (making him hear for the first time a cry that bespeaks) a past that in this case he has unknowingly repeated in its violence. One might observe that her focus on the survivor-victim (indeed, the apparently ambiguous status of Tancred as perpetrator-victim who is termed in passing a survivor) does not explicitly open itself to the formulation of the specific problem of perpetrator trauma which her example seems to foreground, but her prosopopoeia concerning a speaking or crying wound is nonetheless quite evocative. She continues:

If Freud turns to literature to describe traumatic experience, it is because literature, like psychoanalysis, is interested in the complex relation between knowing and not knowing. And it is, indeed at the specific point at which knowing and not knowing intersect that the language of literature and the psychoanalytic theory of traumatic experience precisely meet. The example offered by the poetry of Tasso is indeed, in my interpretation, more than a literary example of a vaster psychoanalytic, or experiential, truth; the poetic story can be read, I will suggest, as a larger parable, both of the unarticulated implications of the theory of trauma in Freud's writings and, beyond that, of the crucial link between literature and theory that the following pages set out to explore. (2–3)

The preceding pages of the present book have explored the crucial link between history and theory with reference to trauma while including occasional allusions to literature. Caruth in the passage I have quoted and elsewhere takes an epistemological turn, but her analysis often exceeds its scope in that "not knowing" for her is intimately related to the role of affect and the unconscious. It is noteworthy that, although Caruth's subtitle refers to history, she approaches history only through the medium of theory and literature, thus not including historiography itself and the contributions or the resistances it might pose to her analysis in both intellectual and institutional terms. Her understanding of the relation of literature to psychoanalytic theory is in terms of excess—with excess on the side of literature.

For Caruth literature (or the literary) goes beyond theory or at least beyond Freud's conscious conception of theory, notably in the case of trauma. The apparent implication is that literature in its very excess can somehow get at trauma in a manner unavailable to theory—that it writes (speaks or even cries) trauma in excess of theory. It is not clear, however, precisely how it does so. Nor is it altogether clear what the relation of theoretical discourse on the literary is to psychoanalytic theory and to literature. It would seem at the very least that this discourse somehow marks (writes? acts out? works through?) the excess of the literary vis-à-vis the theoretical, thereby seemingly escaping or outwitting the limits of theory with respect to excess. Why may discourse on the literary accomplish this extravagant feat while psychoanalytic (and historiographical?) theory does not? Is it because of some special proximity to the literary which is itself defined in terms of excess? Is the very idea of the literary invoked here a rather special one related to the romantic, postromantic, and poststructural movements, notably in their emphasis on what goes beyond limits—that is, excess and the sublime? And is discourse on the literary understood primarily in terms of a relation of participatory, performative enactment with respect to its object of study?

The instability of the nodal point (or decentered, indeed wandering navel) at which literary theory (or discourse on the literary), psychoanalytic theory, and literature intersect is itself indicated by the sentence referring to this point of contact: "And it is, [*sic*] indeed at the specific point at which knowing and not knowing intersect that the language of literature and the psychoanalytic theory of traumatic experience precisely [*sic*] meet."[2] The sentence pauses in an unmotivated way after the first three words, and "precisely" appears in a comparably unmotivated, displaced fashion to (re)mark a meeting—a meeting (possibly a failed encounter?) of literature and the psychoanalytic theory of traumatic experience which itself marks the "specific point at which knowing and not knowing intersect." What is specific about this enigmatic and elusive meeting point that is repeated "precisely" in another enigmatic and elusive meeting point? The language of literary theory—at least Caruth's variant of this language—itself seems to repeat, whether consciously or unconsciously, the disconcertingly opaque movement of post-traumatic repetition in a seeming attempt to elucidate that movement.[3]

2. "There is often a passage in even the most thoroughly interpreted dream which has to be left obscure: this is because we become aware during the work of interpretation that at that point there is a tangle of dream-thoughts which cannot be unravelled and which moreover adds nothing to our knowledge of the content of the dream. This is the dream's navel, the spot where it reaches down into the unknown. The dream-thoughts to which we are led by interpretation cannot, from the nature of things, have any definite endings; they are bound to branch out in every direction into the intricate network of our world of thought. It is at some point where this meshwork is particularly close that the dream-wish grows up, like a mushroom out of its mycelium." Sigmund Freud, *The Interpretation of Dreams,* trans. James Strachey (1900; New York: Basic Books, 1965), 564.

3. As noted earlier, this movement of what might paradoxically be termed precise imprecision prompts the observation that trauma theory in Caruth's rendering might be seen as a fascinating, provocative, somewhat disguised, and often moving rendition (parable?) of de Manian deconstruction. The key notion of "unreadability" is now construed in terms of trauma. Indeed, the "precision" and "force" of "traumatic recall" and the traumatic event's "essential incomprehensibility" or "*affront to understanding*" are seen by Caruth (in line with her interpretation of Bessel van der Kolk and Onno van der Hart) in terms of a "loss" when the event is recounted in "narrative memory" and its telling is varied (153–54), that is, when the victim in some sense begins to work through the trauma. "It is," she contends, "this dilemma that underlies many survivors' reluctance to translate their experience into speech" (154). (It is important to elucidate the complex, often halting and continually

The relation between historiography and theory, in contrast to that between literature and theory, is often understood in terms of the lack of historiography in relation to theory or, conversely, in terms of the excesses of theory with respect to the writing of history. Theory always seems to go beyond what historiography can verify or validate. It seems hyperbolic or speculative in a manner that many historians would reject or find profoundly suspect. Historians rarely point to the complementary extreme—the possible excesses of research which may induce contextual reductionism or "overkill" as well as impede close, critical reading that discloses the ways significant texts are not simply symptomatic of contexts but may also contest them and provide material for a critique of a text's own symptomatic features. Still, historiography is subject to constraints different from those of literature, or at least of fiction, despite the important features these modes of discourse share (notably with respect to narrative procedures). The counterpart is that at least certain forms of literature or art, as well as the type of discourse or theory which emulates its object, may provide a more expansive space (in psychoanalytic terms, a *relatively* safe haven) for exploring modalities of responding to trauma, including the role of affect and the tendency to repeat traumatic events. At times art departs from ordinary reality to produce surrealistic situations or radically

---

renewed movement from traumatized victim to survivor, notably with respect to processes of working through the past, and one might, of course, suggest other reasons for a survivor's reluctance to speak, for example, the sense that one will not be understood, the pain and feeling of shame attached to the event, the sense that one's symptoms are memorials to the dead, and the belief that, by working through those symptoms, one may somehow be betraying those who did not survive a shared experience.) A significant difference in Caruth's variant of trauma theory with respect to de Manian deconstruction is that affect, ostensibly absent in de Man, returns both in theoretical terms and in the movement of Caruth's prose itself. I would further observe that there is an ambiguity in Caruth's use of "literature" and "the literary" which my commentary reiterates. Literature would seem to be the primary site of the literary, which, however, also appears in other areas or discourses. In other words, the literary is both "inside" and "outside" other discourses in ways that call for further elucidation. For example, there are differences between quotation, allusion, the use of tropes, and free indirect style in rendering "the literary" as well as in the latter's role as a "difference within" discourses such as those of psychoanalysis (which, of course, does not itself speak in a unified voice). Moreover, a discourse may embody more or less explicit resistances to, and various modes of framing, the literary, however the latter may be conceived.

playful openings that seem to be sublimely irrelevant to ordinary reality but may uncannily provide indirect commentary or insight into that reality. At other times, art may more directly engage and illuminate social reality and have a mutually provocative relation to it—exploring its problems and possibilities, testing its norms and conventions, and being in turn tested by it. One might even speak of the emergence of a traumatic realism that differs from stereotypical conceptions of mimesis and enables instead an often disconcerting exploration of disorientation, its symptomatic dimensions, and possible ways of responding to them. One would thus seem to have a complex, supplementary relation between literary or artistic practice, related theoretical discourse, and historiography which goes counter to formalistic or sociological conceptions of discrete spheres of activity and instead calls for inquiry into mutual interactions and resistances.

The foregoing discussion may serve to evoke the distinction between writing trauma and writing about trauma. Writing about trauma is an aspect of historiography related to the project of reconstructing the past as objectively as possible without necessarily going to the self-defeating extreme of single-minded objectification that involves the denial of one's implication in the problems one treats. Writing trauma is a metaphor in that writing indicates some distance from trauma (even when the experience of writing is itself intimately bound up with trauma), and there is no such thing as writing trauma itself if only because trauma, while at times related to particular events, cannot be localized in terms of a discrete, dated experience. Trauma indicates a shattering break or cesura in experience which has belated effects. Writing trauma would be one of those telling aftereffects in what I termed traumatic and post-traumatic writing (or signifying practice in general). It involves processes of acting out, working over, and to some extent working through in analyzing and "giving voice" to the past—processes of coming to terms with traumatic "experiences," limit events, and their symptomatic effects that achieve articulation in different combinations and hybridized forms.

Writing trauma is often seen in terms of enacting it, which may at times be equated with acting (or playing) it out in performative discourse or artistic practice. In significant ways this equation is active in Shoshana Felman's work and has a complicated role in Caruth's. While it may induce more or less lyrical, pathos-charged writing that moves the reader, it involves a participatory or emulative relation to the typically literary, filmic, or artistic object of study which at times may inhibit more critical analysis. In Claude Lanzmann (one of Felman's principal objects of study) the tendency to enact or relive trauma was itself an acknowledged criterion of selection of individuals as interviewees in *Shoah*. Despite—or perhaps in part because of—his important role in the attempt to help Jewish victims (an element of Polish behavior absent in Lanzmann's film), Wladisaw Bartoszewski did not find a place in *Shoah*. Lanzmann decided not to include footage of this important historical figure who could have provided a firsthand account of the role of the Zegota group in assisting Jews. The apparent reason for the exclusion was that Bartoszewski recounted but did not relive the past.[4] His voice described and analyzed but apparently did not voice or cry the wounds of the past in the manner with which Lanzmann as interviewer and filmmaker wanted to identify. Lanzmann apparently wanted people more like Clorinda or Tasso than like Freud—people who would move him to the point of identification.

Insofar as *Shoah* is a work of art or of fiction, the exclusion of Bartoszewski and his testimony might be defended. But as art or fiction that is addressing a sensitive historical topic, the film might still be criticized to the extent that it represents the past in a misleading and ideologically tendentious manner. As a historical documentary (or in its obvious documentary dimension), the film would in this respect be even more open to criticism.

One may argue about whether art is always open to criticism on the basis of truth claims deriving from historical research or empirical inquiry. I would suggest that there is an inverse relation between the degree to which a topic is still intensely invested with emotion and value and the strictures placed on art in this respect. In brief, the

4. See Neal Ascherson, "La Controverse autour de *Shoah*," trans. Jean-Pierre Bardos, in *Au sujet de Shoah: Le Film de Claude Lanzmann,* ed. Michel Deguy (Paris: Belin, 1990), 231.

freedom of art (or what was traditionally called poetic license) with respect to truth claims seems to be greatest to the extent the issues art treats are dead or neutral (perhaps neutralized) and must be enlivened or revived by art itself. One might also argue that this freedom is great insofar as the issues are ambivalent or undecidable, and art would be significant to the extent that it explored ambivalence or undecidability in the most unsettling and provocative manner possible. Moreover, it might do so in a sustained allegorical or oblique fashion that paradoxically, perhaps movingly, gave a precise form to opacity and did not involve—or involved only in the most complex and disorienting manner—an "aboutness" or referentiality with respect to particular historical events or figures. Texts of Kafka, Celan, Beckett, or Blanchot often seem to engage in this sort of indirection or veiled allusiveness. Still, in certain cases one might want to question unmodulated indirection or allegory and raise historical questions related to truth claims, especially when there are aspects of the writer's context or past which prompt them or when the writer is indeed making claims about politics and ethics if only in nonliterary texts or interviews. Hence one might want to inquire how Kafka's *Metamorphosis* or Blanchot's *Death Sentence* in their different ways relate to the Holocaust, its antecedents, its larger context, and its aftermath—even though one might never arrive at definitive or even convincing answers.[5] One might even con-

---

5. Kafka's *Metamorphosis* is stunning as an early exploration of the equivocal relation between pest control and sacrifice in that Gregor in relation to his family seems to be both vermin or pest whose removal is a matter of social hygiene and a quasi-sacrificial, contaminating object of ritual anxiety whose death signals the liberation, if not the redemption, of the family. On one level, Blanchot's *Arrêt de mort* (1948; *Death Sentence*, trans. Lydia Davis [Barrytown, N.Y.: Station Hill Arts, 1978]) might be read as involving a postromantic opening to the infinite reconfigured, in predominantly negative terms, as absence. ("Blackest space extended before me. I was not in this blackness, but at the edge of it, and I confess that it is terrifying. It is terrifying because there is something in it which scorns man and which man cannot endure without losing himself. But he must lose himself; and whoever resists will founder, and whoever goes forward will become this very blackness, this cold and dead and scornful thing in the very heart of which lives the infinite" [67–68].)

First published in 1948, *Death Sentence* traces minute, often puzzling or bizarre emotional tropisms in the narrator's relation to dying women, who would seem (perhaps deceptively) to be allegorical of France. The novella's minute tracing of the movements in personal intimacy is interrupted at one point by a statement that foregrounds the problem of public

Conclusion: Writing (about) Trauma

tend that inviting such questions is part of the way these texts are unsettling, question-worthy, and perhaps at times questionable. One could address similar questions to philosophy, particularly philosophy in close proximity to, or challenging dialogue with, literature, for example, Heidegger's later writings or Derrida's work in general.[6] As

---

events in which Blanchot participated in at times dubious ways (notably in his prewar, right-wing, occasionally anti-Semitic journalism). A little more than halfway through the account, the narrator states: "I would like to say something else now. I am talking about things which seem negligible, and I am ignoring public events. These events were very important and they occupied my attention all the time. But now they are rotting away, their story is dead, and the hours and the life which were then mine are dead too" (46). One may well wonder whether such a statement is sufficient to account for involvement in, or even preoccupation with, certain public events. Still, with respect to my argument in Chapter 2, I would note again that the text does not conflate or confusingly mingle transhistorical absence and particular historical losses whether private or public; rather, it attempts to articulate their relationship, however obscure that relationship may sometimes be.

For efforts to relate textual analysis, conceptions of literature, politics, and historical context with respect to Blanchot (where more remains to be done on the level of the subtle analysis of how precisely contextual matters inform a close reading of texts), see Jeffrey Mehlman, *Genealogies of the Text: Literature, Psychoanalysis, and Politics in Modern France* (Cambridge: Cambridge University Press, 1995); Steven Ungar, *Scandal and Aftereffect: Blanchot and France since 1930* (Minneapolis: University of Minnesota Press, 1995); Philippe Mesnard, *Maurice Blanchot: Le Sujet de l'engagement* (Paris: L'Harmattan, 1996); Anne Simonin, "Maurice Blanchot tel qu'on peut l'imaginer," *Art Press* 218 (November 1996): 61–4; and Gisèle Sapiro, "Some Overseas Angles on the History of French Literature," *Contemporary French History* 8 (1999): 335–46. Mehlman sees *L'Arrêt de mort* as having as subtext the myth of Iphigenia and as still implicated in Blanchot's dubious right-wing commitments—indicated by Blanchot's role during the Occupation as member of Jeune France, his writing for the Pétainist *Journal des Débats,* and his position as secretary for Drieu la Rochelle's collaborationist *Nouvelle Revue Française.* Simonin notes that Blanchot held the latter position for only a few months and had taken it at the request of Jean Paulhan, who was attempting to have the *NRF* steer an apolitical course and break with collaboration. She sees Blanchot as turning away from his earlier political engagement and toward the autonomy of art. Despite their interest and value, neither Mehlman's overstated reading nor Simonin's general views provide sufficient insight into a complex, at times equivocal, text such as *L'Arrêt de mort.* (We owe to Mehlman the discovery and insistence on the importance of Blanchot's extreme right-wing past, and the disclosures he made as early as 1980—along with the problems they raise for a reading of Blanchot—have not been addressed by some, including Derrida, for whom Blanchot is very important.)

6. Derrida's work might be read as an attempt to validate gift giving even in its most excessive forms while undermining the attempt to constitute the discrete other as scapegoat and victim. As noted in Chapter 2, however, his *Gift of Death,* trans. David Wills (1992; Chicago: University of Chicago Press, 1995) is particularly puzzling in its analysis and

I have intimated, many commentators would agree with Caruth in thinking that the literary (or even art in general) is a prime, if not the privileged, place for giving voice to trauma as well as symbolically exploring the role of excess.

I have indicated the relation of trauma to the sublime notably in terms of the attempt to transvalue the traumatic into an occasion for the sublime.[7] Trauma and the sublime are two vanishing points of an extreme contrast that threatens to disrupt all continua and disfigure all mediation. Traumatization might be taken as another name for the perhaps terroristic excess of abjection which is tantamount to negative transcendence. Hence the temptation is great to sacralize it. The sublime may already be the ecstatic secularization of the sacred in a radically "excessive" or transcendent form, and the question is whether any mode of materiality may only signify or be a paradoxical vehicle for it rather than "incarnate" it. The sublime as a radical secular transcendent would be, in Lyotard's term, "un(re)presentable." (Here debates about the unrepresentability of the sublime would seem to parallel, if not to displace, early modern debates about the Eucharist.) The sublime would also be beyond ethics. Such a status is generally ascribed to sacrifice. Moreover, those involved in sacrifice, at times including the figure who is the (self-)sacrificial victim or the transfigured

---

seeming defense of sacrifice as "excessive" gift (of death) without an attempt to raise and explore critically the seemingly obvious question of victimization and the typical role of victim as gift. Moreover, Derrida employs a middle-voiced writing with respect to virtually all objects of inquiry, at times in relatively unmodulated or even indiscriminately "generous" ways. Hence he has treated Paul de Man's World War II journalism, including a now notorious anti-Semitic article, in much the same deconstructive-disseminatory manner as texts of Plato or Foucault. Such an approach neutralizes or renders inapplicable the question of the extent to which the text or phenomenon under investigation is ideologically saturated or has more or less strong forces of self-questioning and self-contestation which counter its ideological, prejudicial tendencies and provide material for a counterreading or immanent critique. On this question, see my *Representing the Holocaust: History, Theory, Trauma* (Ithaca: Cornell University Press, 1994), chap. 4.

7. James Berger extends this point into the idea that in postmodern culture trauma is apocalyptic as a catastrophe that is also a revelation. The postmodern is for him particularly concerned with what paradoxically comes after the end—its remainders, residues, or abject yet sublimely ecstatic waste products. See his *After the End: Representations of Post-apocalypse* (Minneapolis: University of Minnesota Press, 1999).

signifier, vehicle, or embodiment of the sublime, have been seen as above and beyond the moral law, perhaps transgressing it in a manner that helps give rise to a new order. And the disconcerting proximity of the sublime and the abject is differentially indicated both by the way the sinner becomes saint and by the way the master race requires its *Untermenschen*. What the sublime, sacralizing excess, and the abject seem to transgress or even exclude—and what might conceivably mediate without fully reconciling their interplay—is the role of limits, including those related to the beautiful in both art and ethical life.

Beauty requires the affirmation and recognition of limits—form-giving limits that need not lead to the quest for totalization, indeed limits that are paradoxically exceeded in any such quest. These limits are the basis of what Kant saw as the analogy between art and ethics, and they might be seen as providing normative grounds for social life which are not absolute but open to testing and contestation, including transgression and excess that need not be runaway, generalized, or rampant. Indeed, the romantic, postromantic, and poststructural appropriation of the Kantian sublime has at times ignored the caveat Kant placed at an important juncture in his reflections on the sublime—a crucial caveat for someone like Durkheim in his attempt to socialize and supplement Kantian ethics in devising the bases of a desirable state of society:

> For the most part, nature excites the ideas of the sublime in its chaos or in its wildest and most irregular disorder and desolation, provided size and might are perceived. Hence we see that the concept of the sublime is not nearly so important or rich in consequences as the concept of the beautiful; and that, in general, it displays nothing purposive in nature itself, but only in that possible use of our intuitions of it by which there is produced in us a feeling of a purposiveness quite independent of nature. We must seek a ground external to ourselves for the beautiful of nature, but seek it for the sublime merely in ourselves and in our attitude of thought, which introduces sublimity into the representation of nature. This is a very needful preliminary remark, which quite separates the ideas of the sublime from that of a purposiveness of *nature* and makes the theory of the sublime a mere appendix to the aesthetical

judging of that purposiveness, because by means of it no particular form is represented in nature, but there is only developed a purposive use which the imagination makes of its representation.[8]

One may, of course, argue that in Kant the sublime plays a more crucial role in culture, in which the subjective-objective opposition is more tenuous and the shaping or even projective role of the mind is less impeded, particularly in contexts wherein limits (including those imposed by the past) are exceeded or disparaged. (This role becomes paramount in theories of the sublime which fixate on its putative relation to an endlessly desiring, abyssal subject that terroristically annihilates the given or the past, including traumatized victims, in a fantastic and fantasy-producing bid for creation *ex nihilo*–theories in which Kant becomes the alter ego of Sade.) But one may also contend that Kant's project in elaborating a concept of practical reason was to provide an analogue in ethics and sociocultural life of the beautiful in art which through critical judgment set forth legitimate limits that contained and countered the "sublime" allure of excess and boundlessness. One might also infer from the above passage that the quest for the sublime in ourselves and in our *forma mentis* may go to extremes, especially when the fascination with excess or hyperbole is given free rein and not countered by a concern for normative limits, without which any ethics seems misguided and any viable form of life in common inconceivable. This reading of Kant was clearly crucial to Durkheim in his understanding of the role of legitimate, flexible limits that articulated institutions stabilizing social life and interacting with varieties of "anomic" excess.[9]

8. Immanuel Kant, *The Critique of Judgment*, trans. J. H. Bernard (New York: Collier Macmillan, 1951), 84–85. This passage raises a problem for Kant's quasi-transcendental or noumenal idea of the sublime, which is opposed to phenomenal incarnation and contrasted with "enthusiasm" seen in the degraded form of *Schwärmerei*. If the sublime is a projection of the mind beyond phenomenality—indeed, a paradoxical experience beyond experience— how is it "excited" by natural phenomena? Does this excitement indicate a trace of immanence or incarnation with respect to the sublime?

9. Durkheim's insistently this-worldly perspective allowed for transitory ecstatic phenomena, such as collectively "effervescent" feasts, and situational transcendence (that is, transcendence of one social order which, through a possibly revolutionary passage involving

There have been important reasons for the prevalent suspicion of normative limits—their unwarranted conflation with normalization, their subservience to exploitative systems, their role in scapegoating nonconformists and outsiders, and their deceptively harmonizing way of providing unearned or undeserved consolation.[10] But these historical functions that pertain in certain social and cultural conditions

---

excessive anomie, gives way to another order—in contrast to transcendence as utterly radical otherness or alterity): "All life . . . is a complex equilibrium whose diverse elements limit one another, and this equilibrium cannot be broken without suffering and sickness. . . . Our reason is not a transcendental faculty. It is part of the world and, consequently, it must follow the law of the world. The universe is limited, and all limitation presupposes forces that limit" (Emile Durkheim, *L'Education morale* [1925; Paris: Presses Universitaires de France, 1963], 34, 95–96; my transl.). "In the ordering of life, nothing is good without measure (*mesure*). A biological characteristic can fulfill the ends it must serve only if it does not go beyond certain limits. The same principle applies to social phenomena. . . . It is continually repeated that it is man's nature to be eternally dissatisfied, to advance constantly without rest or respite toward an indefinite goal. The passion for infinity is daily presented as a mark of moral distinction, whereas it can appear only within unregulated consciences which elevate to the status of a rule the lack of regulation from which they suffer. The doctrine of the most rapid progress at any price has become an article of faith" (Durkheim, *Le Suicide* [1897; Paris: Presses Universitires de France, 1960], 233, 287; my transl.). With the passage from nature to culture, biology, for Durkheim, was supplemented by normative limits and deregulated by anomie. For him capitalism instituted runaway anomie in the economy with disastrous social effects, and romanticism, often inadvertently, provided an ideology that might underwrite unlimited striving and self-assertion in social life. See my analysis of Durkheim, which focuses critically on the problem of the relation between excess and normative limits, in *Emile Durkheim: Sociologist and Philosopher* (Ithaca: Cornell University Press, 1972; reprint, Chicago: University of Chicago Press, 1985).

10. These reasons have at times been prepossessing in the post-Kantian animus against beauty in important dimensions of romantic, postromantic, avant-garde, and poststructural thought. Beauty may be called into question by a movement seeking basic or radical transformation in life or in art. Indeed (as at one point for Adorno), it may be seen as something we do not deserve "after Auschwitz." Or, as Lyotard generalizes the point, the postmodern "would be that which, in the modern, puts forward the unpresentable in presentation itself; that which denies itself the solace of good forms, the consensus of taste" (*The Postmodern Condition: A Report on Knowledge,* trans. Geoff Bennington and Brian Massumi [Minnesota: University of Minnesota Press, 1984], 81). But the animus against beauty may also be symptomatic of an all-or-nothing approach related to a more questionable, uncritical advocacy of unrepresentability, sublimity, excess, and radical transcendence or transgression that may at times reinforce runaway change, planned obsolescence, and readily marketable styles. For a recent attempt to rehabilitate an interest in beauty (which may not take sufficient account of reasons why there has been an animus against it), see Elaine Scarry, *On Beauty and Being Just* (Princeton: Princeton University Press, 1999).

should not simply be universalized or hypostatized to obscure more valid functions or to predetermine one's sense of possibility and desirability. One might even contend that the significance of limits and the problem of attempting to elucidate legitimate limits in relation to norms and institutions (like the problem of working through, to which such an attempt is related) have not had a sufficiently important place in the romantic and postromantic tradition that has fed into contemporary forms of poststructuralism in which the role of sublimity, hyperbole, and excess may at times be enacted, acted out, and even celebrated with a symptomatic insistence bordering on obsession. Indeed, in line with this insistence, closure, however limited, may be foreclosed. Yet the preemptive foreclosure of any and every modality of closure is as doctrinaire and open to question as the quest for definitive, totalizing closure.[11]

History faces the problem of both writing about and writing out trauma, and I have indicated that it is subject to certain frames or limits that may be contested but not, in my judgment, abandoned or simply flouted. Yet what these limits are—or should be—is indeed eminently contestable, and existing limits interact with more extreme overtures that cannot be anticipated or legislated out of existence. My own attempt has been to counteract certain binary oppositions that are important in thought about history and to some significant extent in the writing of history itself: the oppositions between objectivity and subjectivity, objectification and empathy, reconstruction and dialogic exchange, cognition and affect, thought and practice, excess and limits. I would rather construe the terms of these and related oppositions as problematic distinctions that pose the task of articulating relations in more critical, self-questioning forms that enable a different understanding and practice of history writing. I have also argued that history is a field of framed hyperbole—a field in which continually challenged and renewed limits play an important role and in which

11. Commitment related to mutual reliability and trust is a form of nonapocalyptic (or non–end-game) closure, excluding certain possibilities and enabling others.

hyperbole may be required to make a challenge register. In other words, hyperbole or going against the grain also requires the resistance of a grain, and if the existing limits are subjected to questioning, then at some point in the process one must confront the issue of how to generate newer intellectual and institutional limits—articulatory practices that discipline in a way that is necessarily constraining but not absolute, "panoptic," or beyond questioning.

I would summarize a principal argument in this book by recalling the distinction between absence and loss. Absence applies transhistorically to absolute foundations; loss applies to historical phenomena. The conflation of absence and loss induces either a metametaphysical etherealization, even obfuscation, of historical problems or a historicist, reductive localization of transhistorical, recurrently displaced problems—or perhaps a confusingly hybridized, extremely labile discourse that seems to derive critical analyses of historical phenomena directly from the deconstruction of metaphysics and metametaphysical, at times freely associative (or disseminatory), glosses of specific historical dynamics. For example, the notion that absolute foundations are unavailable, that the origin is "always already" ruined, or that the position of the Other (or any final, definitive addressee) is vacant may induce the idea that a given historical institution (the university, say) is in ruins or that all politics is a totally open, absolutely risky, aporia-laden venture in which any concrete, pragmatic proposals are disdained. For, in this view, any such proposal, however tentative or open to debate, would be tantamount to an objectionable incarnation or grounding of the un(re)representable, radically futuristic other, hence something beneath (quasi-transcendental) "theoretical" dignity. In another variant of the conflation of absence and loss, a mythical belief in a past-we-have-lost may be combined with an apocalytic, often blind utopian quest to regain that lost wholeness or totality in a desired future, at times through violence directed against outsiders who have purportedly destroyed or contaminated that wholeness. Compressed between past and future, one may also construe lost wholeness nostalgically and link it to a future perfect—what might have been if only those in the past had recognized what we presumably know: how to create a true community that will endure as a radiant polity.

I would also recall the distinction I made between two approaches to historiography. The first I termed a self-sufficient documentary model or research paradigm, of which positivism is the extreme form. In this first approach, referential statements making truth claims are necessary *and* sufficient conditions of historiography. Everything else is marginal. The second approach, which is the negative mirror image of the first, is radical constructivism. For it, referential statements making truth claims apply at best only to events. And they are relatively marginal in importance. Essential are performative, figurative, aesthetic, rhetorical, ideological, and political factors that project or "construct" structures—in stories, plots, arguments, interpretations, explanations—from which referential statements derive all their meaning and significance. In radical constructivism, there is a stress, if not an exclusive focus, on the way history and other forms of literature, including fiction, resemble one another, while in a self-sufficient research paradigm, the stress, if not the exclusive focus, is on the difference between history and other genres, including literature and, especially, fiction.

My own view is that referential statements making truth claims in historiography apply to both the (problematic) levels of structures and events. (For example, truth claims apply to interpretations and not only to events.) Moreover, truth claims are necessary but not sufficient conditions of historiography. A crucial question is how they interact, and ought to interact, with other factors or forces—dialogic, performative, rhetorical, ideological, political—in historiography, in other genres, and in hybridized forms or modes. The issue of the middle voice in relation to representing or writing trauma raises this question in an accentuated manner.

One important discursive instance of the middle voice is free indirect style, or *Erlebte Rede*. The obvious question is its role in historiography and in other genres or hybridized forms. Free indirect style is itself a hybridized, internally dialogized form that may involve undecidability of voice. In it the narrator interacts with objects of narration in various ways involving degrees or modulations of irony and empathy, distance and proximity—at the limit in labile, undecidable fashion. Undecidability takes the free indirect style to its limit in a kind of discursive return of the repressed middle voice. At its most dubious, it may also generalize that voice and use it to treat all problems with a rather unmodulated, often manneristic rhetoric or endless, meandering melody.

At least when used in a certain way, the middle voice may be argued to be most suitable for representing or writing trauma, especially in cases in which the narrator is empathically unsettled and able to judge or even predicate only in a hesitant, tentative fashion. It would not seem to be a vehicle for truth claims or for ethico-political judgments having any significant degree of decisiveness. It would rather more or less radically problematize such claims and judgments and, at its most forceful, be a way of placing basic beliefs or perspectives in an agonistic, possibly fruitful, interaction with one another—hence also a way of placing the self or the subject in question. A discursive variant of the middle voice may at times be linked to an ethos of uncertainty, risk, more or less indiscriminate generosity, and openness to the radically other, who is utterly unknown and may be "monstrous." These traits have recently been prominent in certain forms of deconstruction. As earlier intimated, the fact that essentialism or the belief in absolute foundations has historically been used to justify objectionable practices or to shore up questionable institutions should not lead to the conclusion that the necessary deconstruction of this tendency is also sufficient as a framework from which to derive an analysis and critique of institutions and historical practices that may also have other bases and dimensions. Nor should one take the frequent complement of the deconstruction of absolute foundations—utopian affirmation that recurrently transcends any concrete realization or incarnation—and push it in the direction of an unguardedly hyperbolic stress on the enigmatic call of an open or empty utopia that is always deferred or *à-venir.* When the latter stress prevails, the desirable tension between flexibly pragmatic attempts to realize certain specific goals and the insistence on the unrealizability of the absolute (or on the untenability of blueprints of the future) is distended or dissipated in the direction of a contentless utopianism or "messianicity" without a messiah.

A specific issue that merits further research and critical reflection is the actual and desirable role of the middle voice in historiography and elsewhere. A related problem is how such a voice would "apply" to different "objects" in historiography as well as be articulated with other uses of language. Insofar as implication in (or a transferential relation to) the object of inquiry is constitutive of research, one always in some sense begins with a "middle-voiced" position with respect to the object or the other. The crucial issue is how one responds to or comes to terms with that initial positionality—and here one confronts the issue of how to deploy various modalities of acting out, working over, and working through. Exploratory "middle-voicing" in an accentuated yet internally modulated, self-questioning form would, as I have intimated, seem to be most suitable for the treatment of figures in variously shaded portions of Primo Levi's gray zone—figures who were themselves in double binds not of their own making and who place the empathic historian in a comparable position.[12] Used with proper framing, it might in certain ways also apply to one's treatment of more uncompromised victims, but, given the difficulty in viably controlling its use, the obvious (but often unconsciously undergone) danger would be its propensity to merge with unproblematic identification, the assumption of the victim's voice, and vicarious victimage.

A pronounced middle voice would probably be most questionable with respect to one's treatment of perpetrators even if one acknowledged, but did not indulge in, the kernel of possibility of behavior analogous to theirs in oneself. Hence the rendering of Hitler's voice in free indirect style would be extremely questionable not only in history but in fiction or film. As noted earlier, the broader challenge to the

---

12. Here the question of modulations of proximity and distance in middle-voiced accounts would be crucial, for the gray zone is itself not simply gray on gray but internally differentiated into significantly different shadings. Moreover, aspects of it could, of course, also be addressed in referential or constative terms.

historian-cum-public-intellectual is not to identify with any given set of subject positions in the seemingly fatalistic grid that was active in the Holocaust as well as in other limit events—the grid linking perpetrator, victim, gray zone, bystander, resister, rescuer, and those born later. It would rather be to try not simply to replicate those subject positions or experiences but rather to investigate them and their more complex, hybridized forms with varying modes of empathy and critical distance. It would also be to try to contribute to working out a complex subject position that would not be beholden to victimization and instead might have practical implications in social and political life.

I would like to examine briefly two questionable literary attempts to render the perpetrator's voice and position in a more or less middle-voiced manner: George Steiner's *Portage to San Cristóbal of A. H.* and Bernhard Schlink's *The Reader*.[13] Much of Steiner's novel takes the rather predictable form of a spy thriller or detective story concerning intrigues surrounding the transportation of the aged but spirited Hitler from the depths of the jungle by a group of Israeli Nazi-hunters. When the task proves futile, the trial of Hitler takes place in the jungle itself with an Indian, Teku, as supposedly neutral witness. At the conclusion of the trial and the novel, one has Hitler's long monologue, which refuses to be interrupted by the interjections of his "defense attorney" but into which is woven certain views Steiner himself elsewhere expresses in his own voice, including in the 1999 afterword to the novel itself. (After Hitler's outpouring and in the midst of "loud drumbeats" of hovering helicopters, Teku, who "had not understood

13. George Steiner, *Portage to San Cristóbal of A. H.* (1979; Chicago: University of Chicago Press, 1999); Bernhard Schlink, *The Reader* (1995; New York: Random House, 1998). In this context one may also mention Hans-Jürgen Syberberg's deeply equivocal *Hitler, a Film from Germany,* text trans. by Joachim Neugroschel (New York: Farrar, Straus & Giroux, 1982). On the middle voice, see also Vincent P. Pecora, "Ethics, Politics, and the Middle Voice," *Yale French Studies* 79 (1991): *Literature and the Ethical Question,* ed. Claire Nouvet, 203–30. (Unfortunately, this article came to my attention only after I completed the present book. Its argument in important ways complements, supplements, and at times has a mutually questioning relation to the one I try to make.)

the words, only their meaning," leaps up and cries "Proved"—an equivocal utterance that may apply either to Hitler's guilt or to the idea that his *plaidoyer* carries conviction.)[14]

Hitler's monologue, which might be read in significant measure as the author's ventriloquated, at times projective, middle-voiced rendering of Hitler, presents the latter (somewhat deceptively) as a sophisticated, quasi-Nietzschean ideologue who nonetheless spews forth his apologetic *Ecce Homo* in the form of an assortment of clichéd statements about the Holocaust. Among those Steiner uncritically repeats in his afterword are the ideas that genocide is so banal or com-

---

14. Hitler's monologue, especially in its attempt to elicit the complicity of the reader by showing how the *Führer* at most carried to their "logical" conclusion tendencies that mark the times (such as prevalent anti-Semitism, including among the Allies), is reminiscent of, if not inspired by, that of Jean-Baptiste Clamence as judge-penitent in Albert Camus's *The Fall* (1956; trans. Justin O'Brien [New York: Vintage Books, 1991]). For an analysis of Clamence's monologue, see my *History and Memory after Auschwitz* (Ithaca: Cornell University Press, 1998), 78–88. In his afterword Steiner notes that the "outrage" that greeted the first publication of the book "is not difficult to understand. It centered on what was taken to be the paradoxical, 'agnostic' conclusion. Though the last word in fact belongs to Teku, the neutral witness[,] and, more emphatically perhaps, to the clamor of the helicopters, it was widely felt that A. H.'s rhetoric and challenge had been left unanswered" (171). In his rather unconvincing attempt to rebut this impression, Steiner observes that, although Hitler may appear to have the last word, "Lieber's long monologue of horror . . . *is* the center" of the novel (172).

Lieber's monologue (chap. 6) actually comes about one-quarter of the way into the novel—more than a hundred pages before Hitler's speech (chap. 17). In Lieber's case, it is until the very last page of the chapter not evident who is speaking in a breathless, somewhat ranting radio communication that trails off plaintively at the end ("This is Lieber calling/ this is Lieber/this is" [52]). Lieber warns of Hitler's Siren-like eloquence yet asserts his necessary existence as the anti-Word or God's contrary. He also insists on Hitler's role in the genocide despite the fact that he could not have done it alone ("Oh they helped. Nearly all of them" [50]). There are at times uncanny echo effects in the relation of Hitler's to Lieber's monologue. And it is at best radically unclear whether Lieber's monologue engages Hitler's in an effective manner; it is possible that his words are for the reader but a faint memory by the time she or he gets to Hitler's address. It is all too evident who is speaking when Hitler begins, and his insistent mode of address makes its points in forceful fashion ("Erster Punkt" are his opening words). One issue raised by the Lieber-Hitler relation is the ability of sustained, more or less experimental indirection to counteract, or even come to terms with, forceful, at times vehement, directness. Moreover, the mysterious Lieber's "position" in the novel is primarily that of a hidden or absent center/god, and his (in)effectiveness is similar to that of the long-suffering yet absent deity in a secular world in which the commanding rhetoric and conviction of a Hitler may unfortunately prove to be the more powerful force.

monplace in the twentieth century that "the mind sickens and grows numb" and that Stalin, whose "blood lust had the manic vehemence of Asiatic despotism," committed crimes that dwarf Hitler's. Moreover, for Steiner Stalin committed his crimes with presumably un-Hitleresque "personal pleasure in torture and the signature, on an industrial scale, of death sentences" (173–74). Steiner also asserts that he has (in good libertarian, if not existentially heroic, fashion) chosen to leave to the novel its freedom, including that of "its myopic readers and sometimes hysterical detractors" (172). Steiner does not seem to realize that analogous views were invoked in blatantly normalizing and apologetic fashion by Ernst Nolte during the 1986 Historians' Debate.

Schlink's *The Reader* is an international best-seller distinguished by the fact that it has received high praise from both Steiner and Oprah Winfrey. (Steiner is quoted on the paperback cover as asserting: "A masterly work. . . . The reviewer's sole and privileged function is to say as loudly as he is able, 'Read this' and 'Read it again.' " Winfrey's strong endorsement of the book was important in promoting its sales in the United States.) Although it does not make technical use of free indirect style with respect to a perpetrator, *The Reader* does generate "middle-voiced," equivocal empathy for a woman SS camp guard in a manner that marginalizes and obscures the plight of Jews and other victims. Jews are subjects of periodic allusions, while Hanna is central to the narrator's concerns.

One merit of the novel is that (aside from clearly designating its status as a novel) it does not mingle soft "porn" with Holocaust-related phenomena in the manner of *Sophie's Choice* or the film *Night Porter.* The erotic relation between the narrator as a boy of fifteen and Hanna as a woman of thirty-six takes place in the early portion of the novel situated in the late fifties, while the Holocaust belatedly comes to the fore in the mid-sixties with respect to the trial of Hanna and other woman SS guards. The only recurrence of sado-masochistic eroticism is in the narrator's dreams, which create discomfort in him. Still, the key revelation in the novel—the narrator's discovery of Hanna's illiteracy, which is related to his own erotic-turned-charitable role as

Vorleser [one who reads aloud]—is an implausible deus ex machina that has dubious functions. It seems to make Hanna a victim of society, and it quite clearly makes her the scapegoat at the trial—indeed, someone who seems intent on assuming the guilt of others in self-sacrificial, victim-become-redeemer fashion. Moreover, Hanna's illiteracy is the reason why she "fell" into the role of SS guard (in order to avoid discovery of her illiteracy with a promotion at Siemens, which seems to assume—but on whose part? Hanna's? the narrator's? both?— that there was less chance of its discovery with entry into the SS). Indeed, agency in general seems erased by the final pages of the novel, and illiteracy might be read as a cultural metaphor apologetically alluding to Germans who presumably were not "in the know" about what was happening to Jews under the Nazis.[15]

My comments should not, however, be read as endorsing the bitter irony of a trial of relatively minor SS guards in a postwar Germany that had reintegrated or avoided prosecuting many former Nazis who had held more significant positions. Nor do they imply the invalidation of all feeling for someone in Hanna's pathetic position, particularly after she serves eighteen years in prison. One may nonetheless contend that a series of features are histrionic and at times incongruous, if not ludicrous, touches that strain the reader's credulity. Among these features are Hanna's spending her prison years as if in a convent (engaging in "rather monotonous work . . . as a sort of meditation" [207] and painstakingly learning to read and write), her final suicide, her leaving her money to the sole survivor of a fire in a locked church (used by the SS as a temporary guardhouse) whose doors Hanna and the other guards did not open, and the narrator's gesture, upon delegation by the woman survivor, in donating this money to the Jewish League Against Illiteracy (as if illiteracy had been one of the primary problems confronting the proverbial people of the book!).

It is, I think, important to signal the dubiousness of certain forms of seeming empathy with perpetrators, often attendant upon a labile use of free indirect style or middle voice. Such forms create an objec-

15. I thank my colleague Leslie Adelson for the latter observation.

tionable (or at best deeply equivocal) kind of discomfort or unease in the reader or viewer by furthering fascination and a confused sense of identification with or involvement in certain figures and their beliefs or actions in a manner that may well subvert judgment and critical response. Of course, Steiner's and Schlink's books should not be taken as representative, and their limitations should not become the basis of rash generalizations about the inappropriateness of fiction concerning the Holocaust or the necessity of restricting representation to documentary, indeed minimalist, historiography. Still, the inevitable "aboutness" or referentiality of historiography is a principal limit in the field when compared with art and literature (especially fiction) or even with philosophy—fields in which the imagination or speculation may have freer reign. History is always about something specific, and it necessarily and constitutively involves referential truth claims. Moreover, theory in it must interact with specific problems and truth claims—both testing and being tested by them. Theory in historiography cannot be a self-propelled discursive machine that generates its own resistances or virtual images and incorporates its problems in a self-referential, even involuted, manner that is interrupted only by unforeseen asperities and unavoidable traces of the referential. Reference in history is crucial—what aboutness is about. Indeed, it might be seen as the analogue in historiography, and in its role in the public sphere, of reality testing in psychoanalysis. But reference is itself dual or multiple, and it is not the only problem in historiography.

Reference is dual or multiple in that references to the past involving truth claims—more broadly, readings and interpretations of the past—are intimately and constitutively bound up with dialogue and debates in the present which bear on the future. We inscribe and remember the past only in ways that interact with the present and future even if (in my view mistakenly) we see our present project as understanding the past only in its own putative terms, asking it no questions it did not ask itself, and entirely cutting our understanding of it off from any belated recognitions. Carried to the limit, the latter project would be self-defeating, for it would amount to living vicariously in the past by becoming what one studies—a project that is always dubious and seems particularly bizarre with respect to phenomena like the Holocaust, its victims, and perpetrators. The problem, as I have tried to indicate, is rather how to interrelate an understanding of the past and the questions it posed to itself—an understanding that strives to be both empathetic and objective—to questions we put to the past, with the possibility that what we learn may change our very questions and our understanding. One can read against the grain only if one recognizes and respects the resistance of the grain. Hence one should try to understand how Hitler or Himmler "read" the world in every sense of the word and how that reading was developed and related to their most extreme policies or actions. Reading a Nazi document such as a bureaucratic report or Himmler's Posen speech against the grain, in order to elicit aspects of it which were not manifest to its writers, requires that one begin by not treating it simply as a source for facts or as an ink blot one projectively reprocesses but as a complex artifact that may indeed have a grain or variety of grains with their own dynamic and force of resistance.[16]

The larger question in reading and interpretation is the relation of genres and disciplines to one another as well as to hybridized forms or modes. A closely associated matter is the bearing of genres and disciplines on problems that themselves cut across and may even disrupt generic or disciplinary boundaries. Trauma presents an acute instance of such a cross-disciplinary problem, for it falls within the compass of no single genre or discipline, and how one should approach it in a

16. Richard J. Evans is off the mark when he contends that Le Roi Ladurie in *Montaillou* (Paris: Gallimard, 1975) reads an inquisition register against the grain because he uses it to reconstruct peasant life in the sixteenth century. On the contrary, he uses it rather unproblematically as a source for information about the past even though he subjects that information to various interpretations. He does not recognize the document's "grain" as an inquisition register that stages a dynamic of question and answer (and involves an intricate play of translations from language to language) which must be critically analyzed if any use of it is not to ignore certain of its crucial dimensions, including the way it may pose problems for direct inferences about life in the past in contexts other than that of the inquisition. (Ladurie took a significantly different, more critical approach to the use of an inquisition register in *La Sorcière de Jasmin* [Paris: Seuil, 1983].) See Richard J. Evans, *In Defense of History* (New York: W. W. Norton, 1997), 123. As intimated in chapter 1, Evans' "defense of history" is in general based on a relatively restricted research model of historiography and manifests an at times vapid antipathy to theoretical self-reflection.

given genre or discipline is an essentially contested question. Even more vexed is the question of the extent to which hybridized genres or disciplines are legitimate in the attempt to come to terms with trauma, indeed in the complex effort to work it through at least in symbolic terms. For the excess of trauma which overwhelms the self and disorients society also poses a challenge to modes of understanding and may become the occasion for critiques of disciplinarity which shade into freely associative "enactments" of confused or undisciplined thought.

Historiography, literature, and other areas or fields have distinctive ways of approaching the inscription of trauma—writing about it and writing it. They also generate mutually provocative questions for one another—questions that are more pressing insofar as they touch on sensitive, affectively charged, value-laden issues such as those raised by traumatic limit events. Should historiography rely *only* on standard operating procedures, however necessary some of them (such as footnoting) may be, when it confronts such limit events and attempts to address the problem of trauma in its bearing on different groups or subject positions? What modes of narrative are most suited for rendering traumatic events, especially in ways that do not harmonize, stylize, or even airbrush them and thus border on repression or denial? What non-narrative forms complement, supplement, and contest narrative representations? Does one's empathic unsettlement in the face of such events—an unsettlement that has a different meaning as it bears on various figures or groups (such as perpetrators, victims, and those in the gray zone)—itself have implications for the writing (including the very style and rhetoric) of history? How is historiography in this respect similar to, and different from, literature and other forms of art? How should historiography address hybridized objects—figures, phenomena, or artifacts in various locations of the particularly troubling gray zone—and what does such an encounter mean for the stability and possible hybridization of one's own mode of address? What is the role of the social sciences or even the natural sciences, including neuroscience, in relation to more interpretive approaches bearing on self-understanding and ethico-political practice? Are there cases in which it may be justifiable, even necessary, to go beyond generic or disciplinary boundaries in order to attempt to do justice to the object of study—even if one would want to maintain that boundaries are important not as fixed barriers but as more or less flexible, at times transgressible, yet institutionalized limits? For example, should the historian, pursuing a line of inquiry, engage in extended close reading of a work of art—a novel, a poem, a film, a painting—even if such a reading takes him or her (as perhaps it must) outside recognizable forms of historiography and the established frameworks or protocols for historical research (including synoptic narratives)? How should such a "performance" be evaluated in professional terms, say, with respect to tenure decisions or hirings?

These are some of the disciplinary questions raised in acute form by the study of limit events and their traumatizing course or aftermath. They are troubling questions, but the manner in which they trouble does not entail the obliteration of all distinctions and, with them, the possibility of all discrimination and judgment. I think some questions are easier to answer than others. There are sound reasons, at least of a pragmatic sort, for the existence of departments of history or of literature. At certain times, departments may undergo basic self-scrutiny and may even be subject to significant reorganization or reformulation. Such processes have been occurring recently with respect to German studies, French studies, visual studies, and cultural studies. In certain ways they have affected larger and more impregnable bastions such as departments of English. Compared with departments of literature, history (as well as art history) seems more epistemologically and even methodologically conservative as an institutionalized discipline, but even in it the recent past has brought self-questioning and an openness to initiatives and debates bearing on some basic issues. In addition, I think significant numbers of academics would now agree that a member of an academic department who demonstrates an ability to satisfy generally agreed-on requirements of research and teaching in his or her area should be allowed a margin—in certain cases a wide margin—to explore issues in a manner that may not be readily adjusted to existing modes of research or styles of presentation. Indeed, if a department is based on such an anxiety-ridden, easily threatened image of itself or the discipline it institutionalizes that it cannot be open to certain challenges, then it may be time for it to be placed in question, for it threatens to lose contact both with other developments in the academy and with its own responsibilities to a larger public sphere.

Related questions arise beyond academically institutionalized disciplines. I have noted some of them with respect to Claude Lanzmann's *Shoah* as work of art—perhaps the greatest film yet made on the Holocaust—and as quasi documentary that includes testimonies of survivors, perpetrators, collaborators, and bystanders as well as figures somewhere in the problematic gray zone. One may also raise questions about Lanzmann's role in the film as *metteur en scène,* interviewer, and character. Still, how to formulate relevant questions, stemming in part from historical research, may be extremely difficult and perplexing, especially in certain cases.

If Binjamin Wilkomirski, whose name appears on the cover of *Fragments: Memories of a Wartime Childhood,* was indeed an impostor in that he was never in a concentration camp and instead was a foster child named Bruno Dössekker who was raised by a well-off family in Switzerland, then this state of affairs has implications for one's reading of the book. In that event, Wilkomirski might be a figure in the gray zone—an indirect victim of the Holocaust who so identified or was otherwise distraught by events (or perhaps in good part by a documentary film as well as by his manifest desire for an identity as Holocaust victim) that he may actually have been confused about his own past and to some extent believed that he indeed had been a child in camps. One might certainly empathize with him in his plight, whatever might be one's response to his evasiveness in facing up to charges of imposture. But one might still judge that his book is dubious as a *faux mémoire* and that the disorientation it (in contrast to the individual Wilkomirski-Dössekker) causes in the reader is not desirable. (An overly clinical approach may obscure the distinction between empathy for—even suspending criticism of—the individual or author in his plight and the role of the text in the public sphere, which may indeed warrant criticism.) Here one may argue that it would have been better in a multiplicity of ways, including ethical and aesthetic ways, if the book had been presented as fictionalized or as a hybridized form. Then it would still have troubled the reader, but its ability to trouble would have been more analogous in nature to that of Tadeusz Borowski's *This Way for the Gas, Ladies and Gentlemen,* although in my judgment it would still not be comparable to the latter as an accomplishment—an accomplishment as work of art, as history, and as hybrid that has the power to unsettle in what might be argued to be a more desirable way.[17]

The genre of Borowski's text is explicitly problematic and hybridized. It is based on the experience of the narrator in the camps and told in story form interspersed with commentary and analysis. The tone is one of bitter irony and disillusionment equally distant from Elie Wiesel's religiosity and Primo Levi's humanism. Even the child's-eye approach of Wilkomirski, despite its possible deceptions or disorientations, seems almost sentimentalizing and comforting by comparison. One might be tempted to attribute Borowski's tone to the "brutalizing" effects of trauma in a young man who found himself in one of the darkest, most harrowing corners of Levi's gray zone.

Borowski was a Polish non-Jew incarcerated for vaguely political reasons yet almost by chance. He became a kapo—a prisoner who guarded and was able to persecute other prisoners, a twilight being who was both victim and victimizer. The voice emerging from Borowski is utterly disconcerting and places the reader in an unbearably uncomfortable position—an unceasingly renewed series of double binds in which empathy and revulsion or confusion continually interfere with or undercut each other. The occasionally obvious "novelized" or fictionalized moments—a description of the sun or the trees—which deliver a promise of narrative pleasure seem almost out of place or even offensive in the context of this account. The comparably rare moments of muted idealism or hope-against-hope which manage to

---

17. Tadeusz Borowski, *This Way for the Gas, Ladies and Gentlemen,* selected and trans. Barbara Vedder, intro. Jan Kott (1959; New York: Penguin Books, 1976).

surface in the text—or even the narrative outbursts that disrupt the agonized irony (for example, the concluding line on p. 142)—are all the more remarkable because of their very rarity, the odds against which they have been earned, and the almost miraculous nature of their appearance. Especially remarkable is that Borowski consistently refuses to participate in a quasi-sacrifical or scapegoating scenario; instead, he makes any attempt to validate this scenario—or see the promise of regeneration in its terms—seem utterly impossible.

The upset or unease caused by Borowski's stories is seemingly close to but tellingly different from that caused by Wilkomirski's *Fragments: Memories of a Wartime Childhood.* In Wilkomirski's case, the reader is upset and perhaps angered by the realization that what was taken as fact on first reading is possibly, indeed probably, invented or imagined. In Borowski's case, the hybridized status of the text is explicit, but this status does not assuage one's unsettlement. In fact, the upset or sense of unease comes not only from the excruciating nature of the account but from our very inability to tell whether anything in these stories that are explicitly presented as hybridized is indeed fiction, since there seems no internal way to distinguish what was experienced, elaborated from experience, and invented. Indeed, despite the critical framing and seeming fictionality of Borowski's stories—devices that imply a certain respect for the reader as one who should not be deceived or manipulated (especially not for the writer's benefit)—one is nonetheless tempted to believe that everything in these stories is, if not empirically true, at least too close to fact for the reader's comfort.

One's reading of the stories is inevitably colored by the fact that Borowski committed suicide in 1951, years after his experience in Dachau and Auschwitz, gassing himself three days after his wife gave birth to a daughter.[18] Yet these are stories that have their place as

18. There are indications in the stories themselves that the concentration camp became Borowski's world and that the camp mentality had fatalistic effects he was unable to exorcise. As he puts it in "Auschwitz, Our Home (A Letter)": "But I think that we should speak about all the things that are happening around us. We are not evoking evil irresponsibly or in vain, for we have now become a part of it" (113). In perhaps the most famous and appealed-to chapter of *The Drowned and the Saved* (chap. 2), Primo Levi asserts that the "the

"literature"—literature that makes the theoretical attempt to define the literariness of the literary seem evasive or even altogether beside the point. They form a kind of captivity narrative that has the power to make ordinary life seem difficult to reenter and ordinary explanations appear as placebos for what can be apprehended only with extreme difficulty and with no pretense to complete understanding. The stories in no sense redeem what they discuss and do not provide us

---

hybrid class of the prisoner-functionary" falls into "a gray zone, poorly defined, where the two camps of masters and servants both diverge and converge. This gray zone possesses an incredibly complicated internal structure and contains within itself enough to confuse our need to judge" ([1986; New York: Random House, 1989], 42). Yet Levi is led to distinguish sharply between perpetrator and victim when he discusses the "beautiful and false film" of Liliana Cavani (*Night Porter*): "I do not know, and it does not much interest me to know, whether in my depths there lurks a murderer. I know that the murderers existed, not only in Germany, and still exist, retired or on active duty, and that to confuse them with their victims is a moral disease or an aesthetic affectation or a sinister sign of complicity; above all, it is a precious service rendered (intentionally or not) to the negators of truth" (48–49). In the very next paragraph, Levi returns to the more qualified, measured tone that is typical of his writing: "It remains true that in the Lager, and outside, there exist gray, ambiguous persons, ready to compromise" (49).

One might initially see the turns in Levi's thought as indicating the difficulty of relating a sharp distinction between perpetrators and victims to the complexities and ambiguities of the gray zone. In addressing this problem, one might contend that Levi, like other victims, is not "guilty" in any relevant sense that would justify the camps or the behavior of perpetrators in them and, in that sense, undermine the significant distinction between perpetrators and victims. The gray zone arose in large part as a consequence of perpetrator behavior in putting victims in impossible situations that induced some victims to "compromise," turn on other victims, and serve the perpetrators. I would further note that one may judge undesirable the unfortunate and constrained "hybridized" condition of "prisoner-functionaries" in the gray zone but suspend judgment or express it in only the most tentative of terms with respect to certain persons in that zone (such as Borowski). (Quite unlike Hannah Arendt or Raul Hilberg with respect to Jewish Councils, Levi himself is even led to suspend judgment concerning Chaim Rumkowski of the Lodz ghetto [68–69].) In addition, one may judge quite harshly and with little qualification Nazis who were instrumental in creating the situation that gave rise to the gray zone.

As does Levi, one may bring strong criticism to bear on artifacts or arguments that tendentiously blur certain distinctions, for example, by an indiscriminate appeal to ambiguity or to the role of the gray zone. One may also distinguish between dubious compromises, for example, those serving one's narrow self-interest or betraying the trust of members of a victimized group, and certain compromise formations that one may normatively affirm as desirable, for example, those that actively resist total closure and an absolutist, dogmatic quest for purity or full unity for an in-group typically at the expense of a scapegoated, even demonized, out-group.

with the higher insight that is the recompense we might expect to derive from even the most tragic of accounts. At most they leave one in a state of necessary unease and with the perhaps equally necessary "never-again" feeling—the feeling that anything analogous to the situation in which these stories arose should be prevented from occurring, whatever its relation to "literature" that is overwhelming in its power to challenge the reader.

The experiences of victims and survivors such as Borowski—and even more so those of less compromised figures such as Charlotte Delbo or countless Jewish victims—indicate telling differences between them and those born later, including secondary witnesses. For the survivor of certain experiences, survival itself may be more than enough. Viewing survivor testimonies serves to bring this home to the viewer. Simply attaining a voice able to bear witness or give testimony—to express certain unspeakable injuries, insults, and forms of abjection—is itself a remarkable accomplishment. That a severely traumatized victim-become-survivor may continue to be haunted or possessed by the past is not surprising. What is surprising is that the victim may in some viable sense indeed become a survivor and even, at least for a time, put together a life involving familial and even professional and civic responsibilities.

If we who have not been severely traumatized by experiences involving massive losses go to the extreme of identifying (however spectrally or theoretically) with the victim and survivor, our horizon may unjustifiably become that of the survivor, if not the victim, at least as we imagine her or him to be. In other words we may come to feel that it is enough if we simply survive and, at most, bear witness. Other possibilities may seem precluded or be situated in an ever receding, vague, or vacuous future. We may even undergo surrogate victimage—something that may at times be unavoidable but, in terms of ethical, social, and civic responsibility, is open to question, particularly in its effects in the public sphere. In any case, our sense of possibility becomes severely constricted, especially in social and political terms. We may even blind ourselves to ways our lives are in fact privileged. Hence we may opt out of certain responsibilities because, through more or less projective identification, we seek only to attain a testimonial voice that bespeaks, writes, or cries out unspeakable suffering and loss. But something different may be required of someone who has not lived through extreme events and been severely traumatized, however much we may insist on the significance, value, and effects of empathy with the victim and survivor or the notion that certain "unclaimed" experiences cannot be possessed. Indeed, working through problems for one born later is itself distinctive and closely linked to ethical, social, and political demands and responsibilities that relative good fortune (of course, markedly different for those in different life situations and subject positions) should call forth and enable one to recognize and to take up. In this sense it is very important to distinguish empathy from identification and to explore the specific ways it may and should be articulated with such demands and responsibilities.

The factors that complicate the referentiality or "aboutness" of history are particularly insistent with respect to intensely invested, traumatic events. These are bound up with our transferential implication in the past and its figures—an implication that must be accounted for in order that historiography be objective without succumbing to the deceptive and even harmful project of objectification that denies transference, eliminates the role of critical self-reflection, and suppresses the voice of the other, including its ability to raise questions for oneself and one's assumptions. I have tried to argue that transferential implication should not lead to identification or simply be acted out (for example, in the dubious manner of Daniel Jonah Goldhagen) but worked through in a manner involving an empathic response to the other as other. Empathy, as I have construed the term, is to be disengaged from its traditional insertion in a binary logic of identity and difference. In terms of this questionable logic, empathy is mistakenly conflated with identification or fusion with the other; it is opposed to sympathy implying difference from the discrete other who is the object of pity, charity, or condescension. In contradistinction to this entire frame of reference, empathy should rather be understood in terms of an affective relation, rapport, or bond with the other recognized and respected as other. It may be further related to the affirmation of otherness within the self—otherness that is not purely and discretely other. This affirmation applies to the imbrication of the past in the present as well as to one's interaction with particular others, including the dead, who may exert possessive force in the present and require modes of understanding which combine cognition and critical analysis with more complex responses, including, when appropriate, a discursive analogue of mourning as a mode of working through a relation to historical losses.

It is conceivable that for some, perhaps many, in secular society, a discursive analogue of mourning is all that is available. Modern society is characterized by a dearth of social processes, including ritual processes, which assist individuals during major transitions in life such as marriage, birth, or death. One finds such processes primarily in traditional pockets of secular society which are not unaffected by more general tendencies toward the evacuation of engaging collective forms and rituals. Moreover, a process such as mourning may not be effective on a national level, where commemorations are often experienced as relatively hollow formalities. Indeed, it would be fascinating to know what actually goes on in the minds of people during proverbial "moments of silence," even in various groups in a country such as Israel, where everything is supposed to come to a stop in order to enable remembrance on Yom Hashoah. (One has here the basis of a Joycean novel that would approach mourning somewhat differently than *Ulysses,* in which important traditional resources are still available.) Yet the modern secular context, to the extent it is indeed characterized by a historical deficit of effective social and ritual processes, should not be generalized or hypostatized as a transhistorical necessity that always and everywhere makes mourning impossible or approximates it to endless melancholy—a view that may itself function to block future possibilities. Nor should one automatically assume that such processes are the prerogative of orthodox groups who embed them in dogmatic, at times intolerant, attitudes toward others. On the contrary, one should be alert to whatever signs there are in secular life of the genesis of social, even ritual, processes that may suggest more effective ways of coming to terms with losses as well as other significant transitions—including more festive ones—in social life.

The broader question here is whether empathy and, even more specifically, mourning are both available to anyone and deserved by all others, regardless of subject position. For example, how can former perpetrators develop empathic relations toward former victims and be able to engage in processes of mourning for them which are not simply perfunctory or encased in hollow commemorations? Perpetrators are often inclined self-defensively to deny the need for empathy and mourning with respect to victims, and whatever affective response they express may be confused with self-pity and nostalgia about an earlier state of affairs which was conjoined with acts of oppression. On the other hand, a regime arising after acts of severe, violent perpetration (for example, postwar Austria and Germany or even postapartheid South Africa) may not recognize the importance of providing social contexts in which former perpetrators may acknowledge their past actions and attempt to work out a different relation to former victims and survivors—including the dead—in a manner that enables empathic response and the possibility of mourning, which require self-criticism and even depression but should not be conflated with melancholic or nostalgic forms of self-involvement. Austria has, of course, been much less effective than Germany in openly debating, and attempting to provide, ways and means of coming to terms with the past, and the consequences have been evident in the degree of public support for Kurt Waldheim and Jörg Haider. And even in South Africa, the limitation of the official mandate of the Truth and Reconciliation Commission to investigating gross violations of human rights and the possibility that perpetrators may be prosecuted for acts that are not acknowledged in their original affidavits may inhibit the role of the TRC itself as a site for empathic response and processes of mourning, although in the case of victims and their families or associates the nature of testimony and exchange often goes beyond a limited quasi-judicial inquiry into the violation of rights to allow for more flexible narratives and processes of reliving and attempting to come to terms with dire past experiences. Insofar as the processes of the TRC do not allow for the empathic response and mourning that may be possible, the cycle of revenge and the at times justified demands of victims or their families for strict justice may not be mitigated by the kind of working through problems which is necessary for forgiveness and a viable measure of reconciliation. Of course, any truly viable reconciliation on a collective level depends not only on such processes as empathy and mourning but also on concrete economic, social, and political reforms in a larger context in which mourning itself has a broader, indeed a political, meaning.

In another register, how does one either determine the "right" of people to empathize with and mourn victims or try to understand (without necessarily forgiving) perpetrators? Is mourning, or even empathy, something like an entitlement or at least a right that one has to earn? May certain perpetrators not have earned or deserve mourning (even empathy) but instead warrant modes of understanding insistently related to critique? In more metaphoric terms, one might suggest that the ghosts of the past—symptomatic revenants who have not been laid to rest because of a disturbance in the symbolic order, a deficit in the ritual process, or a death so extreme in its unjustifiability or transgressiveness that in certain ways it exceeds existing modes (perhaps any possible mode) of mourning—roam the post-traumatic world and are not entirely "owned" as "one's own" by any individual or group. If they haunt a house (a nation, a group), they come to disturb all who live—perhaps even pass through—that house. How to come to terms with them affects different people or groups in significantly different ways. But just as no group that was not there is entitled to simple identification with victims, so the problem of response and the difficulty of attempts to come to terms with unsettling after effects and haunting presences are not clearly circumscribed or "properly" the preserve of anyone.

The dubiousness of identification should not eliminate recognition of the importance of empathic response and even modes of mourning, particularly in relation to victims who in life were denied dignity in the regime in which they lived and suffered. Children of survivors confront special difficulties in this respect, but even those (such as myself) who are relative "outsiders" but have worked intensively on certain problems may develop affective relations with those (living or dead) directly involved in events as well as charged responses to various attempts to represent or come to terms with them and their contexts. Here I would simply note in passing that the kinds of criticism Peter Novick levels (at times justifiably) at the uses and abuses of the Holocaust in American life would seem to have little purchase on, say, Art Spiegelman's *Maus* or on Spiegelman as commentator on his work, and I think they do not adequately account for other responses or commentaries in this or in other countries or settings.

I would further note that it is important to try to provide an account of why one does or does not find something moving. Theoretical discussions of affect and its conditions obviously may not themselves be moving, although they may provide insight into how and why one may or may not be moved. (Here one may refer to Freud's works, which generally do not speak or cry out trauma in the tones of Clorinda but may be of value in trying to account for those tones.) Attentively viewing survivor testimonies is often all too moving, but one's response to the procedures of the interviewers or the context of questioning may impede, if not disorient, one's emotional response. With respect to texts, artworks, and commentaries, the question of affective response is complicated. The requirement that an artifact be moving would seem to be most applicable to "primary" works more than to commentaries or critiques relating to them. But even in the latter case one may call for signs of empathic unsettlement even if one comes to suspect identification and the enactment or acting-out of the victim's voice or experience. However, one cannot apodictically legislate what count as signs of empathic unsettlement, and certain evident expressions of emotion may be quite moving for some but kitsch for others. (The primary way in which I am moved by what I see as kitsch is not to empathy but to anger.) Works by Franz Kafka, Paul Celan, or Charlotte Delbo are moving in a manner quite different from the 1979 Holocaust miniseries or even *The Diary of Anne Frank.* I have indicated that I find Borowski more moving than Wilkomirski—a case in which affective response is influenced by critical judgment and cognition, that is, by one's appreciation of the quality of the work and by what one knows of the author and the context of writing. But the role of empathy and affective response in general, including its relation to cognition, argument, and critical judgment, clearly warrant careful, sustained inquiry.

In a post-traumatic context in which a sense of crisis is prevalent in acknowledged or unacknowledged fashion, the temptation of an "all-or-nothing" response is great. On the one hand, one may deny that any problem, particularly any problem of traumatic proportions, ever really existed—or, if it did, that it remains in any significant way relevant to us now. Thus one may feel no need to be concerned with such "esoteric" problems as symptomatic returns, modes of melancholic or compulsively repetitive acting out, or the possibilities and limits of working through. In line with such dismissals, one may have the belief that the past may simply be transcended or that it has already been overly attended to if not worked through. Hence the continual need to come to terms with certain unsettling problems and their after effects in the present may be denied or wished away. Curiously, such an attitude concerning the irrelevance of trauma and the post-traumatic may be found in Teflon-coated Reaganite evangelical capitalism and in existential, voluntaristic, or radically constructivist creation *ex nihilo*. Still another form of dismissing the post-traumatic is found in hard-nosed social or historical realism that denies the relevance of, even sees as diversionary, all "talk" of traumatic disorientation and instead turns steadfastly to presentist concerns, such as the "politics of memory" wherein the past becomes a strategic pawn or a font of "symbolic capital" in contemporary interest-group maneuvering and competitive victimology. Such "realism" eschews traumatic after effects and the role of psychic (including imaginary or phantasmatic) aspects of ideology as well as the need to link understanding of such aspects to necessary modes of social, political, and economic analysis.

On the "nothing" end of the ledger, one may have the nihilating, at times apocalyptic, drive to carry trauma and destruction to the limit by undermining all attempts at reform or reconstruction as well as efforts to work through problems, however qualified by the realization that some limit events and their symptomatic residues may never be entirely overcome. Once "all or nothing" becomes the watchword or the implicit assumption and the "all" of redemption or totalization is recognized as spurious or disastrous, the only alleviation of the "nothing" may be the postulation of minimalist, often hopelessly naive, strategies for living in the ruins. Of course, the "all or nothing" may become an "all and nothing" insofar as uncompromising, all-encompassing criticism is conjoined with the hope-against-hope of a vacuous utopia or at least a messianic, ecstatic, even wonder-struck expectancy whose fulfillment is impossible or endlessly deferred.

In this context there may well be reason to stress the need to develop a non-Pollyanna understanding of working through the past which is alert to its own limitations and pitfalls as well as attuned to the need for linkages with sociopolitical analysis and practice bearing on contemporary problems and possibilities. One might perhaps envision this attempt as a recuperation of the unrealized possibilities of the early Frankfurt-school project of relating psychoanalysis to socially and politically relevant critical theory, but at present such an undertaking would require a rather different understanding of psychoanalysis in its bearing on historiography and critique as well as a critical yet appreciative engagement with various poststructural initiatives in the context of a social world whose changes do not await the reformulations of any theorist.

On less grandiose levels, the approach I have tried to elaborate not only underscores the affective dimension of historical understanding, which takes varying forms with respect to various others. It also helps one to recognize the significance of the tendency to victimize and scapegoat the other, who, as a totally separate identity, is projectively made into the localized origin of anxiety-producing, typically indeterminate or ill-defined forces that one denies in the self. It is important to investigate the role of victimization in history as well as of a scapegoating, quasi-sacrificial construction of it which is linked to a quest for regeneration or redemption through violence. Such victimization is pronounced in limit events involving the repetition of traumatic scenes of violence against the other. Unproblematic identification—more generally, a binary logic of identity and difference—furthers victimization, including at times the constitution of the self as surrogate victim. By contrast, empathy is a counterforce to victimization, and—without giving empathy an exclusive or primordial position— one may argue that its role is important both in historical understanding and in the ethics of everyday life. Indeed, the role of empathy is an insufficiently explored avenue through which one may inquire into the connection between historical understanding, social critique, and ethico-political activity—a key instance of the manner in which interest in the problem of working through may be seen as a renewal of the concern with the relation of theory to practice. In any event, the problem of empathy is a noteworthy, underexplored indicator that there is much remaining to be done in the attempt of historians and others to write about—and in some sense write—trauma. Here the interaction of history with other genres and with hybridized forms (including that complex genre-in-the-making that is the modern testimony) has brought forceful challenges to taken-for-granted disciplinary and departmental formations as well as to conceptions of scholarship and art—challenges that reach to the very foundations of organized thought and self-understanding.

Index

Index

Index

Index

White, Hayden (*cont.*)
  16–19, 25–27; "The Politics of
  Historical Interpretation: Disci-
  pline and Desublimation," 56n
Wiesel, Elie, 18n, 93n, 101n, 208
Wilkormirski, Binjamin, 18n, 32,
  207–9, 216
Windschuttle, Keith, 53n
Winfrey, Oprah, 201
Winnicott, D. W., 50n

Wolff, Karl, 119n
Wood, Philip R., 60n, 62n, 67n
Wood, Sarah, xiiin
Woolf, Virginia, 55, 105, 180

Young, James E., 103n

Zagorin, Perez, 9–10
Zammito, John H., 8n, 12n
Žižek, Slavoj, 71, 84